THE
ISRAELI-SYRIAN
PEACE TALKS

THE
ISRAELI-SYRIAN
PEACE TALKS
1991–96 AND BEYOND

HELENA COBBAN

United States Institute of Peace Press
Washington, D.C.

United States Institute of Peace
1200 17th Street NW
Washington, DC 20036

First published 1999

Printed in the United States of America

The paper used in this publication meets the minimum requirements of American National Standard for Information Sciences—Permanence of Paper for Printed Library Materials, ANSI Z39.48-1984.

Library of Congress Cataloging-in-Publication Data
Cobban, Helena.
　　The Israeli-Syrian peace talks: 1991–96 and beyond / Helena Cobban.
　　　　p.　cm.
　　Includes bibliographical references and index.
　　ISBN 1-878379-98-4 (alk. paper)
　　1. Israel—Foreign relations—Syria. 2. Syria—Foreign relations—Israel. 3. Arab-Israeli conflict—1993—Peace. I. Title.
　　DS119.8 .S95 C62 1999
　　327.569405691—dc21

　　　　　　　　　　　　　　　　　　　　　　　　　　　　　99-044995

*To the loving memory of my father,
James Macdonald Cobban, who throughout the
1980s traveled with me (and enjoyed meeting my
friends) in Israel, Syria, the United States, and
other countries dealt with in this book. He died,
aged 88, on April 19, 1999. He taught me many
things—not only the power of a well-turned pun,
but also the facts that peace is always worth
working hard for, and that a quest for justice
can come in many different forms.*

Contents

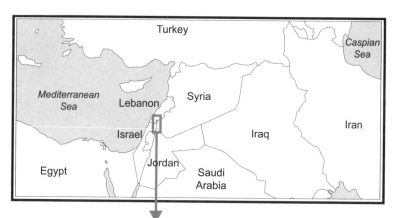

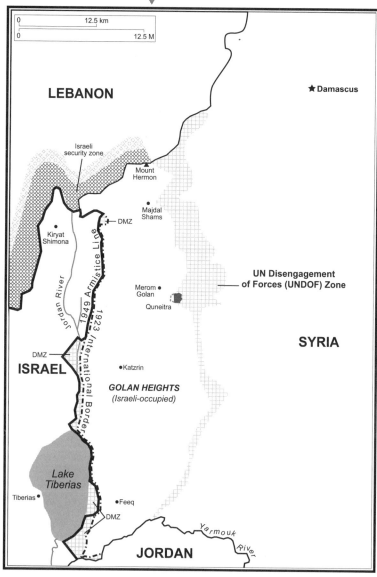

Foreword

"What might the Middle East become," Helena Cobban asks at the very beginning of this study, "if Syria and Israel . . . could reach a stable peace?" After three major conflicts and more than a half-century of a technical state of war between the two regional powers, the question seems oddly rhetorical. Yet as Cobban reveals in this timely work, Israel and Syria appeared to be very close to a peace agreement in 1996, only to see a historic opportunity dashed as a spate of Palestinian terrorist bombings and pressure on then–prime minister Shimon Peres from his own Labor Party forced Israel to suspend talks with Syria on a negotiated peace.

As its title indicates, this book is an examination of the successive rounds of peace talks between Israel and Syria that were facilitated and assisted by the United States between 1991 and 1996. The title's "Beyond" reflects the notion that three years after the disappointing suspension of negotiations in 1996, the leaders of all three countries face the prospect of resuming the negotiations that could lead to not only a bilateral peace treaty between the two Middle East powers, but also to a comprehensive peace that has eluded the region for more than fifty years.

On May 17, 1999, Israeli voters replaced Benjamin Netanyahu with Ehud Barak as the country's prime minister. Although the electorate's discontent had centered largely on economic issues and a general mood for change, the desire for peace lay not so far beneath the surface of the main campaign issues. For years after his electoral defeat of Peres in

1996, Netanyahu seemed to be more adamant than his rightist Likud coalition's position in rejecting concessions for peace with neighboring Arab countries and with Yasser Arafat's Palestinian Liberation Organization (PLO). Indeed, Netanyahu's muscular rhetoric and intransigence on peace initiatives with Israel's neighbors—particularly his stalling on further withdrawals from territory in the West Bank, as called for in the Oslo Accords and the subsequent Wye River Agreements—suggested that any new approaches to end the enduring climate of tension would come only with a change in government.

By contrast, Barak's electoral platform was a welcome sign to those who had lauded the bold peace overtures of his mentor, former Labor prime minister Yitzhak Rabin. Rabin had been assassinated in 1995 by an Israeli extremist opposed to the peace process, but Barak expressed a firm commitment to carry on his mentor's search for peace: "If Yitzhak is looking down on us from where he may, he knows that we together will fulfill his legacy," said Barak in his election victory speech. "We need to strengthen our country's security by moving forward to peace agreements." Barak also signaled that he did not want to waste any time in picking up where the previous Labor government under Peres had left off. In response, there were messages and speeches from Syrian leader Hafez al-Assad and PLO chairman Yasser Arafat welcoming Barak as the harbinger of progress on peace initiatives and agreements that remained dormant under Netanyahu. To solidify that image, Barak held highly visible meetings with Arafat and President Clinton in the months that followed the election. He also brought Peres into his newly formed government, assigning him the portfolio of "Minister of Regional Affairs."

Yet as Cobban notes, Barak has not always been an enthusiastic advocate of an Israeli-Syrian peace, at least with the assumptions and understandings that were taking shape during his service as military chief of staff and foreign minister, respectively, under Rabin and Peres. Assuming the mantle of prime minister, however, Barak at least has heightened the prospect of resuming negotiations with Syria, and there are powerful incentives for an Israeli premier to do so: With a historic settlement between the two countries, Israel would be able to end its occupation of southern Lebanon and claim a comprehensive, regional peace, capping its previous agreements with Egypt, the Palestinians, and Jordan.

While the initiative for a comprehensive Middle East peace, solidified by an Israeli-Syrian treaty, evinced the most progress during Rabin's and Peres's Labor governments, the prospects for such a regional peace were facilitated by another "regional" power—the United States. U.S. involvement in the Middle East has been an enduring component of American foreign policy ever since Israel's independence in 1948. For more than four decades after the British mandate in Palestine ended with Israel's war of independence, the region was perhaps the one most fraught with the dangers and risks of superpower competition: a mostly democratic Israel supported by the United States and surrounded by enclaves of Palestinian refugees and a ring of mostly hostile, autocratic Arab regimes bolstered by Soviet arms sales and influence. Subsequent wars would further change the region's political topography, pushing Israel to establish security buffers by occupying portions of contiguous Arab lands. In the Six Day War of 1967, Israel pushed deep into Egypt's Sinai Peninsula, the West Bank of the Jordan River (including Jerusalem), and Syria's Golan Heights. With its invasion of Lebanon in 1982 to establish a security zone in that country's south, Israel had largely completed construction of a continuous military buffer in the ring of Arab states surrounding it.

Yet the push for that buffer also left an international climate of moral opprobrium, reflected in two UN Security Council Resolutions calling for Israel's withdrawal from occupied territories in exchange for recognition by the Arab states of Israel's right to exist within the pre-1967 borders. But unlike Kissinger's Middle East shuttle diplomacy under President Nixon, or the Carter administration's diplomatic midwifery of the peace between Israel and Egypt in the Camp David accords, President Bush and Secretary of State James A. Baker III took the initiative to achieve a *comprehensive* regional peace in the Middle East. Such was the assumption that led the region's players to Madrid in September 1991.

In this work, Cobban documents Rabin's and Peres's close reliance on the "good offices" provided by the Clinton administration to facilitate communication among the parties in their quest for an Israeli-Syrian peace. How Barak views the American role will obviously be a major factor in the progress of future talks, and Cobban also provides some valuable guidelines in the study's final chapter for maximizing the prospects for success among all actors in their quest for a comprehensive peace.

The political figures in the Middle East peace process all have major incentives for achieving a comprehensive settlement. As the most decorated officer in the Israeli Defense Forces, Ehud Barak possesses the same kind of authority exercised by another soldier-turned-statesman, Yitzhak Rabin. Thus Barak can make bold overtures on the peace front by relying on his credibility as a defender of Israel's fundamental security interests. In frail health, both Hafez al-Assad and Yasser Arafat want the historic mantle of statesman and peacemaker that would come with the return of Israeli-occupied lands to their respective peoples—as does Bill Clinton. Thus in mid-July 1999, Barak proposed concluding the negotiations with Syria before the 2000 elections in the United States and the presidential transition.

If the crucial question now is not if but when the two parties will return to the negotiating table, an equally weighty issue is whether Israeli and Syrian negotiators will pick up where they left off, using the same assumptions and understandings they had acquired during their years of discussions from 1991 to 1996. One problem in this regard is the ambiguity of what exactly was achieved throughout those five years. During Barak's postelection visit with President Clinton in Washington, Secretary of State Madeline Albright devoted her meeting with the Israeli leader to trying to reconcile differences over where the talks stood in 1996. For his part, Barak introduced a new dimension to the Syrian track—"normalization," requiring Syria to end its support to terrorist groups, renounce its official position that Israel is an enemy state, and open its borders.

Helena Cobban, a veteran reporter on the Middle East and columnist on world affairs for the *Christian Science Monitor*, has devoted a considerable portion of her career to studying the personalities and positions of the region's leaders in their fitful quest for peace. Drawing on the recent memoirs of Israeli negotiators, media reports, and her own interviews of major figures in the negotiations, Cobban brings to this study not only a journalist's keen eye for detail and ability to pose penetrating questions, but also a scholar's thorough grasp of regional—and American—politics to give readers a thorough appreciation for just how elusive a comprehensive Middle East peace can be. The shifting venues in her analytical narrative provide a panoramic view of all actors' hopes and concerns, and she demonstrates that progress on the Israeli-Syrian "track" of the regional peace talks (much more than the other tracks) depends on a fragile and often frustrating calculus—in this case, involving geostrategic concerns, Israeli and U.S. domestic politics, the actions of hard-line Islamic organizations in south Lebanon, and Syria's relations with its immediate neighbors and other Islamic powers (notably, Iran).

This study, which was funded in part by the United States Institute of Peace's Grant Program, reflects the Institute's ongoing attention to the various dimensions of conflict in the Middle East. Our objective in sponsoring this work is to provide an extended narrative and examination of the negotiations' course to give analysts and negotiators of a possible new round of Israeli-Syrian peace talks a critical assessment of the approaches that worked—and those that did not—and the domestic and external factors that promoted—and those that hampered—progress on a historic peace agreement between the two countries.

The present work joins a long line of other books published by the Institute's Press that examines the complex interrelationships of the political, social, and ethnic components of the Middle East peace process, including former senior fellow Adnan Abu-Odeh's recently released *Jordanians, Palestinians, and the Hashemite Kingdom in the Middle East Peace Process*, Muhammad Faour's *The Arab World After Desert Storm*, and Mordechai Bar-On's *In Pursuit of Peace: A History of the Israeli Peace Movement*. In addition, the Institute has also examined the vital core of disputes between these peoples at the interpersonal level with the publication of former senior fellow John Wallach's *The Enemy Has a Face: The Seeds of Peace Experience*.

Richard H. Solomon
President
United States Institute of Peace

Preface

The work on this book was made possible through the financial support of two fine institutions: the United States Institute of Peace and the Foundation for Middle East Peace, both in Washington, D.C. The Middle East Institute, also in Washington, D.C., helped to administer both grants. I carried out most of my documentary research in the Alderman Library of the University of Virginia, with the help of the ever-cheerful library staff.

I am very grateful to the above-named institutions, and also to all those individuals in Syria, Israel, and Washington, D.C., who contributed their time and attention to helping push this project forward. Ambassador Walid Moalem, from Washington, and Ambassador Itamar Rabinovich, from Tel Aviv, were both generous in providing their own perspectives on the record of the 1991–96 talks. They both also helped me to set up important interviews with others in their national leaderships. I am particularly grateful for the time and attention that former premier Shimon Peres and Foreign Minister Farouq al-Sharaa gave to answering my questions.

Ambassador Dennis Ross and other serving and former U.S. State Department officials were gracious in their support, and in sharing their insights. Numerous other participants in the talks, and other specialists on the Israel-Syria relationship, also agreed to be interviewed for the project, on or off the record. Professor Moshe Ma'oz, and my fellow scribes Patrick Seale and Ze'ev Schiff, all shared their own expertise, and gave me additional useful ideas on how to push the project further forward. Hosein Agha (from London) and Waddah al-Khatib (here in Charlottesville) gave particular help in the acquisition and translation of materials. I learned a lot from all the people who helped me on the project—those named here and in the text, and those not named—and I am extremely grateful to them.

After I had written a first draft of the text, I benefited greatly from the comments made by Ambassador Samuel W. Lewis, and—as I always do!—from those made by William B. Quandt.

In spite of all the help I have received, none of the above-mentioned individuals or institutions carries any responsibility for the judgments expressed in the text that follows, which must remain my own.

THE
ISRAELI-SYRIAN
PEACE TALKS

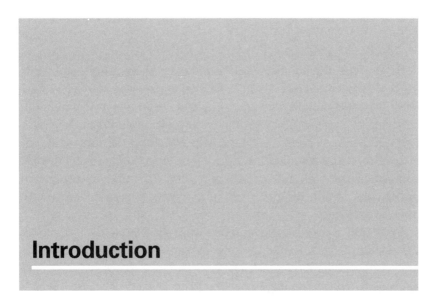

Introduction

What might the Middle East become if Syria and Israel—which have been in a technical state of war since Israel's founding as a modern state in 1948—could reach a stable peace? Obviously, such a transformation would radically improve the strategic situation of both these countries, but the conclusion of a peace agreement on this front could also have much broader positive ramifications throughout the region.

Given Syria's dominant role in Lebanon, it is quite plausible to expect that a Syrian-Israeli peace agreement would be quickly followed by a Lebanese-Israeli peace agreement. That would enable both Lebanon and Israel to heal from the deep traumas caused by Israel's twenty-one-year occupation of a strip of southern Lebanon. In addition, since Egypt and Jordan have already made their peace with Israel, this step would complete the "circle of peace" between Israel and all its neighboring states. For the first time in Israel's modern history, there would no longer be any hostile national armies on its borders. Israel's conflict with the Palestinians might well continue, but this conflict poses no military threat to Israel. Rather, the challenge it poses is the political one of finding a mode of coexistence between the two rival claimants to the Holy Land, and a decent answer to the long-standing claims of the Palestinian refugees. In a situation where Israel and all its Arab-state neighbors are at peace, it may well be easier to find constructive and generous political solutions to this challenge.

Beyond the immediate Israeli-Arab theater, there is also strong evidence that an Israeli peace with Syria might open other doors for Israel in terms of its relations with other major states in the Arab hinterland, particularly Saudi Arabia and the other Gulf monarchies. A Syrian-Israeli peace agreement thus could help transform the strategic situation of the entire Middle East, opening up huge new possibilities for regionwide economic and social development and simultaneously freeing up considerable resources that until now have been tied up in military investments.

Until 1991, people who envisioned what the Middle East might become after the cessation of the state of war between Israel and all the Arab states, or after the conclusion of a Syrian-Israeli peace, perhaps could be accused of daydreaming. But in October of that year, Israel, Syria, and all of Israel's other neighbors sat down together at a peace conference in Madrid, with the avowed aim of reaching final peace agreements among them. Three successive Israeli governments then engaged in bilateral peace talks with Syria. That unprecedented negotiation lasted fifty-two months. It did not get as far as concluding a final peace agreement between the two states, but under Israel's two Labor Party prime ministers of that era, the late Yitzhak Rabin and Shimon Peres, the two sides did break considerable new ground in the effort to build a lasting peace between them. They outlined the main topics that the peace agreement would need to cover. They reached explicit agreement on the aims and principles of a lasting security arrangement between them. They generally concurred on the content of the peace agreement in this sphere of security, as well as in the territorial sphere and in the normalization of political relations, future economic relations, and water—as well as on the linkages among these spheres and the phasing of the successive implementation stages. Among the participants in those talks, and their U.S. sponsors, there was a strong recognition by the end of those fifty-two months that they had achieved a good portion—possibly even considerably more than half—of the work of crafting a final peace agreement.

In March 1996, however, Israeli prime minister Peres abruptly suspended his team's participation in these talks. Shortly afterwards, he was defeated in a general election. His successor, the Likud Party's Benjamin Netanyahu, then refused to resume the peace talks at the point where Peres had suspended them. With Syrian president Hafez al-Assad refusing to resume them at any other point, a three-year hiatus ensued.[1]

As relations between the two countries settled back into a sulky state of no war–no peace, some voices were audible on both sides of the national divide, expressing renewed doubts as to whether a real peace could ever be concluded with the other side. Some of these people—analysts and politicians—tried to base their arguments on the failure of the 1991–96 negotiations: the "fact" that the other side had refused to take that opportunity to make peace just "proved," these people argued, that they did not really want to make peace.

The present study, which is based on interviews with heads of negotiating teams and other actors and analysts in Israel, Syria, and the United States, and on an examination of the documentary record, draws a different conclusion from what happened between 1991 and 1996. Instead of intransigence, this study found a solid (if at times frustratingly slow) record of actual diplomatic progress, as well as an impressive and equally important record of peace-oriented learning on both sides of the national divide. This record placed both countries' leaderships in an excellent position, once peace talks resume, to move toward a speedy and successful conclusion.

In May 1999, Netanyahu was defeated at the polls by Ehud Barak of the Labor-based "One Israel" bloc. Within weeks of Barak's election—and even before he completed the complex, interparty negotiations needed to form his governing coalition—he was signaling a radical new readiness to reengage in the peace talks with Syria. In late June, he gave an interview to the veteran British Syrian-affairs specialist Patrick Seale, in which he stated that, "The only way to build a stable, comprehensive peace in the Middle East is through an agreement with Syria. That is the keystone of peace. My policy is to strengthen the security of Israel by putting an end to the conflict with Syria." Israel's premier-elect used a phrase that Assad himself had coined some years earlier, when he assured Seale that, "I am truly excited to see if there is a possibility to conclude a 'Peace of the Brave' with Syria." And he sent Assad a bouquet of political compliments: "There is no doubt that President Assad has shaped the Syrian nation. His legacy is a strong, independent, self-confident Syria—a Syria which, I believe, is very important for the stability of the Middle East. I see Syria as a pillar opposite us on the other side of the region."[2]

Within days, Seale was in Damascus, where Assad reciprocated Barak's compliments. "I have followed his career and his statements," Assad said of Barak. "He seems to be a strong and honest man. As the election results show, he evidently has wide support. It is clear that he wants to achieve peace with Syria. He is moving forward at a well-studied plan." Assad stressed in this interview that, "It is not a question of starting something new but, rather, now that Netanyahu has gone, of resuming on the basis of what was achieved before."[3] Underscoring his determination to make a fresh start with Israel's new leader, Assad minimized the importance of the indirect contacts he had with Barak's predecessor: "From the moment Netanyahu was elected [in 1996], we realized it was hopeless. Nothing could be done with this man. Many people came to see us with offers of help. . . . After a while we said to them, 'Don't waste your time. It is pointless.'"[4] Thus, in those weeks, Barak and Assad both seemed determined to put the Netanyahu-era stalemate behind them, and to approach the challenge of concluding a Syrian-Israeli peace with renewed commitment and activism.

It was not only with Netanyahu's legacy that Barak was signaling a clear break. His early actions and statements after he assumed office in July indicated that he was also breaking with key parts of the approaches that Rabin and Peres had used toward the Syrian track of the peace talks. Three aspects of Barak's approach, in particular, indicated a break with the precedents established by his Labor predecessors.

First, the speed and clarity with which he acted on this track in his early weeks marked a clear break with the ultracautious, ambiguous way that Rabin had approached the negotiations with Syria during his years as premier from 1992 through his assassination in late 1995—though it is notable that Barak's style did not mark a break with the approach Peres adopted after he succeeded Rabin to the premiership. This apparent discontinuity with the Rabin legacy, and continuity with that of Peres, was all the more striking since Barak was widely recognized as Rabin's chosen political protégé, and always recognized his huge political debt to Rabin.[5]

Second, Barak's stated intention of moving forward simultaneously on all tracks of the peace process marked a clear break with the approach used by both the former Labor prime ministers. At the joint press conference he gave with President Clinton at the end of his inaugural visit to Washington in July 1999, Barak spelled out that, "It is our intention to move the process forward simultaneously on all tracks: bilateral [with] the Palestinians, the Syrians and the Lebanese, as well as the multilateral. We will leave no stone unturned in our efforts to reinvigorate the process."[6] Barak's intention of proceeding simultaneously on all tracks can be seen as naturally linked to the desire for speed in concluding the talks. Rabin's approach of refusing to engage in active negotiations on more than one track at a time was closely linked to the generally slow pace of his negotiations. (This is documented quite fully in chapters 2 through 4.) But moving forward simultaneously on all the key tracks of the talks was also something that Peres, whether through intention or inattention, failed to do during his six months in power. Numerous observers have noted that after Peres opted to give renewed attention to the Syrian track in early November 1995, and moved his main team of negotiators over to that track, he paid insufficient attention to the continued political and diplomatic needs of the Palestinian track—a failure that would cost him dearly in early 1996.

Third, the strong preference for a "command" style of leadership that Barak evinced during his early weeks in office was in clear contrast to Peres's more collegial, more staff-driven approach to leadership—though it looked very similar to the leader-driven way that Rabin had run his side of the negotiations on the Syrian track during his time in office. During the first days after his inauguration, and even before he went to Washington, Barak made a dizzying round of personal visits to the leaders of all his Arab neighbors who would receive him: Egypt's president Hosni Mubarak, the Palestinian Authority's Yasser Arafat, and Jordan's new King Abdullah II. He understood that President Assad was still not ready to receive a personal visit from the head of a state with which Syria was still in a formal state of war—but Barak had already transmitted clear leader-to-leader messages to Assad through Seale, and through at least one telephone call from President Clinton. (At the conclusion of the late-July summit between Barak and Clinton, the U.S. president indicated to reporters that presumably, by prior agreement with Barak, he would again call Assad to update him on the good news from the summit.) In all these actions, Barak was deliberately keeping out of the loop staff members of Israel's foreign and other ministries who had produced such prodigious heaps of paperwork during previous rounds of the peace talks. He was apparently trying to create for himself the opportunity to take speedy and bold decisions in his peace diplomacy with Syria—and unlike Rabin, he was also signaling that he intended to seize the opportunity thus offered.

The primary subject of the present study is the fifty-two-month period of the official talks on the Israeli-Syrian track between 1991 and 1996. This was one of four tracks of bilateral talks between Israel and its Arab neighbors with which it remained in a state of war that were set in motion by the Madrid Peace Conference of late October 1991. (The other tracks were with Lebanon, Jordan, and the Palestinians, with the last of these having some formal linkage, but little connection in practice, with the Jordanian track.)

As noted above, the talks on the Syrian track were unprecedented not only in their taking place, but also in their achievements. The meticulous records that both sides, and the U.S. sponsors, all kept of the points of agreement that had been reached by March 1996 have not yet been made public. Nevertheless, enough of the content of what the parties agreed on has been made public over the years—primarily through leaks within the chronically porous Israeli political elite, including one that was made spectacularly public in June 1995 by then-opposition leader Netanyahu—to indicate the degree of progress that the parties made in key parts of the negotiation. In addition, two of the three men who headed Israel's team throughout the years of these talks, Ambassadors Itamar Rabinovich and Uri Savir, have published memoirs of their participation in the talks on this track.[7]

These memoirs cover the periods when, respectively, Yitzhak Rabin and Shimon Peres were at the helm in Israel. Both authors were notably coy on the important point of how far these Israeli leaders were prepared to withdraw from the occupied Golan Heights in the context of getting satisfaction from Syria in all other areas, as well as on some other important points. Yet they do give a rich picture, from the Israeli point of view, of the tenor, general progress, and main issues discussed in the talks on the Syrian track, while Savir's book also gives some valuable details about the points of agreement reached during the ambitious negotiations that his team conducted during three rounds of talks with Syrian counterparts at the Wye Plantation, from December 1995 through March 1996.

From the Syrian side, the head of the country's negotiating team, Ambassador Walid al-Moalem, gave an unprecedented series of interviews to the *Journal of Palestine Studies* in late 1996, in which he described many important aspects of the talks; these were published early the following year.[8]

The present study builds on these memoirs, as well as on broad documentary research and interviews that the author conducted with those three chief negotiators and with Syrian foreign minister Farouq al-Sharaa; former Israeli premier Shimon Peres; the head of the U.S. "peace team," Ambassador Dennis Ross; and numerous other officials and analysts in Israel, Syria, and the United States.[9] As described in chapter 8, the picture that emerged from this research was one of considerable "learning by doing" in the venture of peacebuilding on both sides of the Israeli-Syrian front line—as well as in Washington, D.C.

In the early months that followed the 1991 Madrid conference, Israel still had a Likud government in power. Throughout those months, Likud's insistence on retaining all, or nearly all, of the territory in Golan that Israel had captured from Syria in 1967 made any peace agreement with Syria impossible. In June 1992, however, Israel's voters brought a Labor government to power, under Prime Minister Rabin. That administration was considerably more favorably disposed than its predecessor to accept that the "land-for-peace" formula mandated by UN Security Council Resolution 242 of 1967 might be applied to the Golan front, as it had been (by an earlier Likud government) to the Sinai front with Egypt. However, despite Rabin's theoretical readiness to entertain a land-for-peace approach with Syria, and despite the considerable understanding he had gained throughout preceding decades of the nuances in Israel's tricky power balance with Syria, he was still not naturally inclined to make any bold or speedy moves on the Syrian track.[10] Nevertheless, by proceeding at a deliberate and measured pace in negotiations with a Syrian leader who was by nature similarly cautious and disinclined to tip his hand, Rabin was able to make substantive progress in the negotiation, and to learn considerably more about the particular sensitivities of his interlocutor and about the broad outlines of what would be possible within any future peace agreement with Syria. Indeed, shortly before his untimely death in 1995, Rabin gave a long television interview in which he revealed a sensitive and realistic understanding of the need for a radical reframing of Israeli attitudes toward Syria, and of the very real benefits that cooperation with Syria could bring to Israel.[11]

The bulk of the present study (chapters 4 through 7) is devoted to the period of negotiations from May 1995 through May 1996. That period started with the successful conclusion (after strong American mediation) of an agreement between the two sides on language for a text concerning the "Aims and Principles of the Security Arrangement." The further progress that the agreement allowed seemed near when the two countries' chiefs of staff met at the end of June 1995 to hold detailed talks on the basis of the agreed text. But rising suspicions inside Israel—fueled by, among other things, Netanyahu's leaking of key army documents—then helped persuade Rabin to put the talks on the back burner, where they still languished when he was killed by an Israeli anti-peace militant four months later.

Rabin was succeeded by his foreign minister and longtime rival for Labor Party leadership, Shimon Peres. There are some indications that when Rabin had put the peace talks with the Syrians on the back burner in late summer 1995, he did so with some thought of holding early elections and then returning to the Syrian track with a renewed mandate for peace. But within days after Rabin was killed, Peres decided to try to reverse the order of these events: He wanted to light a new fire of urgency under the Syrian track and try to bring the talks to a successful conclusion before, rather than after, launching the required election campaign.

It was a bold decision, and one that Peres presumably made on the basis of a full review of what Rabin had already achieved on the Syrian track. Peres also sent urgent messages to Damascus through the United States to ensure that Assad was prepared to join him in the new policy of, as Peres and his advisers put it, "flying high and fast" toward a peace agreement. It is important to note that, in a clear break with the cautious and incrementalist modus operandi that Assad had adopted in the talks until then, he responded very positively to the bold invitation he received from Peres in late 1995.

During the two-and-a-half rounds of intensive, multi-issue talks that the two negotiating teams held at Maryland's Wye Plantation from late December 1995 through early March 1996, the Syrians showed themselves ready to agree to an unprecedentedly broad range of measures in the realms of security arrangements, political normalization, and economic cooperation with Israel—provided that, as they believed the clear trade-off to be, Israel would withdraw its forces to their pre–June 1967 lines. Indeed, through the constructive way that his negotiators performed at Wye, Assad was showing clearly for the first time that he was prepared to proceed to a final peace agreement with Israel even before the Palestinians arrived anywhere close to one, and also that he was prepared for the first time to consider very creative interpretations of Syria's long-standing demands for "balance, reciprocity, and equality" in the design of postpeace security arrangements with Israel. At this negotiation, the U.S. "hosts" played a constructive role as "full participants" in the discussions.

Despite the good intentions of all three parties, Peres's hopes for rapid completion of this negotiation were not crowned with success. Instead, in a series of events reminiscent of a Shakespearean tragedy, Palestinian hard-liners opposed to the Oslo Accords detonated a series of terrorist bombs against primarily civilian targets in Israel in early 1996. The pressure started mounting on Peres from colleagues inside his own party and government—including, notably, then–foreign minister Ehud Barak—to move up the date of elections, deprioritize the Syrian talks once more, and then suspend Israel's participation in the talks completely. On March 4, 1996, this was what Peres finally decided to do.

The weeks that followed Peres's pullout from the talks saw a further dizzying series of developments in the Israeli-Syrian relationship. If Peres had invited Assad to "fly high and fast" toward peace with him in late 1995, after March 4 the relationship between their two governments began to deteriorate rapidly. In a bid to shore up Peres's political position at home, he and the U.S. organized an international conference aimed at demonstrating world support for Israel's fight against terrorism. Unable to do much more to crack down on the Palestinians in the West Bank and Gaza, Peres instead sought to demonstrate his antiterrorist bona fides to Israeli voters by launching yet another in the series of broad assaults against Lebanon that Israel had mounted over the years. Since no reassurance to the contrary came to Damascus—from the United States or anyone else—the Syrians concluded that both these actions were aimed directly against them. It did not help matters that their northern neighbor Turkey chose March 1996 to reveal the existence of a hitherto secret agreement on military cooperation with Israel. Then, in the midst of Israel's massive bombardment of Lebanon in mid-April, an Israeli artillery unit mistakenly targeted a refugee shelter in Kafr Qana, and killed over one hundred civilians of all ages. Syrian television, which just weeks earlier had been airing cautiously optimistic commentaries about the prospects for an imminent peace with Israel, then described Peres as "a killer of children." (Israel's rhetoric against

Syria also had made an intemperate shift during that period.) Peres's decision to launch the April offensive against Lebanon was unsuccessful in bringing about either the desired outcome in Lebanon or his own success at the polls the following month.

The dismal record of those weeks between March and May 1996 seemed to show (as noted in detail in chapter 7) how easy it can be for the dynamics of a high-stakes peacemaking venture to be thrown into a dramatic and damaging reverse gear. Taken together, the period between May 1995 and May 1996 witnessed some of the most dramatic twists and turns of events in the whole fifty-two-month "first act" of Israeli-Syrian peace talks. Can more success be expected from a "second act" led by Barak? At the time of this study's writing, it is still too early to say. Nevertheless, this work has broad relevance for those interested in exploring the dynamics of interstate peacemaking both in this and other parts of the world.

The Syrian-Israeli talks had many features that distinguished them from their better-known counterpart talks on the Palestinian track. For example, since 1974 the Syrians had a stable disengagement agreement with Israel, with whose performance both parties were largely satisfied. Thus, by the time of the 1991 Madrid Conference, it was clear that Syria was interested in concluding only a final-status agreement with Israel rather than any further interim agreements. On the Palestinian track, by contrast, there still remained a strong potential for an interim accord. The Oslo agreement concluded on that track in September 1993 ushered in a series of partial interim steps, while serious engagement in the "final-status" talks was pushed further into the future. In addition, Israel's conflict with Syria is a classic political-military conflict between two established states, while the Israeli-Palestinian conflict is focused more centrally on issues of national identity, national values, and the search for creative formulas of national coexistence than on strictly military questions. A study of the record on the Syrian track can thus provide much rich material concerning such issues as:

▪ the role of leaders in peacemaking;

▪ problems associated with transforming popular attitudes formed through decades of hostility into those more supportive of peace diplomacy;

■ problems associated with conducting diplomacy with an authoritarian interlocutor (as Israel did) or, conversely, with a democratic interlocutor with a highly leak-prone political culture (as Syria did);

■ questions of timing;

■ problems associated with the inevitable intrusion into any bilateral peacemaking effort of other extraneous but politically related conflicts; and

■ the role of a third-party sponsor—in this case, the United States.

This study is prefaced by an opening chapter that locates the Israel-Syria negotiation within the broader peace effort launched at Madrid and provides some essential background on the special features of the Israeli-Syrian conflict. The substantive study of developments in the Israeli-Syrian bilateral talks begins in chapters 2 and 3. Chapters 4 through 7 delve into the events of May 1995 through May 1996 in greater detail. Chapter 8 provides a summary of lessons learned—both those articulated in interviews conducted for this study by former high-level participants in the talks themselves, and those that have become evident through the conduct of the study.

1

The Madrid Conference
and the
Israeli-Syrian Track

MADRID

On October 30, 1991, when Syrian foreign minister Farouq Sharaa sat down at the negotiating table in Madrid, it was the first time that an official from the Syrian Arab Republic had ever, in the forty-three years of Israel's existence as a modern state, sat down openly with Israeli negotiators to discuss a final resolution of the conflict between them. The Madrid conference was also the first occasion in which negotiators from Lebanon and Jordan engaged openly in negotiations with Israel, though various leaders from these countries had participated in clandestine contacts with Israeli officials over the years. From the Israeli side, Madrid marked the first occasion in which any Israeli government agreed to sit down at talks with a delegation openly designated as representing "Palestinians"—though the Palestinian delegation at Madrid was not allowed to claim any open identification with the Palestinian Liberation Organization (PLO), and was present at the table under a formula that made it part of a joint Jordanian-Palestinian team.

The Madrid conference was thus, in many respects, a groundbreaking occasion. Regarding the Israeli-Syrian strand of the peace process that was launched at Madrid, the present chapter will describe what the main issues of contention between them were at that point; what the respective leaders of these two countries represented politically to their publics and what had finally persuaded them to come to the

peace table; the role of the United States in brokering the crucial prenegotiation phase that had brought them to Madrid; and the broader
array of issues at stake within the envisaged negotiation. First, however, it is necessary to set the scene of the Madrid Peace Conference
and describe the broad architecture of the different tracks of peace talks
that were launched there.

The Madrid conference had been convened by the United States,
whose president, George Bush, sat alongside Soviet president Mikhail
Gorbachev at the head of the T-shaped table in the Spanish capital's
ornate Royal Palace. Also sitting at the peace table, along with all those
mentioned, were representatives of Egypt, the only Arab country that
had until then made peace with Israel, and the European Union.

Throughout the day-and-a-half plenary session, each delegation head
delivered one speech. In his presentation President Bush stated, "Our
objective must be clear and straightforward. It is not simply to end
the state of war in the Middle East and replace it with a state of non-
belligerency. . . . Rather, we seek peace, real peace. And by real peace I
mean treaties. Security. Diplomatic relations. Economic relations. Trade.
Investment. Cultural exchange. Even tourism." He called on the Arab
world to show that it was "willing to live in peace with Israel and make
allowances for Israel's reasonable security needs." He also recognized
that "peace must also be based on fairness. In the absence of fairness,
there will be no legitimacy, no stability."[1]

The following day, it was the turn of the Israeli and Arab delegates.
The speech of Israel's seventy-six-year-old prime minister, Yitzhak
Shamir, was studded with rhetoric typical of the Likud Party, of which
he was a historic leader: "To appreciate the meaning of peace for the
people of Israel, one has to view today's Jewish sovereignty in the Land
of Israel against the background of our history. Jews have been perse-
cuted throughout the ages in almost every continent." Where Bush had
made no mention of the territorial aspect of the negotiations, Shamir
referred openly to it: "We know our partners to the negotiations will
make territorial demands on Israel. But, as an examination of the conflict's long history makes clear, its nature is not territorial. It raged well
before Israel acquired Judea, Samaria [the two portions of the Jordan
River's West Bank], Gaza and the Golan in a defensive war. . . . It will be
regrettable if the talks focus primarily and exclusively on territory. It is
the quickest way to an impasse."

Shamir did not hold out the hope of any speedy resolution to his country's long-running conflict with the Arabs. "Today, the gulf separating the two sides is still too wide, the Arab hostility to Israel too deep, the lack of trust too immense, to permit a dramatic, quick solution," he said. "But, we must start on the long road to reconciliation with this first step."[2]

At fifty-three, Syria's chief delegate, Mr. Sharaa, was a generation younger than Shamir, but his performance in Madrid was that of a long-time member of the Ba'th Party, which had ruled Syria since 1963. As Shamir foresaw, Sharaa centered his speech on the need for Israel to pull out of lands it had occupied in 1967. In contrast to Shamir, Sharaa based his argument on modern-day international law, specifically on UN Security Council Resolutions 242 of 1967 and 338 of 1973, "on the basis of which," as he noted, "the peace conference is being convened."

The implementation of these resolutions, Sharaa argued, "should not be the subject of new bargaining during bilateral negotiations. Rather, they should be implemented in all provisions and on all fronts. . . . This means that every inch of Arab land occupied by the Israelis by war and force, the Golan, the West Bank, Jerusalem and the Gaza Strip, must be returned in their entirety to their legitimate owners." He did not spell out what kind of peace Syria might be prepared to offer Israel in return for this withdrawal, hinting only that, "If the objective is truly for the peoples of the region to co-exist, to enjoy security, peace and prosperity, to place their plentiful energies and resources at the service of their . . . development, how can such a desirable objective logically be realized without eliminating occupation and restoring legitimate rights?"[3]

Strong feelings of hostility between Israelis and Syrians were evident inside and outside the plenary chamber. Each side accused the other of falsifying history. At one point, Sharaa held up a "Wanted" poster featuring Shamir, and charging him with terrorism, that had been produced by the British in the era of their pre-1948 rule over Palestine. Binyamin Netanyahu, Israel's deputy foreign minister, countered in a news conference by accusing the Arabs in general of complicity with Hitler, Himmler, Ribbentrop, and Eichmann in planning the Holocaust. He accused Syria of having spoken in terms of "vituperation."[4]

The bad atmospherics between these two parties—and also, to a lesser degree, between Israeli delegates and those from other Arab delegations —augured poorly for the long-term success of the peacemaking venture being launched in Madrid. Another disquieting sign was that even before the end of the first day's speeches, President Bush climbed aboard his plane for the flight home. Veteran *New York Times* correspondent R.W. Apple, Jr., noted that Bush's campaign for reelection twelve months later would effectively begin with a large fund-raiser in Texas later that week. Apple considered it "doubtful" that Bush would want to give sustained attention to the Middle East peace process until after the election, and noted that "without sustained Presidential intervention, a decisive breakthrough in these talks may prove elusive."[5]

Back in Madrid, Bush's able secretary of state, James A. Baker III, stayed on to iron out the numerous remaining problems connected with the peace effort. It was planned that bilateral talks between Israel and each of the Arab delegations would begin within three days—though the location for those encounters had still not been agreed upon when the plenary session opened. It was hoped, too, that multilateral talks on regional issues would get under way shortly after that.

The Americans remained insistent throughout the prenegotiation phase that the negotiations themselves should be conducted separately on a bilateral, face-to-face basis between Israel and each of the other parties involved. (Israel's reluctance to deal directly with the Palestinians was assuaged by wrapping the Palestinians into a joint negotiating team with the Jordanians.) The American insistence on separate, face-to-face negotiations with Israel, which was in line with Israel's long-held preferences, struck directly against the position that Syria had espoused throughout the decades, to the effect that any resolution of the conflict with Israel should be the joint, collaborative venture of a coalition of all relevant Arab states—and one that, preferably, should be conducted through intermediaries or under broader auspices, such as those that the United Nations might provide. Nearly all U.S. officials remained convinced that if the Arab parties approached the diplomacy with Israel jointly, they would be subject to a demagogic, hard-line "lowest common denominator" in their negotiating stance, which would prevent them from ever being able to make real peace, since the concessions on the Arab side that any real peace would require could be made only by each party negotiating with Israel on its own.[6]

Over the years, the Syrians and many others on the Arab side have railed a lot against what they considered to be the divide-and-rule nature of this approach. In a 1998 interview Foreign Minister Sharaa noted that the way his country's negotiators experienced the application of this approach during the post-Madrid diplomacy was "as if each of the Arab parties was in a waiting room, waiting to see the one doctor in town: Each would feel it had to make some concession even to get into the doctor's office, and the party who did get into the office would feel it had to hurry to do its business, because it knew that others were waiting outside."[7] Even though, from this viewpoint, the application of the "separate tracks" approach turned out to be as problematic for the Syrians as they had feared, during the prenegotiation phase, in which the parameters of the Madrid process were established, they did make the concession of agreeing to participate in it on these terms. The Syrians still hoped that effective coordination with the other Arab negotiators could retain some semblance of a common Arab approach, and they still refused to participate in the broader, "regionwide" negotiations over the issues of water, refugees, economic development, and arms control, which they saw as being aimed at normalizing Israel's standing in the region parallel with (but not necessarily dependent on) the pursuit of a final resolution of the Arab-Israeli conflict.

But Syria had agreed to engage in direct, face-to-face talks with the Israelis, starting in Madrid. Who were the Israelis that they would meet with there?

THE ISRAELIS

When Syrian foreign minister Sharaa and Israeli prime minister Shamir encountered each other at the Madrid conference, they represented two political systems that were very different from each other internally but held a number of attitudes in common (although in direct opposition to each other) regarding any future settlement between them. These attitudes included a strong reluctance to concede that any settlement should involve a significant degree of territorial compromise and the need for extreme caution in all stages of approaching any peace agreement.

Israel's political system shares several attributes with the British system, except that the (largely ceremonial) role of the head of state is played in Israel by an elected president, not a monarch. In Israel, the prime minister is undoubtedly the most powerful wielder of executive power. Until 1996, the position of prime minister was filled by nationwide parliamentary elections.[8] A premier's term of office could be terminated by a vote of no confidence within the Knesset (the Israeli parliament) or by the passage of four years since the last general election. In addition, as in Britain, a premier could fine-tune the timing of a reelection bid by calling for new elections at any time prior to the end of her or his full term.

Yitzhak Shamir was born in Poland in 1915. He was considerably more powerful within his political system than the Syrian official whom he would meet in Madrid. By the time he spoke at the peace conference, Shamir had served for more than a year as head of what one pro-Israeli analyst has described as "the most right-leaning government in Israeli history."[9] Before that, he had been Israel's head of government for a few months in 1983–84, and then again from 1986 through 1990. He had been a historic leadership figure in the right-wing, Revisionist movement within the pre-state Jewish community in the area (the *yishuv*), and in the Likud Party that grew out of that movement.

After spending twenty-nine years in opposition in Israel's ever-lively parliamentary system, Likud first came to power in 1977 under another member of the historic leadership, Menachem Begin. In a Nixon-to-China twist of politics, Begin became the first Israeli prime minister to reach a peace agreement with a neighboring Arab state, Egypt. That agreement involved a complete Israeli withdrawal back to the international border and the dismantling of all the settlements Israel had built previously in the occupied zone from which it withdrew—features that Syria would later claim established clear precedents for any future peace agreement on its front.

In the years between 1977 and the convening of the Madrid conference, Likud remained the dominant party in Israeli politics, though between 1984 and 1988 the country's other large secular party, Labor, joined it in a coalition government in which the premiership was rotated between Shamir and Labor's then-leader Shimon Peres. After the elections of 1988, Shamir was strong enough to establish a National Unity Government in which Peres had a much more limited role. But throughout the six years, 1984–90, Labor's other main historic leader, former prime minister Yitzhak Rabin, served in the important position of defense minister. In a significant further twist on this situation, Rabin and Peres had been locked for many years in a bitter rivalry for control of Labor's destiny.[10] By the time the 1992 general elections came around, Rabin would be at the head of the Labor Party.

Throughout the fifty-two months of Israeli-Syrian talks that followed Madrid, the interplay among these three men—all of them major figures in the history of the modern Jewish state—along with Binyamin Netanyahu, the much younger man who would succeed Shamir at the head of Likud, would form the main texture of the domestic political backdrop to Israel's pursuit of a negotiated peace.

THE SYRIANS

On the Syrian side of the table, Farouq Sharaa had been the foreign minister in Damascus since 1984. In that position, he was a trusted representative of, and always answerable to, Syria's very hands-on president, Hafez al-Assad.

Assad was born in 1930, in the northwest Syrian village of Qardaha. In the two decades after he seized power in September 1970, he brought to Syria a degree of internal and external stability that was unprecedented in modern times.[11] Internally, those decades were marked by the increasing consolidation of a ruling coalition made up of four broad sociopolitical strands. The first of these was the membership of the Alawite Muslim community from which Assad's own family stemmed, and which makes up something under 15 percent of the Syrian population. The second was the Syrian military establishment, inside which Assad had received much of his effective political education. Before seizing power he had been a professional, though increasingly political, air force officer: He served as defense minister (including during the 1967 war), and later as commander of the air force. The third strand of the coalition was the broad stratum of men and women of peasant or lower-class urban background whose communities and lives had been modernized and, in the view of many of them, significantly improved as a result of the continuing economic development efforts undertaken by Assad and those who worked with him at the head of the Arab Socialist Ba'th (Renaissance) Party. And the fourth strand was the group of predominantly Sunni Muslim, predominantly Damascus-based, merchants who controlled much of the country's internal and external trade. This latter group assumed increased political importance after a bloody conflict against armed insurgents from the Sunni community, which forms a strong numerical majority within the Syrian population, was brought forcefully to an end in 1982.[12]

By 1991 significant portions of each of these strands had been knit together within the Ba'th leadership. The decision Assad had made a year previously, to contribute troops to the American-led coalition fighting against a sister Arab nation, Iraq, was certainly a controversial one in the context of his and the Ba'th Party's long-standing adherence to the concept of Arab unity. He weathered that controversy with seeming ease. But after the American-led coalition had forced Iraq to withdraw from Kuwait, a clear majority of Syrians seemed to subscribe to the general feeling that now it was time for Washington to repay Syria for its loyalty to the coalition by supporting its demand for speedy implementation of the long-standing UN resolutions on the Golan front and the rest of the Arab-Israeli theater. These resolutions, like those pertaining to Iraq and Kuwait, were all firmly grounded in the principle of the "inadmissibility of the acquisition of territory by force."

Externally, the first two decades of Assad's rule had brought increased stability to Syria's relations with many of its neighbors—including Israel. In 1973, Assad demonstrated the strides he had made in repairing the faults in the Syrian military that had been so glaring in 1967: He joined with Egypt's president Anwar Sadat in launching the surprise attack on Israel whose early hours were so successful. He then showed his ability to react politically to setbacks on the battlefield and to use political and diplomatic means to convert the kudos the surprise attack had given him into a disengagement with Israel. The disengagement stabilized Syria's front line against Israel, and also ensured the support of both superpowers for the continuity of his rule in Damascus. Assad achieved these limited military and political successes at the price of an increased reliance on the Soviet Union—but also by demonstrating, through his participation in U.S. secretary of state Henry Kissinger's shuttle diplomacy, that he understood the reality of the United States' preponderance of power in the eastern Mediterranean.

In the context of the post-1973 diplomacy Assad also, for the first time, expressed Syria's clear acceptance of UN Security Council Resolution 242, which mandated recognition of Israel and the conclusion of peace with it in exchange for Israeli withdrawal from occupied lands. Thus, from December 1973 on, Assad had clearly removed Syria from the group of Arab states that remained rejectionist toward the idea of recognizing and making peace with Israel.

When President Sadat engaged in his unilateral quest for peace with Israel from 1977 on, however, Assad was bitterly critical, judging that by acting alone, Sadat had undercut both his own negotiating position and that of all the other Arab parties to the conflict with Israel. When Sadat was killed by a group of hard-line Islamic activists in 1981, it underlined for Assad how risky the process of making peace with Israel might be. (U.S. secretary of state Warren Christopher would later tell an interviewer that during his long negotiating sessions with Assad, the Syrian president "frequently talked to me at length about precisely how the Sadat negotiations [with Israel] had gone and what he had got, and there seemed to me that he had built a threshold there that he felt he must—. He never said I need a better deal, but I think that was a kind of floor for him.")[13]

Throughout the decades that followed the 1974 Syrian-Israeli disengagement agreement, Israeli analysts and policymakers gained a healthy respect for President Assad's ability to keep the Golan front incident-free. His cooperation with the disengagement regime by no means signaled the definitive ending of the conflict between the two states. But now, instead of continuing to confront each other directly over Golan, they continued their contest for broad regional influence through a series of shadow contests waged in arenas that both of them considered in some sense subsidiary to their own higher-order contest. These arenas included Lebanon, the Palestinian communities spread throughout the countries of the eastern Mediterranean, and to a lesser extent Jordan. (In addition to always remaining keenly involved with developments in these three arenas, President Assad and his diplomats also remained attentive to developments in relations with their other two neighbors: Turkey and Iraq. Both of these relationships were plagued with deep-seated problems. One strategy Assad developed after 1978 to help deal with them was to build a strong relationship with the Islamic Republic of Iran, which also bordered both Iraq and Turkey. This link with Iran remained robust, notwithstanding strong continuing differences between Damascus and Teheran on internal issues like the role of religion in society, or external questions like the Arab-Israeli peace process.)

Of all of the shadow contests between Syria and Israel, that in Lebanon was by far the bloodiest, claiming many thousands of lives between 1976 and 1991.[14] By 1991 a rough and unstable balance of power obtained between the two big neighbors inside Lebanon. Israel kept a troop presence in most of the area south of a Tyre–Kiryat She-mona line as well as in a salient of Lebanon reaching up the southern reaches of its portions of Mount Hermon. Syria meanwhile kept a troop presence in most of the northern two-thirds of the country, and exercised effective political control over the central government in Beirut. It also gave some support to (and exercised some control over the supply lines of) the armed Lebanese movements resisting Israel's continued presence in south Lebanon. These movements were spear-headed by the predominantly Shiite Muslim activists of Hezbollah, which by 1991 had eight elected representatives in the Lebanese parlia-ment and was also represented in the Lebanese government.

By 1991 many Lebanese had come to resent the frequently heavy hand with which the Syrian military exercised its influence over their country. But many, including a good proportion of those who also re-sented Syrian excesses, had come to the conclusion that some form of continued Syrian presence in their country was still needed to prevent any resumption of the broad-scale, internal civil-military disorder that had been an ever-present (and a too frequently realized) threat to their communities and their country since 1975.[15] And many had come to the conclusion, with a greater or lesser degree of reluctance, that President Assad and his advisers had played Syria's hand in Lebanon and the region quite skillfully.

Throughout the Israeli-Syrian peace talks that grew out of the Madrid conference, there was continued tension in south Lebanon. This involved Israeli troops directly, and Syrian troops more indirectly, and frequently threatened to break into a broader regional confrontation. That tension, and the various pacification efforts that sought to dampen it, formed an important backdrop to developments at the peace table.

THE AMERICANS

The Madrid peace conference opened almost exactly eight months after the resounding victory of the U.S.-led coalition in Operation Desert Storm. When President George Bush spoke at Madrid, U.S. leadership of the international community was at an unprecedented high point. Domestically Bush was still benefiting from the political aftereffects of the battlefield victory, and riding high in the American polls (though his administration's poor performance on economic issues was already starting to erode that popularity).

In the minds of George Bush and his advisers, as of political leaders throughout the Middle East, there was always a clear link between that victory and the convening of the subsequent peace conference. In the victory speech that Bush delivered to a joint session of Congress on March 6, 1991, immediately after the liberation of Kuwait, he declared loud and clear that he intended to take advantage of the new balance in the Middle East by using American influence to effect a lasting Arab-Israeli peace. "We must work," he told the assembled lawmakers, "to create new opportunities for peace and stability in the Middle East. . . . We must do all that we can to close the gap between Israel and the Arab states and between Israelis and Palestinians."[16]

The decision that President Bush made to commit his administration to a major new effort to restart and complete all the outstanding business of Arab-Israeli peacemaking was a bold one—especially since, even in March 1991, his domestic political advisers already must have been starting to sketch out plans for the reelection bid that would start in earnest later that same year. Secretary of State James A. Baker III, who had made his name in Republican Party politics through years of tireless political organizing and offering astute political advice, surely must have been aware of these considerations. He was also well aware, from the two years he had spent in the State Department thus far, that achieving a comprehensive Middle East peace would not be easy. But by March 1991, he was, according to his memoir of the time, eager to give the task a try:

> The collapse of my first effort at peace-process diplomacy in the spring of 1990 had left me disappointed and somewhat resigned to the conclusion that there was little hope for progress in the foreseeable future. . . . My own assessment, however, had been fundamentally altered by the war [against Iraq]. As a practical matter, I felt we would be properly criticized if we didn't undertake a renewed effort. In putting together the diplomatic and military coalition against Iraq, I had repeatedly pledged that the United States would address the larger issues of the Middle East after the crisis had been resolved. . . . We had tremendous strength and credibility around the world, and stood at the zenith of our influence in the Middle East. I believed it was time to seize the moment. If we hesitated, we would lose an historic opportunity.[17]

The road that Bush and Baker had to travel to bring the parties to the peace table was not an easy one. In consultation with peace-process czar Dennis Ross and his other advisers, Baker devised the multiple-track structure referred to earlier. One central trade-off within this structure was that between the Israeli-Palestinian track on the one hand, and all the other bilateral tracks on the other. (The peacemaking structure would also, as we have seen, include multilateral talks on various regionwide issues.)

Baker's concept of this trade-off concerned the value of what he termed "parallel reciprocity," which he saw as a way to deal with the fact that if peace were ever to be achieved, all the national leaders involved would have to make concessions that would be hard for their national publics to swallow. Recognizing that the decision makers and publics in the Arab countries considered that they had a strong interest in the resolution of the Palestinian problem, he wrote, "The Arabs would have to justify any moves toward Israel by pointing to Israeli flexibility toward the Palestinians. Similarly, the Israelis would have to put any concessions to the Palestinians in the context of a larger reconciliation with Arab states. Moreover, neither side would be willing to move first. Parallel reciprocal steps, I believed, was the logical solution to this impasse."[18]

Immediately after Bush's March 1991 speech to Congress, Baker started traveling around the Middle East, trying to line up the participants in the envisaged peace process. In a mid-March visit to Israel, Prime Minister Shamir took Baker aside after a social dinner, and pulled from his files a letter that President Gerald Ford had sent then–prime minister Rabin back in September 1975. In it, Ford had promised the Israelis that in planning any future peace settlement between Syria and Israel, the United States "would give great weight to Israel's position that any remaining peace agreement with Syria must be predicated on Israel remaining on the Golan Heights." As Baker recalled it, he then asked his host, "What if there were American troops up there?" Shamir then, as Baker wrote, "paused for a moment, as if he were startled by this notion. 'Then it would be different,' he said."[19]

Baker had for some time been of the view that the Syrians were an important part of any Middle Eastern coalition—whether one convened for war, or one for peace. In September 1990, after President Assad signaled his readiness to join the anti-Iraq coalition, Baker decided to pay a visit to Damascus to meet him—in spite of objections to the idea from Dennis Ross that Baker was later to recall as "vehement" and "adamant." Despite Ross's reasoning, as Baker wrote,

> I felt that the symbolic importance of Syrian participation [in the war coalition] was far more crucial than their literal presence. With Syria represented, the credibility of our Arab coalition partners was immeasurably strengthened. But I had a more long-term purpose in mind. There was no way to move a comprehensive Mideast peace process forward without the active involvement of Syria. . . . I also knew that President Bush was anxious to engage the Syrians.[20]

In the eight months of difficult diplomacy that it took to convene the Madrid conference, Baker continued to give considerable weight to the value of Syria's contribution to the nascent peace process, despite the fact that Syria remained on the lists of those states deemed by the U.S. government to be involved in sponsorship of terrorism and narcotics trafficking. (Syria's generally low standing in the American body politic stood in stark contrast to the strength of Washington's relationship with Israel, which was buttressed by generous aid flows, close strategic and diplomatic coordination, and an active pro-Israeli lobby in Washington.) Baker's insistence on keeping Syria within the emerging peace process did not, however, prevent him from threatening a number of times, in Damascus as in all the other regional capitals that he visited, to leave the "dead cat" of diplomatic failure on his host's doorstep if that was where he felt it belonged.

During those months of prenegotiation, probably the most difficult set of issues that Baker had to resolve were those connected with the Palestinian issue—including the tricky question of Palestinian representation. But finding modalities under which the Syrians and Israelis would agree to talk to each other was also problematic in many respects. In addition, all of Baker's negotiations with Israel over the peace process were paralleled by an increasingly bitter set of disagreements over the terms under which the United States would provide guarantees for large loans Israel wanted to take out to help absorb the hundreds of thousands of new Soviet Jewish immigrants. Bush and Baker were both determined that these funds (which were in addition to the more than $3 billion a year in outright grants that was Israel's norm in the U.S. foreign aid budget) should not be used in any way to subsidize the Shamir government's continued building of Israeli settlements in occupied Arab lands. But Shamir was confident of the support his lobbyists had lined up in the Democratic-controlled U.S. Congress: For many months he resisted the administration's request that in return for U.S. provision of the loan guarantees he agree to stop construction in the settlements. By late September Bush and Baker were proposing that the congressional vote needed on this issue be postponed for a further 120 days; and on October 2, Congress voted for this postponement. "Some said it was only the second time that AIPAC [the American Israel Public Affairs Committee, the main pro-Israeli organization] had ever been defeated on a legislative initiative," Baker later wrote.[21]

In the end, Baker brought off the feat of convening the Madrid conference only by supplying each of the invitees with private letters of assurance from the U.S. administration, along with their more public letters of invitation.[22] In the case of Syria, it was not until October 16 that Baker was finally able to win Assad's agreement to a set of modalities under which the Syrian leader would agree to Syria's participation in the conference. As previously noted, these modalities did not include any expectation from Washington that Syria would be expected to take part in the multilateral talks any time soon.[23] While visiting Syria, Baker also discussed the venue of the upcoming conference with his host. Assad was "not enthusiastic" about Baker's favored choice, The Hague, and preferred Switzerland. Finally, Baker suggested Madrid or Lisbon, and Assad agreed to the first of these. "I knew we finally had a compromise," Baker wrote, "because Madrid was on the list of acceptable venues given to us by the Israelis."[24]

The following day, Baker was meeting Shamir in Israel: "With Assad's participation now assured, Shamir's alternatives were effectively closed off. Unless the Palestinians gave him an eleventh-hour reprieve, Shamir could not say no. Now it was either yes or my dead cat."[25] It turned out to be "yes."

THE ISSUES IN GOLAN

The front-scene action in October 1991 may have been in Madrid, but the core theater over which Israel and Syria have long contended is the half-egg–shaped piece of land that is the Israeli-occupied Golan. A quick drive around Golan can show why this area, spanning roughly seventy kilometers north to south, and twenty-five kilometers east to west at its widest point, lies at the center of the strategic balance in the eastern Mediterranean.

Most of the occupied area is taken up by a broad fertile plateau that slopes gently up from an elevation of three hundred meters above sea level in the south to about twelve hundred meters near the north. The northeastern tip of the zone soars much higher, a further one thousand meters skyward up the southwestern slopes of Mount Hermon (Jebel al-Shaikh). Along most of its roughly straight western side, the Golan is marked by precipitous descents from the plateau, down steep ravines or straight cliffs towards the Upper Jordan Valley or, in the southwest, to the shore of Israel's Lake Tiberias, which lies two hundred meters below sea level. The international border established in 1923 between Syria and then-Palestine (now Israel) lies generally along the bottom of those descents.

From almost any point along the western edge of the plateau, a visitor can look further west across Lake Tiberias or the Jordan Valley, over to the hills of (Israeli) Upper Galilee or the mountainous part of south Lebanon called Jebel Amel. The northern edge of occupied Golan abuts directly onto the strip of Lebanese land that has been occupied by Israel since 1978. If you travel along the eastern side of occupied Golan, near the rusty barbed wire of the disengagement line established in 1974, you can peek easily into nearby villages and towns that are under Syrian control. From certain higher points in the northeast, on a clear day, you can look deeper into Syria—to the capital city, Damascus, fifty kilometers away, or even further north. Or, if you take the road that snakes up Golan's southern boundary from Lake Tiberias to Hammat Gader (home of the biblical Gadarene swine), it seems that at every hairpin bend you risk plunging into the precipices on the other side of the Yarmouk Gorge—all of which belong to Jordan.

The Israeli military seized this area from Syria in a stunningly successful military operation in the Arab-Israeli War of June 1967.[26] In December 1981, the Israeli Knesset voted to annex Golan to Israel, but in the years since then no other state except Micronesia has accepted the validity of that action.[27] For the rest of the world's governments, Israel's status in Golan is still formally that of a "belligerent occupying power," as defined by the Geneva Conventions of 1949. These governments (including the United States) remain committed to the proposition that UN Security Council Resolution 242 of 1967 requires Israel to return occupied land on this front, as on others, to its recognized sovereign owner—in this case, Syria—in return for Syria recognizing and assuring Israel's peace and security.

The strategic importance of Golan to both Israel and Syria has never been in doubt. Prior to June 1967, Israeli officials complained that Syrian gunners perched atop the five-hundred-meter-high escarpments on the plateau's western edge frequently fired on Israeli farmers as they culti- vated land in the Jordan Valley or drained the marshes of the area's for- mer Lake Huleh. What these officials revealed less often was that the Israeli farmers in question were often carrying arms as they worked, in contravention of the 1949 Armistice Agreement that mandated the demilitarization of all areas from which Syrian forces had voluntarily withdrawn.

Israeli General Arye Shalev, who from 1949 through 1952 represented Israel in the Israeli-Syrian Mixed Armistice Commission (ISMAC), has written of the period during which the armistice regime remained intact (1949–67) that

> contrary to the prevailing Israeli view—both countries, and not only Syria, were to blame for the tension and violent clashes. Israel was not always the innocent lamb and Syria not always the wolf. In the first years of the armistice regime it was Israel that tried unilaterally to effect changes in the status quo in the [demilitarized zone]. Syria responded violently.[28]

This demilitarized zone (DMZ)—which in reality is a string of four separate strips and chunks of land, totaling around sixty square kilo- meters—lies *to the west of* the 1923 international border. It comprises those tiny areas of pre-1948 Palestine that the Syrian-controlled forces were able to enter and hold on to in the Arab-Jewish fighting of that year. In the years between 1949 and 1967, civilians from both sides moved into or retained homes and cultivable areas within the DMZ, and there emerged a form of de facto partition of the zone between the two countries where Israel exercised firmer control over around 75 per- cent of it, mainly in the north, and Syria exercised control over the re- mainder, mainly in the south. It is that informal line of partition within the DMZ (but still slightly west of the international border) that has been referred to as "the line of June 4, 1967."[29]

From the Syrians' point of view, the main strategic sensitivity of Golan stems from its closeness to their capital, Damascus, and from the sheer height of the Israeli positions on Mount Hermon, which enables any forces deployed there to dominate the southern and western approaches to Damascus, and to peer forward with radar and other sensing devices into virtually all of the Syrian interior.

The advantages to Israel of occupying Golan were amply demonstrated in the Arab-Israeli War of October 1973.[30] Syria and Egypt had launched that war in hopes of regaining lands lost to Israel six years earlier, and they were able to achieve a large measure of strategic surprise.[31] Notwithstanding that surprise, the strength of Israel's position at the start of the war enabled it to absorb and contain Syria's first assault, and later to launch counterpunches against vital installations in Damascus, along Syria's Mediterranean coast, and elsewhere deep in the Syrian interior. After the Egyptian front had stabilized, Israel pushed forward on the ground in Golan substantially beyond the line it had retreated from, and posed an immediate threat to Damascus. In the diplomacy that followed, Secretary of State Henry Kissinger secured a disengagement agreement that pushed Israel's front line a little further west from the cease-fire line and mandated strict new limitations on the forces each side could deploy along each side of a new UN-controlled "disengagement of forces" zone. After the withdrawal, Israel remained in control of nearly all the area it had occupied in 1967, except for the town of Quneitra.

In addition to its military importance, Golan has two other attributes of key significance in any attempt at Israeli-Syrian peacemaking: its hydrology and its demography.

Hydrologically, successive Israeli governments have pointed to the extreme importance to ensure their control over the headwaters of the Jordan River, many of which rise in or run through the occupied area of Golan. In addition, Israel uses Lake Tiberias (the biblical Sea of Galilee, also known in Hebrew as Lake Kinneret) as a strategic reservoir for its National Water Carrier system, which pumps water from the lake for use in irrigation projects throughout the country, including in the traditionally arid Negev. If, in the context of a peace agreement, Syria regains all of its land up to the international border established in 1923, it would then regain control over a substantial portion of the headwaters of the Jordan and all the terrain reaching to ten meters from the waterline around nearly all the northeast quadrant of Lake Tiberias. A return to the June 4, 1967, line would give Syria, in addition, nearly the entire southeast quadrant of lakeshore, which was included in one of the areas of the pre-1967 DMZ.

The sensitivity of hydrological considerations was strongly demonstrated in the mid-1960s, when a joint Syrian-Jordanian attempt to divert some of the headwaters of the Jordan into the Yarmouk River, south of Lake Tiberias, prompted Israel to fire on the earth-moving equipment being employed. A Syrian plan to continue the diversion efforts was then cited by Israel as one of the causes of the tension that led to the 1967 war.[32] It need hardly be added here that Syria, too, considers its access to the region's relatively generous water supply as important, not least in supporting the reestablishment of Syrian agriculture and other economic activities in Golan after Israel's withdrawal.

The principles of international law and custom give considerable weight to the interest of downstream riverine states in being assured sufficient access to waters on which they depend. However, these principles never give downstream states the right simply to occupy the land of upstream nations in order to ensure such access; and numerous attempts have been made throughout the decades to devise principles for the equitable sharing of the Jordan Basin system among the riverine states.[33]

Demographically, the occupied area's current civilian population comprises roughly equal numbers (about 16,000 each) of Jewish Israeli settlers and Syrian nationals whose families remained in their homes after 1967. These Syrians, who are nearly all of the Druze faith, are clustered in five villages in the far north of the occupied area, on the slopes of Jebel al-Shaikh. The Israeli settlers are spread out in thirty-two settlements throughout the whole of the occupied area. In addition to their pursuit of other activities, the settlers farm many of the rich cultivable lands atop the plateau that until 1967 were farmed by residents of the Syrian towns and villages there.

Prior to 1967, this area contained two Syrian towns (Quneitra and Feeq), 107 villages, and 128 of what Syrian demographers have described as "farms and hamlets." Amidst the turmoil of the Syrian army's collapse in 1967, nearly all the residents of the plateau (unlike those of the five mountain villages) fled their homes; and, according to accounts of the time, the rest of the plateau residents were expelled. After hostilities ceased, Israel prevented these displaced persons, who numbered about 140,000, from effecting any return to their homes and farms. To this end, farmlands, grazing areas, and access routes were sown with landmines, and most of the villages were demolished; their sad remains can be seen in many parts of Golan to this day. One Syrian demographer has estimated that by early 1998, the displaced and their descendants had come to number over 500,000.[34] Syrian policy (backed up by international humanitarian law) reserves for the displaced Golanis the right to return to their homes and lands in the context of a peace settlement.

As early as July 1967, however, the Israeli authorities started building paramilitary settlements in the occupied area. In the decades since then, many of those settlements have assumed an almost totally civilian character. Many of the families of Golan's Israeli residents have come to feel some ownership for the homes, farms, and businesses that they have built up there over the years. In 1993–96, activists who claimed to speak for all the Golan settlers expressed their strong opposition to any Israeli withdrawal from the area. Building a nationwide support network under the name of the Third Way movement (later a political party), these settlers became a powerful political force in the Israel of that period. In the elections of 1996, however, some 50 percent of Golan's Israeli residents voted for Labor leader Shimon Peres, who was known to favor a substantial or even full Israeli withdrawal from Golan, while only 17 percent voted for Third Way.[35] In the elections of 1999, an even higher proportion of Golan settlers voted for Labor, and Third Way lost all four of the Knesset seats it had won in 1996.

In spite of this potentially encouraging showing for the pro-peace forces amongst the settlers, untangling the demographic aspects of the conflict over Golan will remain an important part of the broader effort to build peace between Israel and Syria.

THE STAKES BEYOND GOLAN

As the Israeli and Syrian leaderships approached their encounter in Madrid, were they going there just to try to find a solution for their immediate territorial dispute over Golan? Or was each party also coming to the peace conference to negotiate about far more than that?

It is easy to provide an immediate "yes" to the latter question, since it was probably clear in the minds of all participants in Madrid that no resolution of Israel's continuing security problems in south Lebanon would be possible in the absence of a Syrian-Israeli agreement. Over the decades since 1948, Israeli governments had made numerous attempts to reach out to the government in Beirut behind the backs of the Syrians, in what was called a "Lebanon first" strategy. Those efforts acquired a special urgency after 1982, when Prime Minister Menachem Begin and Defense Minister Ariel Sharon launched a punishing invasion of one-third of Lebanon—and left Israel's forces overextended and subject to continual attacks from nationalist guerrillas. But all attempts to win a "Lebanon first" agreement, including even the formal peace agreement that Prime Minister Begin concluded with Lebanese president Amin Gemayel on May 17, 1983, rapidly fell victim to the stark fact of Syria's superiority over Israel in Lebanon in being able (and willing) to wield effective political influence over that war-torn country. In 1989, the agreement reached in Ta'ef, Saudi Arabia, under which Lebanon's government formally came to accept the terms of its "special relationship" with Damascus, received support not only from the vast majority of Arab states but also from the United States and other major international actors. Therefore, by 1991 it should have been as clear to Shamir as to all the other participants in Madrid that there was little hope of using this new peace process to try to revive the "Lebanon first" strategy, and that the talks with Syria had at least one important potential dimension well beyond the Golan.[36]

From the Syrian point of view, there were, in addition, considerable hopes and expectations that the influence they could wield in the peace process would extend considerably further than just Lebanon. Syria's official rhetoric had for a long time stressed the need for a "comprehensive," as opposed to piecemeal, approach to Arab-Israeli peacemaking. This was evident, for example, in Foreign Minister Sharaa's speech at Madrid, which gave greater space to its references to Palestinian and Lebanese issues than that devoted to "purely" Syrian issues. The emphasis that Syrian governments had continuously accorded pan-Arab issues, even through periods when rival Syrian politicians have disagreed strongly on all other aspects of the country's governance and orientation, has led some analysts to suggest that pan-Arabism is in some way a core component of "Syrianness."[37]

As the diplomacy unfolded in the years after Madrid, considerable tension developed between Syria's hopes for some form of effective coordination with (or, perhaps, veto power over) the actions of the other Arab delegations and the aspirations of those other Arab governments and parties themselves. By July 1994, both the PLO and Jordan had, separately, made their own decisions to eschew any coordination with

Syria and go it alone in their negotiations with Israel. However, Syria did manage to retain a significant degree of coordination in its diplomacy with other actual and potential Arab parties to the peace process. These included, of course, Lebanon; Palestinian opposition elements that could potentially influence or pose a threat to Yasser Arafat's representation of the Palestinians; and significant state actors in the Arab hinterland. These state actors included both Egypt and Saudi Arabia, the latter being a crucial regional power with whose leaders Assad enjoyed numerous long and productive ties.

Given the strategic weight of Saudi Arabia within the Middle East, Syria's ties with it (and with the five smaller Gulf Cooperation Council countries) were often seen as one of the big stakes that the Syrian negotiators brought with them to the negotiating table—whether they were openly laid on the table or not. The Syrians liked to present themselves, however discreetly, as providing a crucial potential key with which Israel could one day unlock its hitherto blocked relationship with the rich Arab hinterland. In this, they ran into some competition from the Palestinians, who also liked to hint that they could provide the key in question. But in 1991, because of its participation in Operation Desert Storm, Damascus was certainly in a better position than the Palestinians to claim that the "key to good relations with Saudi Arabia" was an asset that *it* brought to the table; and this asset was to remain somewhat firmly in Syrian hands from then on.

From the Israeli side, it is probably fair to say that many in Likud did not ascribe much value to good relations with Saudi Arabia and the rest of the Arab hinterland. Once Likud was replaced with Labor, this asset acquired more negotiating value. Eitan Haber, the longtime Rabin intimate who coordinated all the different tracks of the peace process on his old friend's behalf, has said that "Yitzhak Rabin understood immediately that the Syrians are the key to a comprehensive peace, including with Saudi Arabia and with Iraq, even though he understood elsewhere in the world, the peace with the Palestinians would have most meaning."[38]

Even under Likud, however, it was clear that any productive negotiation on the Syrian track was about considerably more than just the Golan plus south Lebanon. Indeed, for Likud in 1991, the negotiation was not even really about the Golan at all, since most Likud leaders,

including Shamir, remained steadfastly opposed to considering undertaking any significant withdrawal from the Syrian front whatsoever.
Instead of "land for peace," their slogan in those days was frequently
"peace for peace."

Assuring military security in a region where Israel had spent its first
three decades totally surrounded by enemy nations has always been a
crucial dimension of Israeli national leadership, and security was almost
certainly the key criterion against which any Israeli government, and
the Israeli people, would judge any future peace agreement with Syria.
By 1991 Israel's military planners were facing a situation in which the
peace on the long front with Egypt, buffered as it was by broad DMZs
in Sinai, had proved durable for twelve years already. The military situation along Israel's security frontier with Jordan along the Jordan Valley
had been stable since late September 1970, including during the Arab-
Israeli War of 1973; and that stability was buttressed by numerous security agreements that had been concluded informally between the two
governments over the years. On the Golan front, thanks to the disengagement agreement, things had been quiet since 1974. In April 1995,
Yitzhak Rabin was to say, "I wish all the lines separating us from the
Arab states were as quiet as the line between us and the Syrians on the
Golan Heights."[39] With the Golan front quiet, the only immediate
threats to the safety of Israeli soldiers (and civilians) in late 1991 arose
from their presence in the occupied Palestinian and southern Lebanese
territories. And neither of those threats ever came close to posing any
significant, let alone existential, military challenge to the security of the
Jewish state.

The major existential military threat that Israel still faced in late 1991
was, in the view of most Western and many Israeli defense planners,
the threat that long-distance missiles carrying either nonconventional
or high-tech conventional warheads might one day be launched against
it from either a neighboring or a more distant state. During Operation
Desert Storm, the Iraqis showed that they indeed had both the capability (albeit fairly rudimentary) and the will to launch such an attack.
And though at the military level Israel showed it was well able to absorb
that strike, the experience that most Israelis had of cowering for long
hours in sealed rooms wearing gas masks was a very traumatic one.
That national political trauma, combined with the paralysis the Israeli

economy suffered as a result of the repeated missile warnings, under-scored to Israel's defense planners the gravity of the damage that such a missile attack could pose to their nation.

One of Israel's responses was to step up (with considerable American help) its attempt to find technical ways to "kill" incoming missiles before they struck. Another response from many Israeli defense intellectuals was to increase their openness to exploring whether indeed a political-diplomatic agreement might now be possible with Syria.[40] For if the victorious Gulf War allies could succeed through the sanctions and demilitarization regime they had imposed on Iraq in stripping it of any effective long-distance missile capability, then Syria would remain the only major state in a formal state of war with Israel that still possessed such a capability. Meanwhile, the Iraqi missile attacks of the Gulf War had also shown that mere possession of a territorial buffer, like that in Golan, could do nothing to prevent the launching or ferocity of such an attack.

If many of Israel's defense intellectuals were starting to think in this way by 1991, it certainly did not mean that Prime Minister Shamir and his government were also thinking in that way, although given Yitzhak Rabin's long-standing ties to the Israeli General Staff, it probably did mean that such rethinking was starting to reach his ears. Shamir, like Begin and Peres before him, was far from a military man. In Shamir's case, the many long years he had spent as a key undercover operative in the Israeli Mossad secret service left him with a fairly Machiavellian view of world affairs but few close connections with the country's military.

Syria's significance as the only neighboring state with which Israel remained in a state of war, and which retained significant military capabilities, could not have escaped anyone's attention in Israel. Neither, therefore, can the potential military benefits of reaching a peace agreement with Syria go unnoticed. In addition, Syria could almost certainly bring Lebanon with it into any postpeace relationship with Israel. Thus, since Jordan had not posed any military threat to Israel for such a long time, the prospect of reaching peace with Syria brought with it the prospect of finally completing "the circle of peace" with all of Israel's neighbors. The only hard question that remained for Israel's leaders was *at what price* could this peace be obtained? When he went to Madrid, Shamir still seemed unwilling to pay any significant price in terms of a withdrawal in Golan. But even in his rhetoric, he admitted that the prospect of a peace with Syria had some value.

For both sides, therefore, the stakes on the table when they met in Madrid were considerably broader than Golan. The way each side would define those stakes would change during the course of their encounter.

But at least, in late 1991, they had finally agreed to talk.

2

From Shamir to Rabin

STALEMATE UNDER SHAMIR

On November 3, 1991, a Syrian delegation headed by veteran diplomatist Muwaffaq al-Allaf sat down as planned for bilateral talks with an Israeli delegation headed by Shamir's hard-line office head, Yossi Ben-Aharon. Meeting in Washington, D.C., the two teams then proceeded to talk with—or rather at—each other for the next five hours. The Syrians' core position was that they wanted to conduct the talks from the starting point that UN Resolutions 242 and 338 both mandated a full Israeli withdrawal from occupied Golan, whereas the Israelis refused to deal first with the territorial issue but sought to identify other smaller steps that could build confidence before any discussion of territory.[1] For his part, Secretary Baker was quoted as commenting, "We're encouraged that the talks took place at all. . . . No one walked out in the conference or the bilateral."[2]

Back in the Middle East, meanwhile, the Israelis were taking steps which seemed clearly to signify that they were not putting all their eggs into the fragile basket of the peace negotiations. On November 4, tough-minded Ariel Sharon, who was now Israel's housing minister, inaugurated another settlement in the occupied Golan Heights. In south Lebanon, tensions also continued to mount. Hezbollah launched some deadly ambushes that killed a number of Israeli soldiers, and the Israelis launched a new spate of shellings and forcibly evacuated civilians from a number of villages north of the Israeli-occupied strip.[3]

Forty years earlier, high-level Syrian and Israeli representatives had sat together in the bilateral sessions of the ISMAC. But those talks had been secret, and aimed only at exploring what level of agreement might be possible in various areas considerably short of an overall peace agreement. In 1952, the two sides managed to conclude a formal agreement regarding return of ships that had accidentally strayed into the territorial waters of the other side.[4] In the talks of late 1991, by contrast, representatives of the two states came together openly to try to conclude a final-status peace agreement between them.

Given the enormous differences that remained between the sides in their publicly stated positions regarding all issues of contention between them, especially the central territorial issue concerning Golan, concluding such an agreement would be an enormous task. To be sure, as long as Shamir's government remained in power, it is fair to say that no substantive progress was made on this track—or, indeed, on any of the other tracks—of the Madrid-launched peace process. In 1999, British writer Patrick Seale recorded the following exchange in an interview he conducted with Shamir:

SHAMIR: Everybody in the world knows that Assad is the enemy of Israel.

SEALE: General Uri Saguy, then head of Military Intelligence, came to you in 1991 and told you there was a change in Syria—that President Assad wanted peace. What was your reaction?

SHAMIR: It's strange to hear such a thing from Uri Saguy. A man of our army. A general. Can you imagine a Syrian general telling Assad, "You have too much Israeli territory"! . . .

SEALE: What was your position when you agreed to enter the Madrid process?

SHAMIR: We wanted to find a compromise.

SEALE: But not a territorial compromise.

SHAMIR: No.

SEALE: You wanted to hang on to everything.

SHAMIR: We are very small indeed to be able to have at least ten million people in the Land of Israel.[5]

Shamir's head negotiator on the Syrian track, Yossi Ben-Aharon, was equally inflexible. Yossi Olmert, the government spokesman who was also a member of the team (until he was removed by Ben-Aharon), reported later that Ben-Aharon had been abrasive and confrontational, deliberately teasing, insulting, and provoking his Syrian counterparts in order to expose their alleged underlying extremism. At the first meeting in Washington, he threw literally in the face of the head of the Syrian delegation a book in Arabic, containing anti-Semitic remarks, written by Mustafa Tlas, the Syrian defense minister. Some of the experts in the Israeli team were appalled by Ben-Aharon's unprofessional behavior, but they could do little. They would meet in the evening in the bar of their hotel and practice throwing books at a target.[6]

The Israeli scholar Moshe Ma'oz noted that, by March 1992, Allaf had expressed Syria's commitment to (1) ending the conflict with Israel, (2) recognizing the state of Israel within its pre-1967 borders, and (3) signing a peace treaty with Israel within the context of a "comprehensive" Arab-Israeli peace.[7] Under Shamir, meanwhile, the Israeli government continued to remain strongly opposed to discussing anything like a full withdrawal from Golan. In 1991–92, Ben-Aharon publicly allowed that, in the context of a peace treaty with Syria, there might be some possibility for "territorial compromise" in Golan. But this formulation—which could be interpreted as referring to reciprocal territorial exchanges between the two parties, rather than simply unilateral withdrawal—went nowhere near meeting the Syrians' base demand for full Israeli withdrawal. Walid Moalem, the affable historian-diplomat who was Syria's ambassador to Washington and who served on Allaf's team in the bilaterals, later described the talks with Ben-Aharon as "not productive." During that period, he said, "the Israelis insisted that Syria give Israel full recognition and end the state of war *before* they would offer any commitment at all on withdrawal."[8]

Events in the ground-floor negotiating rooms at the U.S. State Department, where the talks adjourned after their opening in Madrid, remained more or less static throughout that period. But elsewhere in the same building a slightly (though not wholly) separate conflict was brewing in the United States' bilateral relationship with the Shamir government. The issue—once again—was the question of providing special U.S. loan guarantees for Israel, which the Bush administration had successfully deferred at the beginning of October 1991.

By the beginning of 1992, the 120-day pause that Bush and Baker had insisted on in October 1991 was coming to an end. After some discussion with Senator Patrick Leahy, the chairman of the Senate Ways and Means Committee, Secretary Baker announced in late February that the administration would be prepared to offer the guarantees for the entire $10 billion being asked for—if Israel would freeze all settlement activity in the occupied territories. In addition, under his proposal, the administration would deduct from each year's tranche a sum equivalent to that spent by the Israelis in finishing construction in settlements that had already been started.

Over the weeks that followed, pro-Israeli individuals and groups in Washington lobbied hard to win more favorable terms. Some leaders in the Senate proposed a compromise of which Baker was later to write, "I was sure [it] would drive the Arabs from the peace table."[9] In late March, building on the success he had scored on this issue the previous fall, President Bush threatened to veto this proposal. As Baker wrote, "The President's ultimatum effectively settled the issue. Congressional opposition collapsed under the veto threat, and the foreign aid bill that passed in April did not contain any loan guarantees for Israel."[10]

By April the Shamir government was already in the run-up to a general election at home, and several pro-Likud figures hinted that the Bush administration's robust activity on the loan guarantees might provoke a backlash of nationalist sentiment inside Israel that could easily maintain Shamir in power, perhaps even with a strengthened mandate from the Israeli voters. In the event, just the reverse seems to have happened. When Israeli voters went to the polls on June 23, 1992, they returned a Knesset in whose 120 seats Labor had increased its representation from 39 to 44, while the more clearly pro-peace Meretz Party tripled its representation to 12 seats. Likud lost eight of its previous 40 seats; many analysts attributed its collapse directly to the Bush administration's policy on loan guarantees.[11]

When Baker was writing his memoir of these years, he expressed the judgment that the controversy over loan guarantees "clearly contributed to Likud's defeat." But he strongly denied that it had been the administration's *intent* in pushing the Shamir government so hard on the issue: "This is simply not true. What *is* true is that most of my Middle East specialists believed that the peace process would always be in some peril so long as the Shamir government remained in power."[12]

Whatever the truth regarding American intentions, the outcome was clear. On July 13, 1992, Labor leader Yitzhak Rabin announced a new governing coalition, which drew the left-wing Meretz Party and the Sephardi-ultraorthodox Shas Party (six seats) into the government under the clear leadership of his own party.[13] Rabin announced a shift in government priorities away from Likud's stress on continuing settlement construction in the occupied territories and toward more active engagement in the peace process. He named Shimon Peres as his foreign minister while retaining for himself the defense portfolio, with which he had such long familiarity from earlier years. He also named a new head for Israel's negotiating team on the Syrian track: Itamar Rabinovich, a respected Israeli historian of modern Syria (and also Rabin's trusted protégé and tennis partner of many years). Rabinovich, his new boss decided, would also serve as Israel's new ambassador to Washington.[14]

As for Likud, the campaign Shamir headed in the 1992 election proved to be his swan song. After his leadership was repudiated at the polls, Likud looked for a new leader. The top level of Likud politics was marked by fierce turf battles and deep ideological differences among longtime party activists, in the midst of which a much younger Likud politician who had spent much time in the United States, Binyamin Netanyahu, routed the old guard of the Likud leadership, including Sharon, and seized the leadership of the party for himself.

RABIN'S FIRST FOURTEEN MONTHS

When Rabin took over as Israel's head of government, he brought with him considerable expertise acquired over the years in the conduct of relations with Syria, and in the shadowboxing with Syria that had often taken place in Lebanon.

In 1974, Rabin had been the defense minister at the time Henry Kissinger concluded the disengagement agreement between Israel and Syria. Soon thereafter he succeeded Golda Meir as prime minister. In that position, in 1975, he had been the recipient of President Ford's commitment that in the negotiations over a final-status arrangement with Syria, Washington would "give great weight to Israel's position that any peace agreement with Syria must be predicated on Israel remaining on the Golan Heights."[15] In 1976 Rabin was the main architect of both the "Good Fence" policy through which Israel cultivated friendships with right-wing militias in Lebanon in an attempt to increase Israel's influence there—and of the indirectly agreed upon Red Lines Agreements through which Israel gave its sanction to, but placed strict limitations on, a certain amount of Syrian military intervention in Lebanon. Then, as defense minister in the coalition governments that ruled Israel from 1984 through 1990, he oversaw the arrangements under which Israel undertook its 1985 partial withdrawal from Lebanon, and organized the consolidation of the security zone controlled by the Israeli Defense Forces (IDF) in south Lebanon.

Throughout those years, this risk-averse but steely nerved military man was well able to get the measure of the risk-averse but steely nerved military man in power in Damascus. In addition, by 1992, Assad had a broad reputation among many parts of the political elite in Israel, but particularly among the military echelons from which Rabin sprang, as a man who kept his word and had respected all the agreements concluded with him over the years. In May 1995 Rabin stressed to an Israeli television interviewer, "For seventeen years we have not had an incident along the border with Syria on the Golan Heights, and there has not been an attempted terrorist infiltration. . . . The Golan Heights is the safest place in Israel against terrorist attacks."[16]

During the 1992 election campaign, Rabin and Labor had promised the voters that, if elected, they would strive to win an autonomy agreement on the Palestinian front "within six to nine months." On the Syrian front, they had been decidedly less forthcoming, saying only that "Labor undertakes to hold peace negotiations with Syria without preconditions and on the basis of Resolutions 242 and 338."[17]

Itamar Rabinovich has said that before Rabin was elected, the future premier had given no thought to the role of the Syrian track in the broader peace process.[18] Eitan Haber, the close Rabin ally whom the new premier named as coordinator of all the tracks of the peace process, expressed the judgment that Rabin's views in May 1992 regarding Syria were more actively conflictual than those described by Rabinovich. "You have to understand," said Haber, "that Rabin had served as commander of the northern command [which comprises Israel's fronts with Syria and Lebanon] in the 1950s. And after that, he had something like hatred for the Syrians, because of bad experiences he had regarding that front before and during the Six Day War [of 1967]." As Haber explained it, by 1992 Rabin had for many years harbored a strong feeling that the Syrians had not been punished enough during their successive wars with Israel. Rabin, he said, thought that the Syrians "never considered their wars to be a big failure. For many years, Rabin suffered a 'Syrian syndrome.' He said that one day we have to show them, to teach them a lesson."[19]

In Haber's telling of it, however, "immediately after Rabin came into power, he saw that the key to peace was Syria. And if he could achieve this, then he had no doubt that Lebanon and Jordan would come in as well, and it would satisfy the Egyptians."

In Rabinovich's recollection, the "turning point" in Rabin's change of mind toward Syria was a visit Secretary Baker made to Israel soon after Rabin had completed his government-formation negotiations in July 1992. Baker, Rabinovich said, had assured Rabin of two things: "firstly, that Hafez al-Assad was willing to offer Israel a genuine peace, and secondly, that Baker was willing to commit the American administration to undertaking a serious effort on this track."[20] In his memoir, Rabinovich added that "Both Rabin and Baker saw the advantage of dealing first with an authoritative head of state rather than with the diffuse Palestinian polity."[21]

Haber added that, in his view, Rabin had at that point become inclined to the idea of starting his peace diplomacy with the Syrians, rather than the Palestinians,

> because he wanted to delay the negotiations with the Palestinians, because he understood that this would bring about a clash with the Jews [that is, the settlers and their supporters]. . . . He tried a lot before Oslo to come to a deal with the Syrians. But when he saw there was no chance to do that, and when Peres came with Oslo, he saw that it would take a long time to complete the Oslo process and in the meantime he could do a deal with the Syrians.[22]

From the Syrian side, Labor's victory in the election was seen as offering a welcome opportunity to test whether Israel's new government would be more open than its predecessor to considering Syria's baseline demand for a full withdrawal. With Ambassador Rabinovich now representing the Israeli negotiating team with Syria while serving as his country's envoy in Washington, the role of Syria's ambassador in Washington, Walid Moalem, also started to grow, and he became an important part of the channel through which the Americans conveyed their own and the Israelis' communications to President Assad.

In his very first negotiating round with the Syrians, which started in late August 1992, Rabinovich signaled to them the Rabin government's acceptance of "the applicability of the territorial element in Resolution 242 to the Golan Heights," something which his predecessor had never been prepared to state.[23] The Syrian team responded by presenting a timetable, or agenda, for how they would like to see the talks proceed. As Moalem recalled it, the document was listed under four headings: "Withdrawal; security arrangements; normal peaceful relations; and the timetable for implementation. Mr. Rabinovich considered this positive, as a working paper for the negotiations. This was the first document ever submitted to the peace talks by the Syrians. Thereafter, we held our discussions on the basis of this document."[24] Regarding the *content* of what was in the Syrian paper, Rabinovich has characterized it as offering Israel, "a glorified nonbelligerency in return for full withdrawal."[25] He did however, recognize the significance of Syria having already gone so far as to offer a draft Declaration of Principles for a settlement. And the four agenda items mentioned by Moalem as lying at the heart of this document would soon become referred to by negotiators on both sides as the "four legs of the table" of the peace settlement being pursued—however fitfully—by Syria and the Rabin government.

Although the Israeli side at that point apparently agreed to proceed on the basis of the agenda laid out by the Syrians, throughout the months that followed, Rabin's stance in the talks remained essentially passive rather than proactive. As Rabinovich explained it, once Rabin had formed his government, "his policy for the next year was to let the two tracks [that is, the Palestinian and the Syrian] compete, to see which one would have the breakthrough."[26]

There were other reasons for the hiatus this track experienced in the months after August 1992. On August 13, Secretary Baker had announced that he would be leaving the State Department ten days later to join President Bush's badly faltering campaign for reelection. With Baker went U.S. peace team head Dennis Ross. For the whole of the crucial next five months—through all the diplomatically disabling period of the U.S. election, and then in the lame-duck period after President Bush's defeat at the polls—the U.S. peace team, which was such a vital component of the negotiations, was totally rudderless. Former U.S. ambassador to Israel Samuel Lewis has noted that Rabin always relied deeply on the help of his American "partner" in his pursuit of his diplomacy, and that in 1992, "he knew he was dealing with a lame-duck administration." Rabin's first six months "were wasted because of this," in Lewis's view.[27]

Then, in December 1992, with the Bush administration in the last throes of its lame-duck period, Prime Minister Rabin took a step that cast a broad pall over all tracks of the peace process. The radical Palestinian-Islamic organization Hamas had killed three Israeli soldiers and a border policeman in Gaza. In response, Rabin decided, as Rabinovich put it, to "break the backbone of the Hamas organization in the West Bank and Gaza Strip."[28] He ordered the summary expulsion from the West Bank and Gaza of more than four hundred suspected Hamas and Islamic Jihad activists.

For Palestinians and Arabs everywhere, this move revived terrifying memories of earlier mass expulsions of Palestinians from their native lands. Moreover, the IDF could not, as it had for numerous earlier (though smaller-scale) expulsions of Palestinians from the occupied territories, simply take them into south Lebanon by helicopter, land the choppers briefly, and let them out there. Instead, it took them to Lebanon by bus and tried to drop them at the northern edge of the IDF-controlled security zone inside Lebanon. But the Lebanese authorities had their own fears about large numbers of Palestinians of any political stripe, let alone political activists, being dumped by Israel inside their territory. With the expellees refusing to move any further north away from their homeland, the Lebanese authorities doing nothing to force them to move northward, and Arab opinion everywhere inflamed by the brutality of the Israeli move, the expellees set up well-publicized tent camps along the northern border of the security zone.

The Syrians, and all the other Arab parties, suspended their participation in the peace talks in protest against this move. Thus when Bill Clinton was inaugurated as U.S. president in January 1993, his administration found no Arab-Israeli peace talks under way at all. In its early months, the administration was more concerned with Bosnian matters than with the Middle East. Meanwhile, according to Lewis (who became head of Policy Planning at the State Department under new Secretary of State Warren Christopher), because of its close links to many parts of the American Jewish community, the new U.S. administration was *not* about to do anything to cause an open crisis with Israel.[29] Nevertheless, between January and August 1993 the administration was, "more interested in pushing the Syrian track forward than Rabin was." In pursuit of this, Lewis noted, "We did have discussions about possible carrots for President Assad, including getting Syria off the terrorism

list, the narcotics list, and other carrots related to civilian aviation."
Those carrots were not presented to the Syrians in 1993, however
(though the narcotics list issue was resolved in 1997).[30]

In April 1993, after successive rounds of contacts resulted in an agreed-
upon formula for the very slow return of the Palestinian expellees to
their homes, the Syrians and other Arab parties finally agreed to return
to the peace table. President Assad played a significant role in making
this happen by inviting PLO head Yasser Arafat to Syria, where, during
a four-hour meeting, he persuaded him that the negotiations should
resume. He also publicly offered a new formula to the Israelis: "Full
peace for full withdrawal," though he was still unwilling to spell out in
public what the components of this "full peace" might be.[31] And he made
a gesture to Israel and the American Jewish community by renewing
exit visas for a number of Jewish Syrians.[32] By the second week of May,
however—although the Syrians did not know it at the time—Israeli
foreign minister Shimon Peres was firming up the Israeli government's
connection with the peace feelers to the PLO that well-connected
Israeli private citizens had started in Oslo the previous December.[33]

According to Rabinovich, by early August 1993 Prime Minister Rabin
knew in some detail what the Oslo agreement with the PLO would look
like. "All our efforts until then did not get us anywhere with the Syrians,"
Rabinovich said in an interview. "But before [Rabin] committed himself
to Oslo, he gave the Syrian track one last test with a hypothetical question to the Syrians regarding full withdrawal. He presented the package
of what he would need in return for that: the modalities of reaching
and implementing an agreement, the nature of relations, et cetera. He
was very interested in an Egyptian-type deal [with Syria]. He wanted to
see if he could get that."[34]

In his writings and communications, Rabinovich has nearly always
been guarded in what he would say about the exact content of the early
August 1993 communications with Syria. In his book, he wrote that
during a visit by Christopher and Ross to Israel, Rabin arranged to
have a meeting with them on August 3, at which Rabinovich was the
only other person present. It had been arranged that the Americans
would visit Syria the next day. Rabinovich wrote that, "Rabin asked
Christopher to explore with Assad, on the assumption that his own
demand would be satisfied, first whether Syria would be willing to sign
a peace treaty with Israel without linkage to the pace of progress with

others, second, whether Syria was ready for a real peace . . . and third, whether Syria was ready to offer elements of peace before the completion of withdrawal. Rabin explained to Christopher that he saw the whole process completed in five years. . . ."[35]

From the reference in his interview to "an Egyptian-type deal," it would seem that what Rabin had been talking about in that meeting was a deal involving a full Israeli withdrawal from occupied Golan. From what he wrote in the memoir about, "on the assumption that [Assad's] own demand would be satisfied," the same inference also clearly emerges, since Assad's main demand until then had been for a full Israeli withdrawal—and one not just to the international border, but to the June 4, 1967, line. Thus it is scarcely surprising that, as Rabinovich wrote in his memoir, "Before we moved on to the larger meeting [that is, with more Israeli officials present], I said to Ross that the wings of history could be heard in the room. Rabin's gambit took me by surprise."[36]

Moalem's view of what happened in early August was significantly different from Rabinovich's portrayal. Moalem recalled explicitly that on August 3, "We agreed with the Israelis to the principle of full withdrawal from Golan. The Americans were witness to this."[37] In a follow-up interview, he gave additional details:

> When Rabin was forthcoming on the Syrian track, on 3 August 1993, he told Warren Christopher that he was ready for a full withdrawal. Christopher went to Syria, and talked with President Assad. Assad asked Christopher to clarify if Rabin was talking about a *total* withdrawal; whether Israel would have any outstanding territorial claims after such a withdrawal; and whether Rabin was talking about withdrawal to the line of 4 June 1967. Christopher said he did not know the answers to these questions, and he went to Israel. But while he was there, he gave a negative picture of the Syrian position. In my view, the real negotiation was started then—but the Americans all went on vacation. And then, there was Oslo. . . . The Americans always thought "Syria can wait."[38]

Rabinovich wrote that Christopher reported Assad's response back to Rabin at an August 5 meeting at which, again, he and Rabin were the only two Israelis present.[39] He wrote of that meeting:

> While Christopher and Ross saw Assad's response as positive in that he accepted "the basic equation," Rabin saw it as disappointing. Assad was willing to offer formal contractual peace for full withdrawal and was, in principle, willing to view the agreement as "standing on its

own two feet," but then came a long list of "ifs and buts." Most significantly, Assad did not accept Rabin's demand that the agreement be implemented in a fashion that would offer Israel at the outset a large measure of normalization for a limited withdrawal. Nor did he accept a five-year time frame and offered instead a six-month period for implementing the agreement.[40]

Rabinovich would later recall that after the meeting of August 4, "Rabin had real doubts if Assad was a real partner for peace, because of the response he gave to what was on our side a very real opening gambit. After we got the reply from him, we decided to put this track on a back burner, as we proceeded with Oslo."[41] It seems, however, that after Ross and Christopher took Rabin's reply back to Damascus, Rabinovich was still not aware that his boss had placed the track he headed on the back burner. He wrote that while he was in Washington during those days after August 4, he continued working at trying "to find a way to deal with the new, secret, dimension of the negotiations while keeping the four formal tracks going as usual."[42] He did not learn about the remarkable developments on the Oslo track, and Rabin's decision to pursue them (while placing the Syrian track on a back burner) until around August 20. On that date, Peres called him, in his capacity as Israel's ambassador in Washington, to ask him to help set up the urgent meeting with Christopher, who was on vacation in California, at which news of the Oslo breakthrough would be broken to the Americans.

As Rabinovich had noted, Rabin's expression of a willingness to have Christopher explore a deal with Assad based "on the assumption that his own demand would be satisfied" represented a bold new move (the "wings of history") in the long record of Israeli peacemaking. But how seriously was that new overture pursued? As Rabinovich himself had stated, it was presented in order to give the Syrian track "one last test" before he committed himself to Oslo. And given the timing of what happened over the next two days, the overture certainly seemed to have been thrown out on the basis of a last-minute take-it-or-leave-it communication, rather than the start of a serious exploration of the total parameters of a final peace deal. Ambassador Lewis has pointed out that, although Rabin may have appeared speedy in gauging and rejecting Assad's response to his overture, nevertheless the fact that Rabin might be likely to make such an overture at some time cannot have come as a complete surprise to Assad, since it had been "waved before" him, though in a less definitive way, even before August 1993. "What had not been well considered by Rabin was that the Oslo track would come to fruition so fast," Lewis said. "What he needed was a big signal from Assad."[43]

Another explanation of Rabin's motivation in not following up actively in response to whatever opening presented itself on the Syrian track is that given by the well-informed Israeli-American journalist David Makovsky. He wrote that U.S. and Israeli officials saw Christopher's Israel-Syria shuttle as providing "an opportunity to reignite the stalled Oslo talks by reinforcing PLO fears of being excluded from a separate Israeli-Syrian deal." Makovsky presented further details about the diplomacy of those days that tended to corroborate this view.[44] It is unclear, however, to what extent the Americans were complicit in such a plan, since by all accounts they had no idea at that time how close Rabin and Peres were to completing the Oslo deal.

The important question regarding whether Rabin's August 3 communication to the Syrians constituted a "commitment," as the Syrians understood it, or merely a "hypothetical," as Rabinovich would afterwards claim, is one that became very controversial in Israel after news of it started to leak into the media in 1996. This controversy will be discussed more fully in the next chapter. Suffice it here to note that the ability of the Israelis and Syrians to register significant progress in their negotiation between April and early August 1993 was all the more noteworthy since the talks spanned a period in which there was also a significant flare-up of hostilities within Lebanon.

June and early July 1993 saw an escalation of tensions in south Lebanon, to the point that civilians on both sides of the front line were getting hurt. In early July seven Israeli soldiers were killed in the security zone, and IDF bombardments of areas north of the front line were threatening to provoke Hezbollah to retaliate by firing Katyusha rockets into northern Israel. On July 25 the Rabin government launched a punishing assault against Lebanon, dubbed "Operation Accountability." Rabinovich has written of this operation that "its principal component was a broad-scale expulsion of Lebanese civilians from the southern part of the country north toward Beirut. In this fashion the Israeli authors of the operation expected to generate pressure on the Lebanese government of Rafiq Hariri and ultimately on the latter's Syrian patrons."[45] Over the next six days, Israeli forces launched 22,000 artillery shells and 1,000 air-to-ground rockets against Lebanon, resulting in widespread terror and destruction, and the deaths of 118 civilians and 9 combatants. In the same period, Hezbollah launched 151 Katyusha rockets against northern Israel, killing two Israeli civilians.[46]

In response to the humanitarian crisis caused by the Israeli assault, Secretary of State Christopher launched an urgent round of telephone diplomacy. He has said, "That was my first contact with the Syrians when the Katyushas began to fall into Israel in 1993, and I began to work with Farouq Sharaa on getting the rockets stopped. It became apparent to me early on that the arrangements always had to be trilateral in character, or maybe quadrilateral."[47] On July 31, he was able to secure the agreement of all the parties concerned—which included the governments of Israel, Syria, Lebanon, and Iran, as well as the leadership of Hezbollah—to a cease-fire based on a series of unwritten "rules of engagement" under which all parties would agree to try to avoid causing civilian casualties. The diplomacy involved may have looked complicated, since the United States had relations with neither the Iranian government nor Hezbollah. But Syria clearly played an important role, through the close working relationships it enjoyed with both these parties and the political influence it enjoyed over the government in Beirut. And with its own diplomacy with Israel seeming to be productive in those weeks, the Syrian leadership was evidently inclined to be helpful in regard to calming the situation in Lebanon. One Israeli official was quoted at the time as noting, "I think Christopher had to make only one call—to Damascus."[48]

It was exactly three days after conclusion of the Lebanon cease-fire that Rabin launched his controversial (and short-lived) overture toward Syria.

Then, in the last days of August, came the unveiling of Israel's breakthrough with the PLO.

ACHIEVEMENTS: NOVEMBER 1991
THROUGH AUGUST 1993

In the weeks before and after the Madrid conference, some generally pro-Likud figures inside Israel had expressed interest in exploring whether, by doing some kind of deal on the Syrian front, the Shamir government could lessen the pressure it faced to conclude a deal with the Palestinians.[49] For their part, even after several months' experience with Shamir's negotiating tactics, some in the Syrian political elite continued, as late as early June 1992, to express some interest in the idea that (for essentially this same reason) a Likud government might be better for Damascus to work with than a Labor government.[50] Regardless of such speculation, the fact remains that the Shamir government did nothing effective—on either the Palestinian or the Syrian track—to push relations toward a peace agreement.

By the time Rabin was elected, President Assad and his advisers presumably had come to a realization that Labor would be more likely than Likud to be an engaged negotiating partner, since the welcome that Allaf had prepared for Rabinovich's team at their first encounter was, by Syrian standards, so forthcoming. The "four-legged" structure of negotiations the Syrians proposed in that encounter helped to push the negotiation forward by breaking it into identifiable subsections in an ordering that was agreeable to both sides. It did, however, contain what could be seen as one internal structural flaw. The questions of "normal peaceful relations" and of the sequencing of a phased implementation were two that, if handled creatively, could be more helpful in building support for a potential peace agreement within Israel than within Syria. Thus, leaving discussion of them *until the end* could tend to undercut Israeli public support for an agreement in which a withdrawal component favorable to Syria might already have been—with whatever caveats—essentially agreed upon. Still, the structure proposed by the Syrians appealed to the obsession with security matters that Rabin and Assad both shared. It thus provided a durable template for their negotiations and continued to be used by the two sides for the rest of Rabin's life.

During Rabin's early months in office, there is considerable evidence suggesting that the views of different members of the Labor leadership toward conduct of the different bilateral strands of the peace process, and their analysis of the relationship among these strands, were by no means fully thought out, far less mutually agreed upon. The main actor in Israel's new government was undoubtedly Rabin himself, but as the assessment from Rabinovich cited above seems to indicate, Rabin did not come into power with any firm strategy of his own regarding which track he would prioritize. What Rabin had decided upon, instead, was essentially to sit back and let the interlocutors on all the various tracks compete among themselves for his attention.

While the diplomatic stance he chose for himself during his early months in power was essentially passive and reactive, in his command of the considerable instruments of force at Israel's disposal Rabin initiated significant, proactive operations in both the Palestinian and, later, the Lebanese arenas. But the nature of these actions revealed how scant his understanding was of the political dynamics within his country's neighboring societies. In the Palestinian arena, he clearly did not understand that his attempt to expel the four hundred suspected Hamas supporters would trigger the scale of furor and diplomatic crisis that ensued. In the Lebanese arena, he presumably hoped that when he launched the large-scale assault of July 1993, it would solve Israel's Lebanese problem for the foreseeable future, which it did not.

In the case of the crisis triggered by the Palestinian expulsions, Rabin did show the capacity to learn from his mistake. He realized that in dealing with the Palestinians he would now need to supplement his long-used recourse to force with a more actively engaged political strategy; hence, his endorsement of the Oslo contacts with the PLO. The limited utility of his use of force in the Lebanese arena seemed to take a little longer to become evident to him.[51]

If Rabin did not seem to have a very clear understanding of the political dynamics within Palestinian or Lebanese society, he nevertheless retained at the diplomatic level enough of a reliance on divide-and-rule tactics among his various Arab interlocutors so that by the end of his first fourteen months in office he seemed to be bringing clear diplomatic advantage to his country. His summer 1993 breakthrough with the PLO brought plaudits from all of Israel's traditional friends around the globe—and also from numerous former enemies and governments previously wary of too close an identification with a seemingly intransigent Israel. Meanwhile, he had given away nothing tangible at all in the Syrian track.

Disclosure of the Oslo contacts' existence—and achievements—came as a difficult blow to a Syrian leadership whose intelligence apparatus had apparently totally failed to pick up any scent of what was going on in Norway. It is quite possible to guess that President Assad felt he had been doubly deceived—by both the PLO leaders (with whom he had an old feud that dated back at least to the early 1980s) and an Israeli government that at the beginning of August 1993 had been making an undoubtedly intriguing overture to Damascus. That overture was not followed up on immediately by the Rabin government. But later, it proved to have been a worthwhile initiative for Rabin to have launched: When he (and the Americans) sought to return to the Syrian track in late 1993, they would find Assad still intrigued enough by what he had already heard that he was willing or even eager to resume the negotiation.

What, meanwhile, of the record of the American cosponsors during the Shamir and early Rabin periods?

It is hard to form a simple judgment on this score, because the period in question was one punctuated in a major way by the turnover of power within the U.S. political system. In early 1992, the Bush-Baker team still seemed to have the same degree of commitment to bring about the successful completion of the peace process that they had displayed throughout 1991 toward its launching. But Shamir proved intransigent, and Bush and Baker were forced to expend a great deal of political capital in dealing with his intransigence on the critical settlements issue. Then, after Rabin came to power in summer 1992, the American body politic entered a long period of presidential-level transition. Between Bush's prolonged lame-duck period and Clinton's inevitable learning period after taking office, it probably would be unrealistic to have expected any clear-cut U.S. initiative on any aspect of Arab-Israeli diplomacy before March or April of 1993—even without the crisis provoked by the Palestinian expulsions.

The style of diplomacy that President Clinton and Secretary Christopher brought to Arab-Israeli peacemaking was markedly different from that of their predecessors. Dennis Ross, who headed the peace team under both administrations, has noted that during the period of getting the sides to open the negotiation in the first place, "Baker was much more willing [than Christopher would prove to be] to use an 'in-your-face' approach. Under Secretary Christopher, we took the approach that these were bilateral negotiations between the parties."[52] The fact that —at least after the Palestinian expulsion crisis had been resolved— bilateral negotiations were under way certainly did not obviate the need for the skillful passing and interpretation of messages by a third party which itself had a strong interest in the talks' success. By all accounts, this was a role that, each in his own way, Clinton and Christopher seemed well suited to carry out.

Between 1993 and 1996, there were numerous occasions on which Clinton spoke on the telephone with Assad—and even more occasions on which he talked to Rabin.[53] (The experienced diplomatic writer David Remnick has written that after the two men first met, during Clinton's 1992 election campaign, "Clinton gravitated to Rabin as to a kind of father figure." He quoted Rabin aide Eitan Haber as saying, "It looked to me that Clinton saw Rabin as mentor. . . . They spoke on the phone constantly, coordinating every step before anything became a problem, even the smallest step. Even their agreement not to kiss or hug Arafat on-stage at the White House—to make it just a handshake—was coordinated.")[54] Alongside his phone relationship with Rabin was a series of twice-yearly, face-to-face meetings, many of which were keyed, as Rabinovich has noted, to Rabin's schedule of visits to meetings of leading American Jewish and pro-Israeli organizations. At the end of 1993, Clinton would then hold the first of two face-to-face meetings with Assad as well.

Meanwhile, between Clinton's personal meetings with these two leaders, Christopher would maintain the texture of a personalized carrying of messages between them, an undertaking that was seen by both Rabin and the Clinton administration as desirable, given the need to deal as directly as possible with Assad rather than with his officials.

In their interactions with Rabin, did Clinton and Christopher ever question the priorities and judgments the veteran Israeli politician made? Samuel Lewis has judged that President Clinton was very good at "sympathetically challenging people to reconsider tough issues," and that he did this with both Assad and Rabin. Lewis noted that the Americans (though he did not specify at which level) tried to remind Rabin, for example, that he was not the only one who faced political constraints on what he could do in the negotiations, "but he didn't want to hear about them." Neither Rabin nor Rabinovich, he said, ever took seriously people who told them that Assad was running big political risks connected with the negotiations: "Rabin saw himself as having a one-vote majority in Israel, and asked how could Hafez al-Assad as an absolute dictator for thirty years think that *he* has problems?"[55]

The Americans also occasionally tried to question Rabin's absolute judgment that the Israeli political system could digest progress on only one track of the peace process at a time. One senior U.S. official recalled of that era that some American officials sought to persuade Rabin to reframe his view of the peace process into one more embracing of a comprehensive, regionwide vision of peace that might allow active engagement on more than one track at a time. But though the issue was raised, "We were very mindful of the political constraints on him [Rabin]. . . . The president and the secretary of state were very mindful of what Rabin said on this issue. In addition, especially after Oslo, they felt he had already done a lot to reframe his views, and that Hafez al-Assad was not doing as much reframing in this regard."[56]

In September 1993 nearly all the world's attention turned to the path-breaking new developments on the Palestinian track of the peace process. But by the end of the year, the Syrian track would also start to revive.

3

Slow Progress between Oslo and May 1995

FROM OSLO TO THE "AIMS AND PRINCIPLES" DOCUMENT

On September 13, 1993, Prime Minister Rabin and PLO chairman Yasser Arafat met on the White House lawn in Washington, D.C., for the public signing of their groundbreaking agreement—the first ever concluded by Israel with a party that claimed to represent "the Palestinian people."[1]

For the Syrians, the news that the Palestinians and Israelis had been negotiating secretly behind their backs for all these months and had reached a formal interim agreement came as a double whammy. It undercut both the hope they had expressed widely in their public rhetoric that, in their peace talks with Israel, they could enjoy productive "coordination" with the other Arab parties in the peace diplomacy, and their hope that they were near a breakthrough in their own diplomacy with Israel.

"We were taken by surprise by Oslo—we did not even know about the secret talks until the agreement was announced," Moalem has admitted.[2] Explaining how seriously the Syrians, from their side, had all along taken the responsibility of "coordinating" with the Palestinians, Moalem has noted in the paper that he presented to the Israelis shortly after Rabin's election that "two pages of the five were dedicated to the Palestinian people's rights. . . . When the Palestinians and Israelis surprised the world with Oslo, Rabinovich told Allaf that we could not be Palestinian more than the Palestinians."[3]

59

On September 11, *New York Times* journalist Thomas Friedman reported on an interview he had held with Clinton the day before. The president had explicitly talked about the need to prepare the Israeli public for sizeable further concessions, in addition to those envisaged in the Oslo accords, that they would need to be ready to make, particularly toward Syria. But he was evidently confident that Oslo could help that process: "Each successive day that the [Oslo] agreement builds up in strength I think that enables the government in Israel to engage Syria," he said. Clinton recounted that he had called Assad on the telephone on September 9, and had reassured the Syrian president that he remained committed to "the whole process" in the Middle East and that he really believed that "you got to solve these interstate conflicts." He also recounted how he had persuaded Assad, during that conversation, to allow Moalem to represent Syria at the White House signing ceremony.[4]

At the time, official spokesmen in Damascus explained that their government was "neither opposed to nor supportive" of the Oslo accords, and that it was up to the PLO leadership to bear responsibility for their implementation. But Moalem did attend the ceremony, after which he joined other Arab diplomats in shaking hands with Rabin and Peres.

Rabinovich has written that immediately after the signing ceremony, while many Arab and Israeli dignitaries were fraternizing at a lunch at the State Department, Rabin attended a private lunch at the White House with President Clinton. According to Rabinovich, Rabin had been quite alarmed by what Friedman had reported about the president's views. If the "reassurance" of the Israeli public that Clinton had talked about "was simply meant to prepare the Israeli public for an almost simultaneous major concession to Syria, then Rabin was worried. He explained to Clinton that there was indeed only so much the traffic could bear. . . . He told the president that he was still committed to the notion of an agreement with Syria but he needed a few months, and asked the president's help in persuading Assad to wait until the end of the year."[5] Rabinovich noted that Rabin "returned elated from his lunch with the president. As he saw the meeting, the president, a very political man, understood Rabin's perspective and concerns and was very attentive to them. President Clinton then called President Assad a second time to brief him on his discussion with Rabin, to assure him of his administration's and Israel's commitment to move forward with

Syria as well in a few months, and to ask him specifically to restrain the 'rejectionist' Palestinian leaders residing in Damascus."[6] (Samuel Lewis has noted that the Israeli leader's remarkable breakthrough on the Oslo track had, in fact, "convinced Clinton that he was on the right track in letting Rabin take the lead on peace process issues. It was also very popular with the American Jewish community.")[7]

The Syrians were not happy at all about having had their track of the talks put on a back burner—especially given that, after Rabin's August 3 communication, they had felt it was at such a hopeful stage. But they had no better option than to wait out the "few months" that Clinton had said Rabin needed before serious reengagement.

By December or so, the Clinton administration was finally signaling that it was ready to inject the ingredient of presidential power into the task of restarting the talks on the Syrian track. It did so by arranging a January 16 meeting in Geneva that was the first summit-level Syrian-American encounter since Assad had met President Jimmy Carter, also in Geneva, in 1977. Part of the Syrian president's preparations for this meeting included, some weeks beforehand, lifting the provision that until then had forced Syrian Jews who wanted to travel outside the country to leave one or more family members behind. With that and other restrictions lifted, by mid-January only some four hundred members of Syria's once-thriving Jewish community remained in the country. Most of the rest had joined the large Syrian Jewish community in Brooklyn. Of those who stayed in Syria, a *New York Times* reporter wrote that most were, "either elderly people who believe they are too old to start over again, or well-placed business people who feel they cannot afford to leave."[8]

During the postsummit news conference in Geneva, Assad said, "[W]e want the peace of the brave, a real peace that thrives, continues, guarantees the interests of all, and gives rights to their owners. If the leaders of Israel have enough courage to respond to such a peace, a new era of security and stability and normal peaceful relations among all will emerge in the region." He added, "We are ready to sign peace now."[9]

If President Assad seemed buoyant at the end of his meeting with Clinton, his hopes of fast progress toward conclusion of a peace agreement were considerably dampened the very next day, when Israeli deputy defense minister Mordechai Gur announced on his government's behalf that "in the event the territorial price demanded from us on the Golan Heights is significant, the government will put the issue to referendum."[10] Rabinovich has written that, by bringing the notion of a referendum out into the open, Rabin was trying to achieve several goals, including "calm[ing] down the Israeli political system." Rabinovich wrote that Rabin's message to the Clinton administration was "that by making a public statement in this matter [Rabin] was underlining the seriousness of the negotiations with Syria. Our American interlocutors, I felt, did not quite see it that way."[11] Neither (to say the least) did the Syrians.

Four days later, another setback struck at the heart of President Assad's family, and at his hopes for a political stability in Syria that might survive his own life. His beloved son, Basil, whom the president had for some years been grooming to succeed him in office, was killed in a car accident near Damascus.

A month later Israeli-Arab tensions flared again throughout the Middle East after Jewish-Israeli extremist Baruch Goldstein slaughtered twenty-nine Palestinian civilians who were praying in Hebron's hotly contested Ibrahimi Mosque.[12]

Despite this series of setbacks, the momentum provided by President Clinton's direct involvement in the Syrian-Israeli talks was such that the discussions continued throughout those months. By July 1994, according to Moalem, the Syrians had finally received from Rabin satisfactory answers to the questions Assad had posed (through the Americans) the previous August. In particular, according to Moalem, Rabin had now finally confirmed that the "full withdrawal" discussed the previous August could be construed as a withdrawal to the June 4, 1967, line.[13]

Here, again, exists a disparity between what the two lead negotiators have been prepared to say in public about the nature of this communication. Rabinovich has written that the Israelis had heard much, throughout the negotiations with Syria, about their insistence that the end point of withdrawal should be the June 4, 1967, line. He noted that in a meeting with Rabin on July 19, Christopher then

> returned to the June 4 issue. Could he [on his upcoming trip to Damascus] give Assad "clarity with regard to the end of the line"? By now Rabin had clearly decided that he could actually fit the issue into the paradigm built on August 3 [1993] as long as it was a "clarification" and not a "commitment," and told Christopher that he could tell Assad that this was his "impression."

On July 21 Christopher and his team returned from Damascus. At a small meeting in Rabin's office he told us that Assad knew that he had no commitment from Rabin but that he was willing to proceed on the basis of the clarification.[14]

According to minutes of the July meeting that were later obtained by the Israeli daily *Ha'aretz*, Rabin did tell Christopher at that July 1994 meeting that "he could accept Syria's demand [regarding withdrawal] . . . if President Assad accepted strict conditions set by Israel in other areas."[15] Rabinovich's explanation of this was that Rabin had told Christopher during that meeting that "he could consider" a peace with Syria in which Israel would withdraw to the June 4, 1967, line. But any promises Rabin may have made to Christopher in that regard were, Rabinovich stressed, made under the express understanding that they not be presented to Assad as Israel's negotiating position. Instead, they were intended to allow Christopher to present "very real ideas" as mere hypotheticals, and then gauge the Syrian response.[16]

Whatever the nature of the ex post facto spin from the Israeli side, during the entire period that Rabin and his team were negotiating with Syria, there seems to have been broad understanding between the two sides that the structure of the agreement they were aiming at was, in the metaphor commonly used by both parties and by the Americans, "like a table with four legs that cannot stand until all four have been constructed."[17] The depth of the Israeli withdrawal was understood to be the first of these legs. Therefore, the parties agreed not to disclose the content of the conditional agreement they had reached on this leg until they had reached agreement on the other three as well.

By July 1994, the Syrians considered that they had received a satisfactory commitment from Rabin regarding withdrawal. It was on this basis, therefore, that after July 1994, they started preparing their positions regarding the next leg of the table.[18]

For his part, Foreign Minister Sharaa noted in a 1998 interview that, though he could not say there had ever been "full confidence" between the Israelis and Syrians, from either side of the negotiating table, nevertheless, "I can say there was a good measure of mutual confidence after Rabin gave the [July 1994] commitment that the withdrawal would be full, to the 4 June 1967 line. This made a lot of changes, and enhanced the confidence of both sides."[19]

But once again, as had happened the previous August, news of an agreement approaching a breakthrough on another track immediately intervened, diverting much of the Israeli leadership's attention from dealing with the Syrian track. This time it was the Jordanian track that registered the progress. On July 25 Israeli and Jordanian negotiators in Washington signed a declaration laying out the principles according to which their governments would conclude a formal peace treaty, and pledged themselves to achieve this within two months.

In the event, it took the Jordanians a little longer than this to conclude their peace treaty with Israel. The Syrians used the intervening time to do what they could to push matters forward on their track. On July 29, Moalem was given a mandate from Damascus to open small exploratory discussions with Rabinovich, which could help iron out problems and could potentially allow the negotiations to proceed much more speedily than in the more formal setting of the "big team" meetings.[20] (These meetings were held in the presence of Ross and Martin Indyk, the chief U.S. National Security Council staff member on Middle East issues at the time.) On September 4, Moalem presented Rabinovich with a second major Syrian document that reportedly detailed his government's views on the issues that made up the other three legs of the table. He also at this point signaled Syria's agreement that Israel's withdrawal from Golan could take place "in two stages."[21]

At the end of October, Rabin and Jordan's King Hussein met on a windy airfield in Jordan to sign the peace agreement between their two countries. From Rabin's and the Americans' points of view, things were progressing well in the peace process at that point. But Clinton still seemed determined not to stop with the Jordan-Israel treaty but to consider actively pursuing the possibility of a counterpart peace agreement between Israel and Syria. Therefore, after presiding in avuncular fashion over the festivities in Jordan, he undertook a quick side visit to Damascus—the first by a sitting American president since Richard Nixon.

According to some indicators, by now the Syrians seemed more open to engaging with the "public reframing" aspects of peace diplomacy than they had been during the signing of the Oslo accords. During the Jordan-Israel treaty signing, Syria's state-controlled television station aired much or most of the signing ceremony without hostile or defensive comment, including shots that showed Israeli leaders smiling and laughing with their Jordanian hosts. Veteran Syrian journalist Ibrahim Homeidi has recalled that these kind of media reports were very different from earlier references to Israeli leaders as heads of "Zionist gangs" and so on, and that they had the effect of helping Syrian citizens to start thinking of the possibility of Israel's presence as a neighbor in the region one day becoming an acceptable thing.[22]

While Clinton was in Syria, he spent a total of two hours alone with President Assad (including time driving to and from the presidential palace), and more than two hours in discussions with aides present. The two men gave a news conference afterward, in which Assad spoke of Syria's commitment to "the objective requirements of peace through the establishment of peaceful, normal relations with Israel in return for Israel's full withdrawal from the Golan to the line of June 4, 1967, and from the south of Lebanon. . . ." For his part, Clinton referred to some principles that would later become an important part of the conceptualization of postpeace security arrangements between Syria and Israel. "Peace must also be secure for both sides," Clinton said. "Security for one side should not come at the expense of the other's security. Peace must guarantee security against surprise attack by any side."[23]

After returning to Israel that evening, Clinton said of his time in Damascus: "I went there because I was convinced that we needed to add new energy to the talks, and I came away convinced that we had."[24] During this encounter, however, Assad was not as forthcoming as many in the American and Israeli press had hoped he would be. He did not express in public the regret that Clinton said he had expressed in private, regarding the "killing of innocents" (in reference both to a recent terror explosion on an Israeli bus and to the killings in Hebron earlier that year). And when Israeli-American reporter David Makovsky asked the Syrian president what assurance he could give Israelis that it would be safe for Israel to pull out of the Golan Heights, Assad replied with what one *New York Times* reporter described as "a lecture in which he said security concerns could never justify any effort 'to preserve the lands of other states.'"[25] According to the *Times* reporter, Assad "went on to mock the importance of an official visit [by himself to Israel, as Sadat had undertaken in 1978], saying that adversaries throughout history have 'not put conditions for achieving peace that one party should visit the other or not visit the other.'"[26]

According to Moalem, while Clinton was in Damascus he informed Assad that Rabin wished to start discussing the security arrangements leg of the table; and he proposed that these discussions be conducted by the two countries' military chiefs of staff, who would travel to Washington for the negotiations.[27]

These talks were preceded by one set of meetings in which Moalem became acquainted with the thinking of Israel's chief of staff, Ehud Barak, and Rabin's military aide, Danny Yatom, and another in which Rabinovich met Syria's longtime chief of staff, Hikmat Shihabi. According to Moalem, his preliminary meetings with Barak seemed to proceed well. "When I reported to him about Rabin's commitment to withdraw to the line of June 4, 1967, he said the role of the military was to fulfill the position given to them by the political leadership and find a solution to any [political] decision," Moalem recalled.[28] For his part, Rabinovich found Shihabi "dignified, polite, and reserved."[29]

On December 21, the two chiefs of staff finally got to meet each other. According to evaluations expressed subsequently by both sides, these talks were not a success. Moalem and Rabinovich were still the formal heads of their countries' respective delegations at these talks. Moalem said that Barak "had only four days to prepare" for the breakthrough meeting with his Syrian counterpart. He charged in addition that "it was impossible to continue in that format because Barak was focusing more on his political future, so he was exaggerating his demands."[30] (Barak was due to retire at the end of December. Even at the time, his future career was already widely—and, as it turned out, accurately—judged in Israel to have enormous potential, not least because he was considered to be a favored protégé of Prime Minister Rabin.) For his part, Rabinovich stated the following June that, from the Israeli side, "we failed to carefully prepare for the [Shihabi-Barak] meeting, which was held almost spontaneously."[31]

In Damascus, according to Foreign Minister Farouq Sharaa, the Israeli-American request that the security arrangements be negotiated between the military chiefs had all along looked like an Israeli tactic to delay the negotiations "because officers on their own cannot reach a decision."[32]

Dennis Ross has recalled that there were "points of convergence" at that first chiefs of staff meeting (COS I): "There was no disagreement between Barak and Shihabi about the *aims* of a security arrangement.

But Assad wanted to reach agreement on principles, as well."[33] As Rabinovich wrote, "Thus Ross proposed that we combine discussion of aims and principles."[34] And that was, indeed, what ensued. Given that the late December meeting had pointed up the apparent limitations of the military-to-military approach, the parties thereafter returned their negotiations to the level of the political leadership on both sides, with the purpose being to hammer out some agreed language at the political level concerning the "aims and principles" of the security arrangement. Those negotiations began in early 1995.

In March 1995 Secretary Christopher traveled to the Middle East in an attempt to give the Israel-Syria talks more momentum. Starting as he usually did in Israel, he met with Rabin. According to Rabinovich, the Israeli leader "began his meeting with Christopher by saying that he was aware of the fact that the question was being raised whether he wanted to or could conclude an agreement with Syria. 'I want and I can,' Rabin said, 'and the time is now.'"[35] Christopher then undertook a prolonged Israel-Syria shuttle, and contacts between the parties multiplied over the two months that followed. In early May, Foreign Minister Sharaa made a rare visit to Washington, where he had a meeting with President Clinton and provided high-level Syrian input into the drafting venture. Sharaa's visit was followed by one from Rabin; and on May 22, the Israeli prime minister signaled his final approval of an agreed-upon text titled "The Aims and Principles of the Security Arrangement."

THE "AIMS AND PRINCIPLES" DOCUMENT

It was agreed among all three parties at the time that, as with Rabin's earlier communications concerning the extent of an Israeli withdrawal in return for peace, the exact text of what was being agreed to, and even the existence of this agreement, would not be publicly revealed. However, some news about its existence did surface within Israel's ever-loquacious media at the time, and thereafter the Israelis and Americans used a feat of rhetorical legerdemain to refer to it in public as "a non-paper," or even "a non-paper paper." Dennis Ross's explanation of the status of this particular text is that "it was not meant to be a formal agreement. It was designed to create a base line, or provide a framework for the ensuing discussions." Along with the text of the

"Aims and Principles" document, the parties also agreed to the sequence of events that would follow. According to Ross, this sequence was: "Firstly, I'd go out to the region and talk to the two chiefs of staff. Secondly, they would both come to D.C. to meet with each other. Thirdly, security experts from both sides would then follow up."[36]

Though the existence of the text became widely known at around the time its terms were finally agreed on, its content did remain secret —for a short while. But later, in the course of developments to be described in the next chapter, a document referring almost explicitly to the text of the May document was made public in Israel (see chapter 4). The disclosure of this text has since then provided a fascinating window to see just how much agreement the Syrian and Israeli negotiators were able to reach at the conceptual level by May 1995, regarding the basis for a postpeace security arrangement between their countries.

A close reading of the leaked document allows a nearly full reconstruction of the original text of the "Aims and Principles" paper, as follows. The aims (or "objectives") were, in the order listed:

— "to reduce, if not to almost totally *eliminate* the danger of a surprise attack,"
— "preventing or limiting daily friction along the border," and
— "to reduce the danger of a large-scale offensive, invasion, or comprehensive war."

The agreed "principles" were as follows:

1. "The legitimate need of each of the parties is that the security of one party or the guarantees thereof should not be achieved at the expense of the other. . . ."
2. "[T]the security arrangements will be *equal, mutual, and reciprocal on both sides* . . . [and] if in the course of the negotiations, it transpires that the implementation of equality, from the geographic dimension, proves impossible with regard to specific arrangements, then experts from both sides will discuss the problematic aspects of the specific arrangement and solve them—whether through *modification* (including additions or subtractions) or through some other agreed upon and acceptable solution with a single variable. . . ."
3. "Security arrangements must coincide with each party's sovereignty and territorial integrity. . . . [T]he arrangements will be confined to the relevant areas on both sides of the border."

(In addition, the document presented this additional sentence that purported to have been taken from the "principles" part of the document: "The purpose of the security arrangements—to ensure equality in overall security in the context of peace between the two countries.")[37]

It was on the basis of this document that the two sides agreed that the chiefs of staff would meet again, one month later, at the end of June 1995.

A DELICATE STRUCTURE IN THE MAKING

By the end of May 1995, thirty-three months of negotiation between the Rabin government and the Syrians had resulted in the construction of essentially one-and-a-half legs of the table of the peace that they hoped to conclude between them. That process had been considerably more drawn out than, for example, the Israeli-Egyptian negotiations at Camp David in 1978, when thirteen days of intense, summit-level negotiations, with the continuous engagement of the U.S. president, had crafted the first breakthrough set of agreed texts that within months led to a full peace agreement between Israel and an Arab neighbor.

The "Aims and Principles" document represented the "half-leg," having set the stage for completion of the more detailed agreement on the transitional and postpeace security arrangements. One of the notable features of this document's text is the ambiguity that is embodied within it. Many Israeli analysts have expressed the view that, under the structure of the document as agreed upon, the "Aims" part of it, broadly speaking, meets Israel's most pressing concerns, while the "Principles" part of it is more clearly sensitive to long-held Syrian concerns.

Such a distinction would hold unambiguously only if one assumes that the Syrians have no reason to fear a "sudden attack" from the Israeli military, which is not really a valid assumption. However, the fact remains that, territorially and in many other respects, Israel is the status-quo–defending party in this unresolved conflict, so therefore the Syrians generally may be assumed to have the greater interest of the two countries in keeping alive—at least, pending the satisfactory resolution of the territory issue—the possibility of a "sudden attack."

It was in the heart of the "Principles" part of the May agreement, however, that the text's deepest ambiguity was buried—namely, in the contrast between the second half of the second principle and the rest of the

"Principles" section. How could the "modifications" mentioned in the second principle be actualized on the ground in a way that would also satisfy the other three-and-a-half principles? Would that not depend centrally, indeed, on exactly where the mutually agreed, final-status border between the nations would end up being located? Those were the issues that Rabin's military planners, under his new chief of staff, Amnon Lipkin-Shahak, and Syria's military planners under General Shihabi started working on as May turned into June 1995.

In fact, the ambiguity built into the heart of the "Aims and Principles" document was an integral feature of Rabin's whole approach to peacemaking on the Syrian track. Deliberate ambiguity was also a distinguishing feature of all the communications that Rabin made, in public at least, regarding the depth of the Israeli withdrawal that he was considering.

The central problem for Rabin in this regard was that the Syrians had made absolutely clear throughout their whole participation in the pre-Madrid prenegotiations and the post-Madrid diplomacy that, while in the abstract they favored the conclusion of a peace with Israel, they would not be prepared for one second to consider any peace settlement that might involve making any lasting territorial concessions to Israel whatsoever. They based their position firmly both on the precedent of the peace agreement that the Egyptians had won with Israel in 1978–79, and on the preamble to UN Security Council Resolution 242, which refers to "the inadmissibility of the acquisition of territory by war."

Soon after he came into office in 1992, Rabin reportedly had become intrigued with the possibility that he might achieve a full peace with Syria before the regional military balance should change against Israel. But once he started exploring this window of opportunity, he immediately came up against the hard fact that, in order to take advantage of it, he would have to start, at the very least, considering the possibility of a "full" Israeli withdrawal from Golan. There was no other way. The Assad regime had signaled in every way it knew that it had zero interest in talking about anything short of a final-status agreement that would involve a full Israeli withdrawal. It had no interest in any further disengagement agreements or other transitional arrangements. It wanted to discuss only a final-status agreement (which could, the Syrians came to admit, be implemented in more than one phase, provided the final outcome was known in advance—as had been the case in the implementation of the

Egypt-Israel treaty). And Syria had no interest in discussing any final-status agreement involving anything short of full Israeli withdrawal.

But the moment Rabin started even countenancing the idea that Israel might withdraw fully from the Golan, he knew full well that this would be a controversial step inside Israel. Controversial, moreover, not just in a political sense, from the point of view that Likud and the other right-wing parties would be opposed to it, but intensely controversial within the Labor Party, too.

Eitan Haber knew Rabin's mind on such issues as well as anybody. When asked if he thought Rabin would have been prepared to commit Israel to a "full" withdrawal from Golan when push came to shove in the context of a satisfactory peace agreement, Haber said yes (although he remained of the view that this would not have been back to the June 4, 1967, line).[38] Thinking about the idea of such a withdrawal was indeed a difficult issue within the Labor Party, Haber noted, "because many of the settlers had gone to the Golan *by the orders of the Labor leaders* over the past thirty years." The day Rabin decided he needed to make a territorial deal over Golan, Haber recalled, he traveled to the area and met with seven hundred people there: "Many of them told him not just that they were Labor supporters but that they came from *his same camp* inside the Labor Party."[39]

One of those at the meeting may well have been Yehuda Harel, a veteran Golan settler who with seven comrades had gone to the Golan Plateau to found the first Israeli settlement there, Merom Golan, as early as July 1967. Harel had certainly been closely associated with Rabin's camp inside Labor for a long time. The only time before the 1990s that he left his daily work in the kibbutz movement (first in Galilee, then from 1967 on in Merom Golan) had been in the early 1980s, when he went to work in Rabin's political office for a couple of years in the fierce leadership battle Rabin was waging at that time against Peres. In the mid-1990s, when it started to look as though Rabin might be planning a significant degree of Israeli pullback from Golan, Harel was one of the leading organizers of the antiwithdrawal grouping within Labor that was known as the Third Way movement. Later he recalled, "I used to talk to [Rabin] every two or three weeks during the negotiations on the Syrian track. He hesitated a lot on the withdrawal question—and we can never know now what he actually would have done. But I believe he would have done it."[40]

It should be noted that by 1991—the year before Rabin became premier—the move that Likud had taken so boldly a decade earlier, to annex Golan to Israel, had come to seem entirely natural to many Israelis. By that year, most Israelis had come to consider Golan as naturally part of their own country, and this was emphatically not a partisan political sentiment. So for Rabin to be perceived in Israel, and in Labor, as actively pursuing a peace agreement with Syria that would involve the return of Golan to Syrian sovereignty was without a doubt a position that involved some degree—though not necessarily an unmanageable degree—of political risk.

As far as one can reconstruct his thinking and actions in this regard, Rabin tried to deal with that risk by using a combination of three tactics in his conduct of negotiations on this track:

▪ First, the creative use of *ambiguity*. He wove successive layers of ambiguity around the nature of the core deal he was pursuing with Damascus.

▪ Second, a resort to extreme *secrecy*. He tried to hold the details of what it was he and Rabinovich were negotiating as tightly and secretly as possible within Israel's notoriously leak-prone political system, pending completion of the whole four-legged table of the peace accord.

▪ Third, use of a very *slow and carefully modulated pace*. The hope here being, presumably, that as the Israeli public became more and more used to the idea of peacebuilding as a worthwhile national goal, the value of territorial holdings might erode.[41]

From the standpoint of the Assad regime, there was a strong predilection to be amenable to use of the second and third of these tactics. Like Rabin, Assad was a leader who always clearly placed a very high value on employment of secrecy and a cautious pace in his conduct of diplomacy. The Syrian leadership also seems to have been quite prepared to collude to a great extent in Rabin's use of creative ambiguity in the negotiations.[42] For though Syria had a strong interest in Israel being as clear as possible on the issue of withdrawal, it also had its own strong interest in the utmost ambiguity and secrecy being maintained regarding the other three legs of the table—primarily, the nature-of-peace leg, but also the security-arrangements leg. Therefore, a sort of informal tit-for-tat agreement seems to have developed between the two sides: Pending total agreement on the whole four-legged structure, Syria would do nothing that would publicly undermine Rabin's ability to keep intact his ambiguity regarding withdrawal—if Rabin would do nothing to undermine Syria's parallel need for utmost discretion regarding what it was the Syrians would be prepared to offer regarding the nature of the peace.

By the end of May 1995, however, the sides had not even reached the point of discussing the nature of the peace. In accordance with the strong preferences of both Rabin and Assad, the negotiations on withdrawal and security had been given precedence. It was in regard to Rabin's communications concerning withdrawal that his use of ambiguity was most clearly evident. As we have seen previously, that ambiguity concerned both the exact content and the status of his communications on this issue.[43] Had Rabin merely presented the idea of full withdrawal as a hypothetical, as Rabinovich claimed, or had it been a more solid commitment? Or was it, rather, a conditional commitment —with the condition in question being that Syria provide satisfactory answers to him regarding the other three legs of the conceptual table?

One factor that came to cloud the record on this issue was that, over the thirty months that followed August 1993, some of the parties (including the United States) would on occasion reportedly use the term "commitment," even in the negotiating room, to describe the nature of Rabin's communications regarding full withdrawal. "It was used, sometimes, as a kind of shorthand," one ranking U.S. official admitted.[44] According to Moalem, there was in addition one much more unequivocal occasion in early 1996, when Rabinovich himself blurted out to him in the negotiating room: "We even promised you that we would withdraw to the 4 June 1967 line!" (By then, Rabinovich was no longer the head of the Israeli delegation but merely a regular member of it. As Moalem recalled it, immediately after Rabinovich's outburst, the new Israeli delegation head, Uri Savir, got into a vehement argument with his teammate. Moalem, meanwhile, asked U.S. team leader Dennis Ross to enter into the minutes what Rabinovich had said.)[45]

One interesting dimension of any study on the nature of Rabin's 1993–95 communications concerning withdrawal is the role played by the U.S. mediators. In a very real way, the Americans formed the glue that was expected, in near-neutral fashion, to hold the table-legs of the ongoing negotiation securely in place pending completion of the whole table. By all accounts, for example, it was Secretary Christopher to whom Rabin entrusted any commitment he was prepared to make regarding the depth of a postpeace Israeli withdrawal. In addition, the text of the "Aims and Principles" document was "deposited with" (in Moalem's words), or entrusted to the American side, pending satisfactory completion of the whole structure. The United States thus came to play various different roles in holding the broader structure of the peace agreement intact. More than that, they had also been instrumental in finding much of the language for the "Aims and Principles" document, and indeed some of that language was already being previewed in Clinton's statements during his October 1994 visit to Damascus.

Some Israeli observers have charged that during the many shuttle visits he made between Israel and Syria, Secretary of State Christopher on occasion came to exaggerate to Assad just what it was that Rabin was ready to offer. For his part, U.S. peace team head Dennis Ross has stated categorically: "There was nothing that either Secretary Christopher or I conveyed to President Assad that we had not previously been asked [by the Israelis] to convey. I always did this precisely. We always drew a distinction, as well, between what we were asked to convey, and our own interpretations of it."[46]

Regarding Rabin's recourse to secrecy, it seems quite probable that in Israel *only Rabin and Rabinovich* knew the full details of what their precise negotiating position on this track was. Did Rabin even keep his foreign minister, Shimon Peres, fully informed? It seems fairly clear that he did not. In fall 1996, Israeli journalist Orly Azulay-Katz wrote that while Rabin was alive he kept all the important details of the diplomacy he was conducting with Syria secret from his foreign minister, and that Peres learned about such matters as Rabin's conditional offer of full withdrawal from Golan only *after* he succeeded to the premiership in the wake of Rabin's killing.[47] Peres strongly denied that account and averred that nothing he learned about the Syrian-track negotiation after Rabin's death caused him any surprise at all.[48] Dennis Ross has said, however, that in November 1995, ten days after Rabin's funeral, he went to Israel for four days and had what seemed like "fifty-five hours of discussions [with Peres] on the Syrian track. He wanted to know everything that had gone on."[49] If Peres had felt fully briefed by

Rabin while the latter was still alive, one might infer that his need to be briefed by the United States might have been somewhat less.

Rabinovich has noted that he had tried to conduct his job according to an agreement Rabin and Peres had reached with him, whereby he would report to Rabin regarding his work on the Syrian track and to Peres regarding his work as ambassador in Washington. According to that agreement, it would be up to the two principals themselves to decide when and how to keep each other informed of these respective missions. Therefore, Rabinovich was supposed to refrain from informing Peres about what was going in the Syrian track. Any informing that would be done, Rabin made clear, would be done by him himself.[50]

The last significant feature of the negotiating style that Rabin used on this track was his very slow, drawn-out timing.[51] By the end of May 1995, he and the Syrian leadership had devoted thirty-three months of at least partial attention to the talks on the Syrian track. But the parties' active engagement in these talks was by no means continuous throughout this period. One can identify three clear hiatus periods, during which either the Israeli side deliberately put this track on the back burner, or the talks were for other reasons not being actively pursued. The first of these hiatus periods lasted from August 1992 through March 1993, with the pause mainly attributable to U.S. disengagement throughout the election and transition era, to the step (or misstep) Rabin made regarding the attempted mass expulsion of Palestinians in December 1992, and to the Syrians' reaction to the expulsion. The second pause lasted from September 1993 until January 1994, and had been requested by the Israelis to allow them to "digest" the Oslo agreement. The third pause was a shorter affair, in the direct aftermath of the conclusion of Israel's Declaration of Principles with Jordan. Between them, the three pauses ate up around twelve months of time that the parties to the Syrian-Israeli track of the peace talks otherwise could have been using to pursue their own agreement.

From the Syrian point of view, the foot dragging they saw Rabin engaging in (as Shamir had done before him) engendered continuing questions regarding the seriousness of Rabin's intention to conclude a comprehensive peace agreement with the Arabs. In an interview Farouq Sharaa noted:

> It seems that the Israelis have not made up their mind firmly, and haven't committed themselves to a comprehensive peace. This is an

important reason in them dragging out the negotiations. . . . This is the strategic reason; and at the tactical level, they want each Arab party to feel that it is in a waiting room, and it needs to make further concessions if it wants to get a chance to see the doctor.[52]

Despite the slow pace of the talks, by the end of May 1995, Rabin had registered some considerable diplomatic achievements with the active help and involvement of the United States. He had succeeded in detaching both the PLO and the Jordanians from the embrace of any effective coordination with Damascus. And the four-legged structure of Syrian-Israeli peace looked as though it was being crafted into shape— slowly and carefully.

However, the very combination of tactics that Rabin had employed to get this far on the Syrian track still carried within it the threat of back-firing—or exploding. For the longer the negotiations dragged on, the harder it would become for Rabin's other two key tactics of extreme secrecy and deliberate ambiguity to be maintained intact. How long, indeed, could he hope to keep the whole delicate structure, woven around as it was with barriers of secrecy and ambiguity, from crashing to the ground?

4

Chiefs of Staff II: Inside and Outside the Negotiating Room

GETTING TO CHIEFS OF STAFF II

After they had reached agreement on the text of the "Aims and Principles" document, it seems to have been the intention of all three parties —the Israelis, the Syrians, and the United States—to move relatively speedily to the actualization of its terms by holding a second set of chiefs of staff talks (COS II).

On the Israeli side, part of Rabin's preparation for moving the Syrian track forward was to start, in his usual ultra-cautious manner, to prepare Israeli public opinion for the possibility of an eventual and extensive withdrawal from Golan. After the end of Rabin's late May 1995 visit to Washington, it became clear to members of the Israeli political elite that something was indeed happening on the Syrian track: Media interviewers and Rabin's own cabinet colleagues immediately began raising questions regarding the extent of the widely suspected Israeli withdrawal. On May 26, for example, an Israeli television reporter confronted Rabin with a map of Golan and asked him, "as a veteran military man," to clarify on the map "the points of dispute with Syria. Where do we want the border to be demarcated and where do the Syrians want it?"[1] At that point, Rabin was still unwilling to admit to his own public that, at least according to the sole hypothesis on which he was building his ongoing diplomacy, this issue had long since been decided. So he attempted to reframe the discussion by pointing out that the dispute with Syria was over all four dimensions ("legs") of the negotiation, and not just over the extent of the withdrawal.

In this interview, too, Rabin referred directly to the possibility that Israeli settlements in Golan might have to be evacuated. Specifically, he said that during the transitional period, one settlement might have to be "uprooted."[2] This proposal was mentioned in the context of "confidence-building" moves that the parties might make during the transitional period. But Syrian foreign minister Farouq Sharaa immediately signaled that his country had no interest in pursuing the idea.[3] Rabin quickly dropped it. But already, even the mere mention he had made at this point of evacuating one settlement galvanized into further action all those, settlers and others, who were firmly opposed to any talk of withdrawal from Golan.

If Rabin remained circumspect in his references to the territorial issue on Golan, by now Foreign Minister Peres was becoming far more outspoken on the possibility that Israel might have to effect a total pullback. "The price we will have to pay Syria in exchange for peace is the same price we paid Egypt, though it does not need to be identical," he was reported as telling a meeting of the Labor Party Standing Committee on May 25.[4]

The author of the article that reported Peres's words may or may not have been present at the meeting, but in Israel's very leak-prone political culture, it is quite likely that a participant in even a supposedly private gathering might have passed notes or a tape to a journalist. (It is also possible that Peres, and even Rabin, may not have been unhappy with such leaking.) In the paragraph that follows are further extracts from what Peres was reported as saying.

Noting that the precedent in Egypt had been determined by Likud, he said, "I do not know any Syrian that is willing to receive less than what Egypt received." He "sharply criticized" the position presented at the meeting by the Third Way movement, the grouping of activists inside the Labor Party who were opposed to any withdrawal from Golan, and responded to them by saying, "This is tantamount to making peace without the Arabs, or making peace without peace." He expressed the opinion that it would be easier to reach a peace agreement with Syria in 1995 than in 1996. And he previewed what would later become some of his most common additional arguments regarding the desirability of peace with Syria: "I am convinced we must not hesitate and must not allow the chances for a comprehensive peace in the Middle East to slip between our fingers. None of us will be forgiven if our children one day learn that it was possible to put an end to war in the Middle East and that we stuck to slogans and escaped the big decisions. There are no tricks here, we have here two truths and we must choose one: remaining on the Golan Heights means giving up peace." He also likened the Golan Heights to Gaza, saying that neither of them was "sacred land."[5]

By May 27, Peres was in Morocco, where one press correspondent reported him as saying to King Hassan: "We do not wish to keep holding on to Syrian land. The Golan Heights is Syrian land, and we are sitting on the Syrians' land."[6] Almost immediately, Peres denied the specifics of that report, saying that he had merely been clarifying to the correspondent that the Golan Heights had never been part of Eretz Yisra'el (the biblical Land of Israel), and that the issue "never came up" in his talks with his Moroccan host.[7] What Peres did or did not say on the issue, and to whom, thus remained murky. Rabin meanwhile said nothing in public either to help clarify what the government's actual position on the territorial question was, or to slap down any of Peres's increasingly explicit hints that the withdrawal from Golan might eventually be total. The prime minister thus seemed quite content to have his old rival for Labor leadership act as a kind of lightning rod on this question in front of the Israeli public.

The official Syrian reaction to the shifts in Rabin's and Peres's rhetoric was to quote very forthcoming versions of their statements, without comment but with apparent approval, on the official radio station. On May 31, for example, Syrian Arab Radio reported from "Occupied Palestine" (Israel) that "Israeli prime minister Yitzhak Rabin has said that any person who says that peace can be achieved while keeping the entire Golan Plateau, or the major part of it, is lying. . . . Meanwhile Israeli foreign minister Shimon Peres yesterday said that peace with Syria and Lebanon will be different from peace with other states because this peace will mean the end of war in the Middle East. . . ."[8] One intention of such broadcasts was presumably to help persuade Syria's ever-skeptical public opinion that this Israeli government was indeed one that could be trusted to make an honorable peace with Syria. The broadcasts can be viewed, therefore, as evidence that the Syrian leadership, like that in Israel, was also preparing to engage seriously in the planned negotiations.[9]

On the American side, preparations for the upcoming chiefs of staff discussion were carried out at numerous levels. The chairman of the Joint Chiefs of Staff, General John Shalikashvili, had nominated General Daniel Christman, a veteran of arms control talks with the Russians, to prepare the U.S. military's participation in the talks. At the political level, President Clinton conducted personal telephone calls in the first week of June with both Assad and Rabin. On June 7, according to one well-informed Israeli reporter, Rabin told associates that in his recent phone conversation with Clinton, the president said, "I have never heard Syrian president al-Assad so optimistic about the prospects for an arrangement with Israel as he was during our conversation this week."[10] During these conversations, too, Clinton invited the two other government heads to send their chiefs of staff to Washington for a second attempt at direct talks, starting June 27.

While the principals on all three sides continued with their preparations for deeper diplomatic engagement, trouble was (again) brewing within the Israeli political system. Once again, it was not only from the political opposition parties that strong criticism of the government's pursuit of the Syrian talks was being voiced, but also from deep within Rabin's own party, Labor—including from Labor ministers in his cabinet. On May 28, for example, Qol Yisra'el Radio reported that "Ministers Tzur and Shetrit sharply attacked Foreign Minister Peres's remarks that the Golan Heights belong to the Syrians. Minister Shetrit told our political correspondent Shlomo Raz that the foreign minister acted with intellectual dishonesty. . . ."[11]

For his part, opposition leader Binyamin Netanyahu was eager to use this issue—along with the government's controversial plans to undertake its first substantial withdrawal from West Bank cities under the terms of the Oslo agreement, scheduled for July 1—to help whip up opposition to the government.[12] In this effort, he was aided by anti-withdrawal activists from among both the Golan settlers (or "residents" as they preferred to call themselves) and the nation. In May, for example, a body called the Golan Residents' Committee (GRC) was able to boast on its Web page that "[Knesset members] Binyamin Netanyahu and Ariel Sharon pledged their support for the Golan before a gathering of over three thousand Likud leaders and members during a rally in the ancient [Golan] city of Qatzrin during hol hamo'ed Pesah [Passover week]."[13] Not surprisingly, the Syrians were watching what was happening. Syrian state radio reported: "Our kinfolk in the occupied Syrian Golan have warned Binyamin Netanyahu, leader of the Likud bloc, and other Israeli officials against paying provocative visits to the occupied Golan."[14]

In the United States, pro-Likud activists, led by Yossi Ben-Aharon (who had been head of the talks on the Syrian track before Rabinovich), had been busy since May 1994 in a campaign to try to undercut the Rabinovich team's ability to complete an Israeli-Syrian agreement. In particular, the campaign sought to build opposition in Congress and elsewhere to the idea of U.S. peacekeeping troops being stationed on the Golan in the event of a peace settlement, an element that the negotiators all agreed should be part of any eventual peace agreement. In November 1994, the pro-Likud campaign had gained increased momentum after the Republicans won control of the U.S. House of Representatives.[15] In May 1995, the GRC Web page boasted that among the numerous international visitors the GRC had hosted in the past month was Congressman Benjamin Gilman (Republican of New York), chairman of the Committee on International Relations, who "repeated his conviction that Congress should hold open discussions concerning the deployment of U.S. troops to the Golan before the negotiations proceed any further, when he met with Yehuda Harel [of the Third Way and GRC] this month. Gilman and others from the Foreign Affairs Committee hope for a June meeting to discuss the issue and invited Harel to join them in Washington, at that time."[16]

In Israel, the antiwithdrawal activists were campaigning at several different levels. Politically, they were pressing for introduction of a bill in the Knesset that would require a special two-thirds majority to allow the passage of any amendment (or, presumably, any annulment) of the 1981 Golan Law, that had "extended Israeli law to," or in effect annexed, Golan. At the end of May, Labor faction chairman Ra'anan Kohen agreed—against Rabin's wishes—that this bill could be submitted for a vote during the current Knesset session.[17] In terms of popular organizing, meanwhile, on June 20 the activists rallied hundreds of Golan residents to what was described as "a giant demonstration at the Gibor junction in Qiryat Shemona, protesting the arrival of Prime Minister Yitzhak Rabin for the celebrations marking Metulla's 100th anniversary which started yesterday." The demonstrators, *Ha'aretz* reported, "blocked roads and clashed with the police."[18]

The antiwithdrawal activism on behalf of Likud, the Third Way movement, and some of the Golan settlers was certainly intense, but it was carried out against a background of a recognizable openness throughout early 1995, on behalf of a significant portion of the Jewish Israeli public, to the possibility of a full pullback from Golan in the context of a satisfactory peace agreement. Researchers from the Tel Aviv University's Tami Steinmetz Center conducted two polls at the end of May—one before and one after the statements Rabin and Peres had made about full withdrawal. Spelling out further what might be involved in a "full" peace agreement, interviewers asked on May 25 whether respondents would support a peace agreement that included "full recognition on the part of Syria, including diplomatic relations, commercial ties, and open borders in exchange for a withdrawal from the Golan." To this question, some 16.7 percent replied Yes, 34.8 percent favored a partial withdrawal, 46.5 percent objected to a withdrawal, and 2 percent did not reply. (When the same question was asked four days later, after Rabin's and Peres's declarations, the number saying Yes rose to 20 percent.) The poll also found that 65.6 percent of those asked said that "on the withdrawal question the most important position is that of the IDF and the security establishment, then that of the public, and only then that of the prime minister and the government ministers."[19]

In addition to the prospect of a substantial or even full withdrawal from Golan, another aspect of the government's peace diplomacy with Syria that bothered many Israelis in these weeks was the question of Syria's relationship with the continuing tension in south Lebanon. On May 15, Rabin had admitted before the Knesset that the July 1993 Operation Accountability "did not bring about an end to terrorism from Lebanon."[20] In that speech, he seemed to be implying that the best way to respond to Muslim fundamentalist–related violence in general, including in Lebanon, was through an acceleration of the existing peace process, as well as through military counteractions.

At the end of May, the tension in south Lebanon had escalated to the point that once again, as in the run-up to Operation Accountability, Hezbollah rockets were being targeted against northern Israel.[21] On June 18, three Israeli soldiers from the elite Giv'ati Brigade were killed in a Hezbollah ambush inside south Lebanon.[22] By then Rabin seemed to be even more prepared to spell out in public the view that Israel's continuing woes in south Lebanon could not be resolved through purely military means but required a political-diplomatic breakthrough with Syria as well. The following day, the excellently informed journalist Aluf Ben reported that Rabin,

> believes that only a peace agreement with Syria will solve Israel's security problems along the border with Lebanon and put an end to Hezbollah's guerrilla warfare against Israel. Two reports which reached the prime minister's desk in recent years have strengthened this assessment. One report quoted Syrian sources as saying that as soon as the Golan Heights issue was resolved, the Syrians would stop all anti-Israeli activities from Lebanon by Hezbollah and the Palestinian rejectionist groups. The second report noted the practical steps Syria had taken to restrain Hezbollah activities in Lebanon, such as confiscating weapons.[23]

Over the past two months, Ben reported, there had been "an exacerbation in military activity in south Lebanon," but he noted that this exacerbation had occurred "from the part of both sides." He wrote that Chief of Staff Amnon Lipkin-Shahak had told the cabinet the week before that Hezbollah had changed its "reaction mode to *SLA* [South Lebanese Army] *and IDF strikes against Shiite villages* in south Lebanon and now retaliated by firing Katyusha rockets."[24] This latter wording was notably different from the way that Israeli officials usually describe only their own side's escalatory or hostile actions (including those of the Israeli-backed Lebanese militias in the South Lebanese Army) as "retaliations," while portraying those of the other side as unprovoked.

In the (unwritten) set of understandings reached at the conclusion of Operation Accountability in 1993, all the parties had undertaken not to target, or otherwise entangle in the hostilities, civilians or their villages. (That constraint was generally in line with the duties imposed by international humanitarian law on commanders of combatant forces, to the effect that they should not target noncombatants or their facilities and should take active steps to avoid, wherever possible, the occurrence of collateral damage to noncombatants and their facilities.) Now, Ben attributed to unidentified "Israeli officials" the judgment that "Hezbollah is being very careful to refrain from any gross violation of the understandings reached following Operation Accountability, which prohibit any attacks against civilian settlements on either side, whether in Israel or outside the security zone. The Katyushas were *in retaliation for SLA attacks on Lebanese villages.*" Israel, he wrote, "has made great efforts to rein in the SLA and maintain tighter control over it. Hezbollah, for its part, fears an angry response by Syria, which is committed to the Operation Accountability understandings." He added that

> Israel has made some enticing proposals to the Syrians. Foreign Minister Shimon Peres said that Syria will receive control over Lebanon and that "al-Assad will get more than al-Sadat did." Rabin has reluctantly accepted Syria's demand to put off negotiations with Lebanon until the issue of the Israeli withdrawal from the Golan Heights is resolved; however, Israel continues to propose reaching bilateral arrangements with Lebanon.[25]

As the time for COS II drew nearer, the Lebanon issue continued to simmer—and Rabin stepped up his efforts to keep a lid on it. On June 25, Israeli radio reported that Rabin, "in his capacity as defense minister, has ordered IDF troops to be deployed in SLA outposts in south Lebanon to oversee SLA activities and to make sure no excuses are given to Hezbollah to fire Katyushas at northern Israel."[26] That evening, Israeli television showed Uri Lubrani, Israel's longtime coordinator of affairs in Lebanon, saying, "We have to do all we can to make sure the SLA does not violate the understandings. Sometimes it works and sometimes it does not. I do not think we can restrain them totally. . . . *The IDF sometimes also fires in an uncontrolled way. That happens in war.*"[27]

In the complex conflict under way in south Lebanon, another party clearly involved—along with the various Lebanese parties, Israel, and Syria—had for a long time been the Islamic Republic of Iran. For the Assad leadership in Syria, ever since the attempt to conclude a formal alliance with Iraq came to an acrimonious end in 1979, the relationship with Iran had been a mainstay of its desire to find an alternative source of strategic depth in the continental hinterland. The relationship had survived since then despite significant differences between the two regimes on a number of issues (see chapter 1). On the important topic of the Madrid-launched peace process with Israel, Iran had always remained opposed to it from the very start, on the grounds that it was another vehicle for American domination of the region, and one that would leave the rights of Muslims significantly curtailed by the "Zionist entity"—Israel.

President Assad had found a variety of ways to deal with this significant difference of opinion with Teheran regarding the peace process. One of the means he employed was recourse to an informal but very evident division of labor. Sharaa, his English-speaking foreign minister, handled Syria's relationships with Washington, the Israelis, and the peace process in general. Vice President Abdel-Halim Khaddam, who had preceded Sharaa as foreign minister but was not as fluent in English as Sharaa, handled most of Assad's relationships with Teheran, the pro-Iran parties in Lebanon, and the Arab countries of the Gulf.

The pro-Iran parties in Lebanon certainly included Hezbollah, an organization that had grown up in the aftermath of Israel's large-scale 1982 invasion of Lebanon and whose founding ideology had been the need to free south Lebanon from the occupying presence of the Israeli military. As noted previously, by 1995 Hezbollah had eight members in Lebanon's parliament and was represented in the Lebanese government. In mid-June 1995, some U.S. officials began expressing the hope that after the conclusion of an Israeli-Lebanese peace accord (which they reportedly judged could not be done until an Israeli-Syrian agreement was reached), Israel would pull all of its forces out of Lebanon and Hezbollah would become a totally political movement, decommissioning its paramilitary wing.[28] However, they must have realized that such a development would require either that the Syrians be able to secure the acquiescence of Teheran (as they had secured Teheran's acquiescence to the 1993 cease-fire in Lebanon) or that Syria be prepared to force a break with Teheran over this issue, which seemed unlikely.[29]

On June 23, with only four days to go before the COS II meeting, Khaddam was in Teheran, where he discussed Syria's engagement in the peace process with his official hosts. During Khaddam's visit, an interviewer from the Iranian state radio station asked him whether the talks with Israel had made any progress. Carefully, he replied that the talks "have not taken us to a point where we can say serious progress has been made." But he was not totally negative. Asked how he viewed the future of Syrian-Israeli relations, he replied: "This is linked to the results of the talks. If the talks lead to the Israelis accepting a withdrawal to the 4 June [1967] lines and withdrawal from all Lebanese territory, then we can say that the negotiations are on a positive course. If, on the other hand, the Israelis continue their intransigence. . . ."[30]

One Arabic newspaper represented in Teheran meanwhile cited unidentified "sources" there as saying that Syria had "informed Iran of 'its fixed desire' to push the peace negotiations with Israel toward a 'positive conclusion.' The sources added that Syria is seeking to obtain a confirmation from Iran of [its acceptance of] a plan to disarm the Lebanese branch of Hezbollah after a comprehensive agreement has been reached with Israel." Khaddam's mission was not, according to this report, an easy one. The report noted that the official Iranian radio had urged Syria "in strong language to 'stand fast against the U.S. pressures.'" Syrian sources were quoted as describing Khaddam's mission as "'the most delicate mission' in his long political work."[31]

Khaddam returned to Damascus June 25; shortly thereafter, General Shihabi left for Washington for the encounter with General Shahak which would start June 27. On the day the talks opened, Syrian state radio aired a commentary in which it declared:

> It is clear to all observers that Syria is not taking part in the Washington talks from a weak position. On the contrary, throughout more than three and a half years, Israel has failed to force Syria to budge, even an inch, from its declared position toward the peace process and toward the need for this process to lead to the Israeli troops' full withdrawal to the June 1967 lines.
>   . . . Syria has exhibited adherence to the principles of evenness [ta'adul], equitability [takafi'], and balance [tawazun] in any proposed security arrangements.
>   The current talks are yet another test of Israel's intentions and credibility as regards peace.[32]

From the Israeli side, one of the fullest public expressions of Rabin's hopes as he prepared for COS II had come in an impromptu news conference he gave on June 10, shortly after meeting in his Tel Aviv home with Secretary of State Christopher. "This government," Rabin told a reporter for Israel's Channel 1 television

> wants to reach a peace which will provide us with real peace—a peace which every Israeli will recognize as such, wherein every Israeli will be able to travel to Syria, to Damascus or anywhere else, in order to forge commercial or cultural relations. Second, peace itself is a component of security. A situation where there is no motivation for war is the best

basis for peace. We must, however, establish security arrangements that will satisfy us in case, God forbid, there is a change in the situation.[33]

Rabin told Channel 2 on that same occasion: "I believe that the public wants peace, and whoever says that we can reach peace while preserving the entire Golan Heights or most of them is simply lying. It is legitimate to claim that the Golan Heights are more important than peace. But whoever believes this should say this outright. To claim, however, that peace is attainable while preserving the entire Golan Heights is lying, especially where the Likud people are concerned."[34]

Shortly before COS II opened, Rabinovich told an Israeli radio interviewer: "We have a window presently in which a comprehensive Syrian-Israeli agreement is negotiated. The window, I think, will close at some point in early 1996. . . . We have several more months ahead of us. Technically speaking, the issues can be negotiated and agreed upon and finalized within this period." He assured his interviewer that the Israeli side at the talks would be raising the south Lebanon question with its Syrian counterpart there. But Rabinovich defended the government's decision not to make a cessation of hostilities on Israel's northern border a precondition for continuing the talks with Syria: "The problem with presenting conditions," he said, "is that you may legislate yourself out of the game."

Rabinovich also referred to plans the parties had already agreed on for what should follow the COS II talks: "There is a second [that is, further] round already determined for the security talks. It will take place next month. Two delegations headed by the Syrian ambassador to Washington and myself, and including military experts other than chiefs of staff, will continue the work begun by the chiefs of staff."[35]

CHIEFS OF STAFF II: IN WASHINGTON AND BEYOND

At 2 P.M. on June 27, at the National War College in Fort McNair, Washington, D.C., Syrian chief of staff Hikmat Shihabi and his delegation met and shook hands with Israeli chief of staff Amnon Lipkin-Shahak and his delegation. Secretary Christopher chaired the meeting that ensued, aided by General Christman and Dennis Ross. Christopher told the participants, "We attach great significance to these discussions."[36]

According to Moalem's recollections, the agenda at COS II was organized to consider, in turn, three major issues:

1. The security regime for the "relevant areas" along the Golan front line, as referred to in the "Aims and Principles" document,
2. Early-warning systems,
3. The role of international forces.[37]

During the first day of discussions, the Syrian negotiator said the parties reached agreement on the first of these items, that on both sides of the eventual border there would be security arrangements consisting of both demilitarized zones and zones of reduced armament. The chiefs of staff then moved on to the second agenda item, and agreed on the use of satellites and aircraft for early warning, as well as some input from "international technical help" in this field. Moalem believed at that point that the parties had agreed that, between them, these features would be *sufficient* to provide the early warning they felt they needed.[38]

In his 1998 memoirs, Rabinovich does not give any specific information regarding points that may have been agreed upon during the first day's discussions. He does, however, give an interesting portrayal of some of the texture of the talks:

> The meeting began inauspiciously. Shihabi was the first to speak. He warned that a failure of this second meeting could have dangerous repercussions, and proceeded to present a modest set of security arrangements that grew directly out of the agreed "principles." On both sides of the line demilitarized zones would be established in which international forces and local police could be deployed. Depth would be added to them by contiguous areas of limited deployment. Monitoring would be implemented by satellites, airborne radar, and other "non-intrusive" measures. Syria was also ready for mutual transparency afforded by prior notification of large-scale exercises and reserve call-ups.[39]

As Rabinovich described it, it was then the turn of the Israelis to make their prepared presentation. This was done not by Shahak but by General Tzvi Shtauber, the head of the IDF planning branch. Very soon after Shtauber made this presentation in Washington, a seventeen-paragraph document, which almost certainly was the talking points for the presentation, was leaked to the Israeli press. This text, which came to be known as the "Shtauber document," stated:

> Our concept of the components of the security arrangements is based on several tiers: a. The objective and principles of the security arrange-

ments as formulated to date [that is, the "Aims and Principles" document]. b. An analysis of the military possibilities of both sides, and the threats and military answers that each side can present. . . . c. The need to have security arrangements contribute to a solid sense of security and to the conduct of normal life both in Syria and in Israel, and to help create relations of confidence between the two sides.[40]

The Shtauber document spelled out the security-enhancing features that it considered Israel gained from its existing military presence on the Golan Heights. It noted, "These assets, which may not be sufficient, as proved by the 1973 war, are supposed to provide us with the time required to mobilize reserves. . . ." Therefore, the document stated, in the context of the envisioned peace agreement, the IDF would "withdraw and cede an excellent defense line. . . . We do not think that such a withdrawal should be used to improve the positions of the Syrian Army. Therefore, our first principle is that any area vacated by us should be demilitarized and remain clear of any military infrastructure and presence."[41]

The document also proposed the following four additional elements:

- The continued presence of a foreign force (regarding which it noted, "It is very important that this force should include a conspicuous American element").
- The establishment of "thinned-out areas" on both sides of the demilitarized zone.
- The establishment of *complementary and overlapping arrangements* about early warning, verification, and supervision measures.
- Attention to broad-scale restructuring of both sides' armed forces.[42]

In regard to early warning, the document notes that "the IDF should continue to receive information which can only be obtained by a presence on Mount Hermon. (We will have to discuss the various possibilities to exercise this ability.)"[43]

The document also dealt with the need to "ban hostile military cooperation against the other side"; to increase transparency and trust between the sides; to establish naval and aerial regimes; to avoid friction in third countries, including Lebanon; and the need for "isolating and preventing aid from elements carrying out hostile and violent activities against the other side and against the peace process."[44] In the final section, the text refers again to the need for transparency and confidence-building, and proposed two immediate steps that could be taken in this context: "We are hereby inviting Syrian officers to join UN officers in the check-up patrols they conduct on the Golan Heights. I also think that agreement to cooperate in searching for MIAs [troops missing in action] will largely contribute to creating a positive climate in the negotiations."[45]

According to Rabinovich's memoir, Shihabi "responded strongly" to Shtauber's presentation,

> and rejected the plan on grounds of principle without getting into detail. He objected to four aspects of the plan: first, it was not predicated on the assumption of Israeli withdrawal to the lines of June 4, 1967; second, it included an Israeli ground station on the Golan; third, it expanded the notion of "relevant areas"; and fourth, it interfered with the size and order of battle of Syria's armed forces.[46]

The Israeli diplomat wrote that General Christman then offered some "bridging questions," and there was a discussion of airborne early warning systems. "Part of the discussion was specific, professional, and at points impressive," Rabinovich wrote. "At other moments the discussion was still plagued with slogans like 'full peace will bring full security.'"[47]

Far away from Washington, however, at the exact same period that the two chiefs of staff were holding their meeting, there was sharp controversy inside the Israeli political system over the basis on which the talks were being held. Israel is seven time zones ahead of Washington, D.C. On June 27, even before the talks opened, antiwithdrawal activists attracted a number of demonstrators estimated at several thousand to a protest rally against the talks. During the rally, police once again arrested several protesters who tried to block a major northern highway.[48]

Several hours before Shihabi and Shahak sat down together in Washington, Israeli radio reported that Likud chief Netanyahu had told a meeting of Likud's Political Committee that "senior sources" had leaked details to him "from the position papers the chief of staff will present to his counterpart in Washington." These details, he claimed, involved "Israeli concessions on four issues."[49]

Almost immediately, Rabin's deputy foreign minister, Yossi Beilin, derided this claim, and questioned the reliability of Netanyahu's sources. Anonymous staffers in Rabin's office described Netanyahu's allegations as "sheer nonsense."[50]

In the morning session of the Knesset on June 28, Netanyahu upped the ante by disclosing *inside the Israeli parliament* the text of a document he had received, which he described as, "a document of concessions [given] to the army chief of staff, General Amnon Shahak, for the talks in Washington."[51] (This was the text of the Shtauber document, the talking points for the presentation General Shtauber had given in Washington some fourteen hours earlier.) While Netanyahu was doing this, Rabin and Peres pointedly walked out of the session. Rabin's first reaction to Netanyahu's disclosure was to say that he had given Shahak no written guidelines for the talks in Washington.[52] But that evening, it became clear that Israel's usually vigilant censorship would be unable to prevent the publication of the text of the document in question, since Netanyahu's disclosure of it in the Knesset had invested it with parliamentary immunity. In what was described as "a rare late-night joint statement," Rabin and Peres then said that, "if in fact the Netanyahu document is an internal army working paper, as they believe it to be, then both the Likud chairman and whoever gave it to him broke the law and something must be done about it."[53] The following morning, the full text of the leaked document was duly published in at least one Israeli newspaper.[54]

Rabinovich described the impact of the leaks on the Israeli negotiating team as follows:

> Back at Shahak's hotel [on the evening of June 27], we found out that political life and public opinion in Israel were agitated over what came to be known as the "Shtauber document.". . . As we know, the claims made by the head of the opposition [concerning the document] were unsubstantiated and the episode, awkward as it was, failed to obstruct the negotiations (or, to put it differently, it was not the publication of the Shtauber document that obstructed the military discussions between Israel and Syria). . . . The "Shtauber episode" also vindicated Rabin in his insistence that the details of the Syrian negotiation be kept within a very small and narrow circle.[55]

He wrote that during the second day of meetings, "Shahak agreed with Shihabi that part of what both states required by way of early warning could be obtained from the air."[56] Clearly, that was somewhat different from Moalem's impression that the two sides had agreed that airborne systems (and foreign technical help) would provide *sufficient* early warning.

Rabinovich recalled that the chiefs of staff parried a little regarding the comparability of the depths of various proposals for DMZs, and that

> The discussion moved to the issue of the "relevant areas." It was in this context that Shihabi made an interesting gambit when he pointed to the fact that according to the Syrian definition of, "from Quneitra to Safed" (as against Rabin's original "from Damascus to Safed"), the proportion was 10:6. This statement was a clear departure from the mechanical approach to the notion of equality and an invitation to make a counter offer.
>
> Shahak was in no hurry to make that counter offer, but he did present what came to be known in the parlance of the peace process as "the Shahak question.". . . [He] asked, "Why would you need to keep so many of your divisions so close to the Israeli border after we make peace? Syria has a territory nine times larger than that of Israel and it has common borders with five states; why should such a proportion of her military be kept on one border?" Shihabi did not respond directly to the question, but he did say that in the event of an Israeli withdrawal Syria's "strike units" would not be moved forward from their present positions.[57]

Rabinovich was probably right to pinpoint the breakthrough nature of the 10:6 formula that Shihabi offered for the "relevant areas." Moalem's recollection of what happened during the second day of talks was, however, notably less upbeat. He has said the following:

> News came to us during the meeting of the two chiefs of staff about the leaking of the military document from Israel concerning their military study on the "Aims and Principles" document. . . . Netanyahu was like a crazy man, going with it to the Knesset at the time the two chiefs of staff were discussing.
>
> We felt at the time, reading of this, that the Israelis are *not* serious. Why was it leaked? And why, with this timing? This was a question-mark in front of us. We doubted *who* was leaking it. Generals opposed to the peace process—or Rabin himself?
>
> A second event gave us more than doubts. When the two chiefs of staff came to discuss an early-warning regime from air and space, we felt we had made a step ahead in this complicated negotiation. And all of a sudden, Shahak came up with a demand to keep a monitoring station on Mount Hermon!
>
> So these two things poisoned the atmosphere. Rabin could have stopped the leaking. And we believe that he ordered Shahak to come up with the new demand regarding the ground station. . . .
>
> We felt we had ended the agreement on monitoring from air and space, and should have moved to new areas of discussion. But then Shahak came up with new demands regarding the ground station.[58]

Moalem recalled that the chiefs of staff never got around to considering the third agenda item they had planned (the role of international forces), because they had now become deadlocked on the discussion of the second item—the question of Israel's demand to retain its own ground-based early-warning capability in Golan even after conclusion of the peace. "They mentioned that they wanted to keep their existing early-warning system on Mount Hermon. We refused this totally. We consider it against our sovereignty, and a type of spying on us even after peace. We are sure they could do what they need to do with satellites or planes," Moalem said. (On the issue of international forces, which was not discussed, he noted that Syria preferred that these be UN forces, while the Israeli side preferred a U.S. or U.S.-led force.)[59]

Foreign Minister Sharaa has commented that Shahak's seemingly unexpected introduction of the ground station issue—in addition to Rabin's earlier promise to the Knesset that he would submit any peace agreement with Israel to a national referendum—served to seriously dent the "good measure of . . . confidence" that the Syrians had gained in the Rabin government's intentions in July 1994. "We felt suspicion when he insisted not only on a ground early-warning station, but when he [subsequently] insisted on our sending officers to Washington to talk on details before the broad outlines of the security arrangement had been agreed," Sharaa said.[60]

Senior U.S. negotiator Dennis Ross recalled that he had met both Shihabi and Shahak separately, during visits to their countries prior to COS II, and that those meetings had revealed "some flexibility on each side." At the end of COS II, Ross said, he himself wrote down and presented to the participants a summary of the points on which the two sides had now reached agreement, which in his recollection totaled fifteen separate points—as well as a list of those points on which there was not yet any agreement. He said both chiefs of staff concurred with his lists, and that at the end of COS II they agreed that there remained disagreement on the question of ground early-warning stations.[61] The U.S. diplomat presumably secured the explicit endorsement from COS II participants regarding what had and what had not been agreed upon in an attempt to avoid the disappointments and confusion that had followed COS I. This technique of summarizing at the end of each meeting the points on which the parties had reached agreement is one commonly used to good effect by mediators. Ross continued to use the technique throughout the Wye Plantation talks of early 1996, but the Israeli side was never happy to have him produce such a written record.[62]

No U.S. official would offer details of what the fifteen points of agreement had included, save to note that one of them was that the two sides would give each other advance warning of military exercises. "There was no question," one official concluded, "but that COS II went well. Each side said so privately to us afterwards. Shihabi even seemed *more* upbeat [than Shahak]."[63]

On June 29—while the talks were still in session in Washington— a second key document was leaked to journalists in Israel. This text was described as also having been authored by General Shtauber.[64] The following day, it too was published in full in the Israeli press. Its title was "An Analysis of the Document of Understandings." It provided an analysis of the "Aims and Principles" document agreed to by Israel and Syria the month before, and had presumably been prepared as part of Shtauber's and Shahak's preparation for the COS II encounter.[65] As an introduction to each portion of its analysis, the document uses quotation marks to cite clauses purporting to be the successive clauses of the "Aims and Principles" document. Thus it is quite a straightforward task, using the text of this document, to re-create the text of the original "Aims and Principles" document relatively fully (as was done in chapter 3).

The Shtauber document, which had been disclosed earlier, had studiously avoided any mention of the actual location of the final line to which the IDF would withdraw under the envisioned peace agreement. However, the "analysis" document, as published in the Israeli press, spelled out in its final section that one provision of the May document had been that "Security arrangements must coincide with each party's sovereignty and territorial integrity." It concluded that this wording "seems to lead to a claim that the zero line is the border (whether the international border or the 4 June 1967 borders), according to which Israel will carry out a full withdrawal."[66]

Asked about this second document, Peres did not try to dispute its authenticity, only its status. "It is only natural for the General Staff to prepare numerous working papers," he told an IDF Radio reporter. "There is nothing new about this. It is really scandalous on the part of these people, who gained possession of these papers illegally, to reveal their contents to the Syrians in the very midst of the negotiations;

and then to seek to increase confusion . . . by claiming that these are the prime minister's instructions to the chief of staff. This is truly a terrible combination."[67]

From the Syrians' point of view, news of the leaking of the two military documents in Israel had come as a bombshell that raised serious questions for them about the credibility and seriousness of the Israeli leadership with which they were trying to negotiate over these delicate security issues. In public, the immediate reaction from Syria's official radio was merely that "the uproar being raised by extremists in Israel over the existence of an Israeli military document on a total withdrawal from the Golan is absolutely meaningless. Peace with Syria is linked to a total withdrawal."[68]

But for the Syrian negotiators—and also, presumably, for the man who directed their effort from the Presidential Palace in Damascus—the leaks clearly cast an unwelcome pall over the whole negotiation. As Moalem saw it, "From the end of June [1995] until we went to the Wye Plantation talks in December, the talks were frozen."[69]

ANOTHER PAUSE

On the Israeli side, the officials involved in the COS II talks tried bravely to continue with their work, regardless of the political storm that had erupted back home after Netanyahu's spectacular leaks. After the talks had finished on June 29, Rabinovich gave a lengthy interview to the generally pro-Labor daily *Davar,* in which he gave a cautious evaluation of the talks' achievements: "We are treading a path which could lead to a peace arrangement. The last three days somewhat brought us closer to our objective."[70] General Shahak, still in Washington, cautiously told an interviewer for IDF Radio: "I do not know if one could call it negotiations. On the other hand, it was not a show. It was a dialogue that included an exchange of information, views, and thoughts."[71]

Meanwhile, according to Rabin aide Eitan Haber, a high-level investigation was launched in Israel to try to ascertain the source of the politically explosive leak. "Many of us were asked to undergo a polygraph," he said, "but they didn't find anything."[72] From the Syrian side of the negotiation, it was seen as significant that—given the degree of questioning that the leaks had sparked in their minds regarding the trustworthiness of their interlocutors—they received no assurance from the Israeli side at the time (or, indeed, later) that any such investigation had been launched in Israel.[73] One high-level U.S. official concerned with the negotiations has also stated that he had "no recollection" about any Israeli investigation into the June 1995 leak.[74] Therefore, it seems that nothing was done from the American side either to reassure the Syrians that the leak had been unauthorized and was being fully investigated by the Israeli authorities. Thus the doubts that the leaks raised in Syrian minds remained unassuaged.

In the two weeks that followed COS II, another set of issues also came to cloud the atmosphere between the parties to the negotiation: the thorny question of whether Syria was or was not ready to consider the idea of a ground early-warning station to be operated on Mount Hermon by a non-Israeli third party as part of the long-term security arrangements, and the linked question of the role of this issue within the broader negotiation. In the view of the Israeli and U.S. participants in the talks, this issue came to assume much more importance than the erosion of trust that had been caused on the Syrian side by the affair of the Israeli leaks.

In the second week of July, U.S. negotiator Dennis Ross headed back to the Middle East to hold talks related both to the planned next meeting (of lower-level military experts) on the Israeli-Syrian track, scheduled for later in the month, and to the drawn-out negotiations on the Oslo II agreement, which was supposed to be concluded between Israeli and Palestinian negotiators before a deadline of July 26. (This latter agreement, which was over modalities for Israel's pullback from the centers of most major West Bank cities, was not concluded until late September. It was extremely controversial inside Israel.) Rabinovich has written that while he was in Israel, Ross presented to Rabin his "summary" of what had happened in the COS II talks— which presumably included the same list of fifteen "agreed points" that he had presented at the end of the COS II meeting. Rabinovich wrote that Rabin "was not pleased with Ross's summary; it did not dovetail with what he had heard from Shahak."[75]

On the morning of July 11, Ross traveled from Israel to Damascus. He has recalled that shortly before he arrived there, Syria's official radio broadcast a commentary noting that while the Israelis could not maintain any long-term presence on Golan, perhaps a third party could do so instead.[76] The exact wording of this broadcast was the following: "Even if it is necessary to have warning stations on both sides of the border, it would be possible to assign this task to international and friendly forces which guaranteed the implementation of any peace agreement reached by the two sides."[77] Another portion of this same text, which may seem to have ruled out the flexibility noted by Ross, stated: "It is natural for Syria to reject the presence of warning stations and Israeli soldiers and officers in the Golan, especially since such a presence means the continuation of occupation of this small part of Syrian territory." This reference to Golan constituting a "small" part of Syrian territory was new, but it became quite frequent in official Syrian commentaries during those days. The intention seemed to be to signal that, although the Assad regime had labored long and hard on the Golan diplomacy, still it was not such an important issue for them that they were currently prepared to make further concessions in order to regain the Golan.

In the event, the radio commentary's earlier reference to the idea of third-party early-warning stations caused a definite rise in U.S. hopes that such a solution indeed could be found to the ground station problem. But one U.S. official said that when he met President Assad shortly thereafter, the Syrian leader himself raised the issue of the broadcast—in order to *deny* firmly that from Syria's point of view, a third-party presence for the purposes of early warning might be at all permissible. The official recalled that,

> After this, Assad remained immovable. Why? Had he seen that possibly he was going too far. . . ? Or perhaps something else happened. What? He was always asking: What am I gaining from this process? He must have seen something that indicated to him that the Israelis were not ready to move. There had been an Israeli press story, perhaps, indicating that Rabin was not ready to move until after his elections? Although, at the time, [we] had just seen Rabin and gotten his agreement to do a shuttle to see if we could put together a new agenda.[78]

If that was indeed what the United States was hearing from Rabin, and what it was seeking to convey to Assad, it was a message somewhat at variance with what the Syrians had heard, for example, on the Israeli state radio station's news broadcast of July 10. In that broadcast, the radio quoted Rabinovich as saying that "the negotiations between Israel and Syria have been put on hold until understandings are reached at the military level."[79]

By the time of the Syrian radio's mid-afternoon broadcast on July 11, Assad's information apparatus was taking no chances whatsoever of being misunderstood on the issue of foreign ground stations: "Syria rejects any formula for the presence of early-warning stations on the Syrian territory."[80]

One possibility regarding the apparent turnabout in the Syrian leadership's position on third-party ground stations that the U.S. official did not mention (although Rabinovich, in his memoirs, did) was that the July 10 radio commentary's reference to the issue had been a mistake—either an outright mistake, or the mistaken disclosure of a concession that, according to Assad's planning, should not have been made that early. From his perspective, Rabinovich would later describe the commentary as "strange."[81] And given the formalistic and highly secretive manner in which the Assad regime conducted all aspects of its negotiation with Israel, it would indeed be strange if a Syrian change of heart on an issue as sensitive as this were to be signaled first of all through the public media rather than inside the negotiating room. Another possibility was that the July 10 radio broadcast had been used to float an authorized trial balloon, but that as a result of debate and reconsideration within the Syrian leadership, its terms were withdrawn soon after. (Indeed, a U.S. or other third-party role in providing early warning, even with the use of human operators, could perhaps be said to be permissible under the rubric of the "foreign technical help" that Moalem said Shihabi had agreed to.)

During Ross's meeting with Assad, the Syrian president also made it clear that he was not prepared to go ahead with the military-to-military talks, as previously planned, until he had received satisfaction on the ground station issue. Moalem has explained that after Shahak introduced the idea of an Israeli-manned ground station on Mount Hermon on the second day of the COS II talks, "We felt this had been introduced by the Israelis to blow up the negotiations after the Netanyahu exposé. It had previously been agreed that after COS II, the military experts would meet. We refused, because this demand [for an Israeli-manned ground station] blew up the negotiation. We asked how military experts could agree if their superiors could not?"[82]

Asked to describe his view of what had happened in the discussions on the ground station issue, one senior American official would say only that "It is hard to say what happened regarding the ground stations." He confirmed that Assad did not want to go ahead with previously agreed military-to-military talks, but said he wanted to return instead to the "ambassadors channel." "Rabin saw that as bad faith on Assad's part," the official recalled.[83]

Rabinovich has confirmed that Rabin was angered by the Syrians' insistence that they could not proceed with the military-to-military talks until the issue of the Israeli ground station was resolved to their satisfaction. "Rabin had to remind them that they had agreed on a whole series of modalities for conducting the talks," he said. "Their inflexibility on this was unacceptable."[84]

From the Syrian side, Israel's negotiating stance in the weeks after COS II also fueled further suspicions, for instance "when [Rabin] insisted not only on ground early-warning stations but when he insisted, too, on our sending officers to Washington to talk about details before the broad outlines were agreed," Foreign Minister Sharaa has recalled. "This insistence delayed things, because the officers on their own could not reach a decision. They wanted to have lower-level officers to stay a long time there talking, to pretend there were negotiations, but [the negotiations] were in fact dead."[85]

FALLOUT FROM COS II

In retrospect, Netanyahu seems to have achieved a lot with his coup of acquiring and then releasing into the public domain the texts of the two military documents. On the Syrian side, he succeeded in damaging the trust that had been built up in the integrity and seriousness of the Israeli negotiating partners. The Rabin team's failure to communicate anything to the Syrians that would mitigate this effect merely compounded the Syrian side's suspicions about the provenance of the leak—as well as raising broader questions about the degree of Rabin's commitment to building a long-term relationship of trust with Syria, as would be required in any viable peace regime. By the end of July, Foreign Minister Sharaa was to refer, in a speech given to welcome Saudi Arabia's visiting foreign minister, Prince Saud al-Faisal, to Israel's "premeditated foiling of the Washington talks between the chiefs of staff."[86]

On the Israeli side of the negotiating table, the disclosures instigated by Netanyahu succeeded in stripping away the layers of ambiguity and secrecy in which Rabin's negotiating strategy up to that point had been swathed. Rabin's main reaction to the furor raised by the Netanyahu leaks was (yet again) to come to a broad tactical decision to put the Syrian-track negotiations on the back burner in his scheme of leadership priorities. Anyway, by mid-July the negotiations on the Palestinian track were starting to absorb a lot more of his attention and political capital than he had perhaps intended.

Those negotiations would lead to the September 28 signing of the Oslo II agreement in Washington, D.C., mandating further Israeli withdrawals from the West Bank, the holding of elections by the Palestinians in the occupied territories (but not Palestinians still living as refugees in Syria and elsewhere), and an Israeli handover of additional powers to the Palestinian Authority for the remainder of an interim period whose final point was still to be negotiated. Like the first Oslo agreement, this one was also extremely controversial in Israel and among many Palestinian refugees. With the right-wing parties starting to mobilize in the early stages of the election campaign that by law had to be conducted sometime on or before October 1996, the tension on the streets of many Israeli cities rose to fever pitch. Leah Rabin has nevertheless written that "On the fifth of October [1995], the Knesset debated and ultimately approved the second Oslo agreement. The way seemed clear to tackle the next item on the peace agenda—peace with Syria."[87]

To add to Rabin's pressures, by the end of October serious trouble had arisen within Labor's ranks with the announcement by those Knesset members and others associated with the Third Way movement (whose members were predominantly from within Labor's ranks) that they would "continue to prepare to run in the elections." According to a Qol Yisra'el radio report, this move was interpreted by Third Way members as "a practical announcement on the establishment of a new party."[88]

The United States doggedly continued to try to restart the talks on the Syrian track, but Rabin remained reluctant. Later, when Rabinovich recalled that in late October Rabin had agreed that Ross could return to the region to discuss doing something on the Syrian track, he described Rabin's agreement as constituting a "concession" to the Americans. "He was having terrible problems in his coalition, especially with the Third Way people. He was having problems getting Oslo II through the Knesset, and problems with the budget. He was moving towards elections, anyway," Rabinovich said by way of explanation.[89]

One U.S. official has recalled of this period that, "Rabin always wanted to have two tracks in play—from August 1993 on. At this point, he had something going with the Palestinians, but he didn't want the Syrian track to wither. He wanted to have them both going, so he could use it as a lever—and he might have a breakthrough. But by this time he didn't compare Assad favorably with Yasser Arafat. He saw Arafat as prepared to take hard decisions, like himself, but he thought Assad was not yet prepared to do that."[90]

When Secretary Christopher went to Damascus as part of his late-October shuttle, he found Assad apparently equally dubious about Rabin's intentions. One official has said that at the meeting, Christopher told the Syrian leader that "history may record that you had an opportunity [for peace], and you lost it." Assad paused and then said only, "Perhaps."

For his part, Rabin aide Eitan Haber has said that, finally, in early November, "I called [U.S. ambassador to Israel] Martin Indyk on Rabin's orders and told him that we had decided to postpone everything with the Syrians because we were now in an election period. . . . Rabin was hoping to get a stronger mandate [in the negotiations] from the elections, but he was still planning for a referendum as well."[91] Rabinovich has confirmed that it was Rabin's intention to resume the talks on the Syrian track after his hoped-for victory in the election. "I think he thought an agreement with Syria would be more likely in his second term than in his first term," he said.[92]

In retrospect, Rabin's decision to impose yet another pause on the Syrian track at this time may seem particularly regrettable, since despite the continued gaps between the two sides, some significant progress had indeed been made at COS II. Syria's public propaganda, for example, had always dwelt at length on the need for basic concepts of "equality," "evenness," and "equitability" to govern the restriction placed on both sides in the security arrangements. So the 10:6 formula that Shihabi was offering for the "relevant areas" signaled the start of a new phase of negotiations.[93] On July 3, an Israeli television report noted that the Israeli cabinet had rejected the specifics of this formula —but it described Israeli officials as being pleased "with Syria's very readiness to accept the principle of geographical disparity in the security arrangements."[94] From Damascus, an editorial in a government-backed daily warned on July 5, "Any talk or press leaks about arrangements through which Israel realizes gains at the expense of Arab security and the security of Syria are aimed to make way for the Israeli allegations and pretexts or even market them in order to undermine the Syrian position. . . ."[95] But the editorial notably did not refute the report outright.

Two other indicators in the period surrounding the COS II talks may have signaled that the atmosphere was ripe for further progress on this track. In a little-noticed move in late June, Syria sent its first-ever delegation to take part in one of the multilateral gatherings held under the auspices of the Madrid-launched peace process.[96] And in Israel, on July 1, despite the fact that the controversy sparked by Netanyahu's leaking of the military documents was then at its peak, a nationwide opinion poll showed Rabin now pulling ahead of Netanyahu in the polls.[97] During the four months that followed July 1, the Israeli domestic political scene became very heated. Extreme nationalists opposed to any Israeli withdrawal in the West Bank or Golan openly called Rabin a "Nazi," and so on. But still, public support for his general peace diplomacy remained surprisingly solid. A poll that sampled all Israeli citizens, Jewish and Arab, at the end of October revealed that the pro-Rabin "left-wing bloc" could be expected to retain 57 seats after a general election, while the right wing would have 55 seats, with eight seats still "undecided."[98]

THE LESSONS OF SUMMER 1995

Reaching agreement on the "Aims and Principles" document had been a breakthrough for both sides. In particular, with both leaderships now actively entertaining the ideas of mutuality contained therein, they were starting to turn away from a zero-sum view of the relationship to one that contained some degree of cooperation in security affairs. That this was the case was shown in the shifts that both sides made in their public rhetoric before the convening of COS II. On the Israeli side, in addition, the prime minister and those around him were displaying a new attitude toward the implications of the tensions in Lebanon: They showed themselves prepared more than ever before to discuss in public the need to rein in the actions of some of the ground-level hotheads on their side (whether from the IDF or from its allies), rather than milking the actions of these hotheads for its supposed "deterrent" value. On the Syrian side, meanwhile, the decision to authorize the unprecedented participation of a Syrian scholar in an event conducted under the aegis of the multilateral talks, and the regime's apparent decision to start reconfiguring the relationship with Iran, also provided additional evidence that the leadership was actively exploring some of the ramifications of a future peace with Israel.

During this period we also see the United States becoming more active as a *mediator* on this track, moving somewhat beyond its previous, more passive role as a mere *facilitator* to one that involved nudging the parties along toward spelling out their areas of agreement.

To an important extent, the Israelis and Americans were still not treating the concerns of their Syrian interlocutor with the seriousness that they deserved. This was shown by the failure of either of these two to take any step to reassure President Assad that the leaking of the military documents had not been authorized. But still, the conclusion of the "Aims and Principles" document had generated enough momentum that, even though the Israeli leaks caused some pause for reconsideration in Damascus, the Syrians felt they had a serious potential interlocutor in Rabin nevertheless.

In a different world, Rabin might perhaps have taken the evidence provided by the polls during the summer of 1995 as vindication of the rightness of his peace diplomacy, even in tough times, and as a mandate to pursue it further with some dispatch. As it was, he did not take that path. He chose instead to put the Syrian talks on hold while completing the Oslo II negotiations with the PLO and starting his electoral preparations. By the end of October, the Israeli media—and even Syria's foreign minister—were talking quite openly about a message having been conveyed indirectly from Rabin to Assad, asking for the resumption of the talks to be delayed until the following April.[99]

We will never know whether that strategy of Rabin's would have succeeded—or how the talks on the Syrian track might have proceeded if it did.

On the evening of November 4, an extreme Israeli nationalist named Yigal Amir assassinated Prime Minister Rabin.

5
Peres Takes Over

THE FIRST FOUR DAYS

"On that terrible night," Mrs. Rabin wrote in her memoir, about the evening of November 4, 1995,

> When the first bang was heard, Yitzhak looked back, as though he were thinking, Just a minute, what is going on here? and then I saw him drop down as others piled on top of him. I thought, and later so strongly wanted to believe, that he was thrown down as an act of protection.
>
> I heard three short bangs. Could they have been firecrackers? Noise-makers?
>
> Suddenly, I was standing alone.[1]

In Damascus, according to one unconfirmed report, when President Assad heard the first news of Rabin's killing that evening, he placed his country's military forces on full alert. Tension had been running fairly high in south Lebanon for some weeks, and there was always the risk of another suicide bomb from Palestinian hard-liners. Under those circumstances, Assad may have feared that Rabin's assailant had been an Arab—and that some in Israel's leadership would seek to respond by hitting Syria.

U.S. negotiator Dennis Ross visited Damascus less than two weeks later. According to him, Assad still seemed "stunned" by what had happened to Rabin. Previously, Assad told Ross, he had thought that Rabin always exaggerated the domestic political problems he faced on account of his peace diplomacy. But now, according to Ross, the Syrian leader "realized that the opposition in Israel was serious." Ross said that Assad seemed "somber. . . . He seemed to agree that Rabin had paid with his life for his pursuit of peace. He seemed regretful about it, and he was ready to see Peres as sincere in his desire for peace."[2] Assad did not say anything in public that expressed this regret.

If Assad was stunned and regretful in response to Rabin's death, these words are nowhere near strong enough to describe the reactions of those who had worked closely with Rabin in the Israeli political scene. For Shimon Peres, Rabin's killing came as a particularly tough blow. Over the previous few months, the two men had worked closely together in their handling of the peace diplomacy with the Palestinians. According to both Ross and Rabinovich, over that period the two Labor leaders had finally come to appreciate each other's gifts, and to feel comfortable and confident working together.[3] On the night of November 4, Rabin had taken the unprecedented step of taking part in a huge public peace rally in Tel Aviv, making a large gesture of public solidarity with a constituency in Israel that traditionally had been much more supportive of Peres's leadership than of his own: the peace camp. Minutes before the shooting, Rabin had been standing at Peres's side behind the rally's podium, singing—for the first time ever—the peace camp's signature tune, "The Song of Peace."

And then he was dead. When Ross saw Peres at the funeral a day-and-a-half later, he said Peres "looked like his whole world had been shattered."[4] In the hours and days that followed, Peres had to come to terms with his own shock and grief. He had to step into Rabin's shoes as acting head of Israel's government and start figuring out how to compose his own new government team. He had to launch a speedy investigation into the shooting and assess and reduce the degree of the risk that remained to others, including himself. He had to oversee the organizing of a massive state funeral that attracted heads of state and government from scores of countries, including Presidents Clinton and Mubarak, King Hussein, and many others. Along the way, he had to rapidly prepare himself to take charge of all aspects of Israel's ongoing peace diplomacy with its neighbors, including those parts of it that Rabin had not shared fully with him.

Some portions of the challenge Peres faced on this latter score had to be addressed immediately. Once Rabin's funeral was over November 6, Peres would be meeting with Clinton. Rabinovich considered it so urgent that he brief Peres in person on the nuance involved in the Syrian track—and that he do so *before* the meeting with Clinton—that he approached Peres while they were all still at the cemetery to plead for thirty minutes alone with Peres. In the short meeting thus arranged,

> We went through the essential record of the negotiation and of the American-Israeli exchanges in that regard. It was all done under immense time pressure, but I did make a point of warning Peres against the term "commitment," that, I suspected, might be used in the discussions with the president. It would be one thing for Rabin's successor to express a commitment to the late prime minister's policies and undertakings. But this would be different from implying, as the very term might, that an actual commitment had been made with regard to withdrawal.[5]

Other, broader aspects of the conduct of the peace process perhaps did not have to be dealt with quite as rapidly—but Peres and his closest aides seemed eager to tackle them anyway. In particular, within the two or three days immediately after Rabin's killing, Peres was coming to a major decision to reverse the priorities Rabin had seemingly decided on earlier, whereby he had (once again) deferred the talks on the Syrian track, this time until after the upcoming Israeli elections. On November 7, two Israeli journalists were already reporting that in Peres's private meeting with Clinton the day before, the acting prime minister "said Israel is willing to advance toward an arrangement with Syria, that he is not deterred by the upcoming elections, and that we must forget past controversies, regain our composure, and 'talk business.'"[6]

Was that report informed by something more than the wishful thinking of those around Peres? It seems so, because two days later IDF Radio was reporting (based on an interview with close Peres aide Uri Savir) that Peres had told Clinton that "over the next few weeks, we should examine the possibilities for advancing the negotiations with Damascus." On that broadcast, Savir also expressed the view, "If Syrian president al-Assad really wants peace, he will find an Israeli partner." The negotiations with Syria up to that point had been, Savir said, "too slow, indirect, petty, and narrow."[7]

Already, in the weeks preceding Rabin's death, Peres had gone on public record in Israel and elsewhere that he considered reaching a peace agreement with Syria more important than a Labor win in the coming elections.[8] Over the days that followed his meeting with Clinton, it became increasingly clear that going all out for a peace agreement with Syria before rather than after the elections was indeed a step that Israel's new premier was actively considering. On November 8, he told a visiting Egyptian television team that "any attempt to contribute to bring the parties closer and to really pave the way for peace with Syria by an Egyptian-supported contribution will be appreciated by us."[9]

That same day, British foreign secretary Malcolm Rifkind, who had been in Israel for Rabin's funeral, made a small shuttle visit to Damascus to talk with Assad. He found encouraging news there to bring back. In a joint press conference at the end of Rifkind's visit, Foreign Minister Sharaa commented on the prospects for the negotiations in the aftermath of Rabin's assassination: "Something good might result from something bad. The Israelis may feel in these moments that peace is in their interest and in the interest of all parties." Syrian television attributed to Rifkind the comments that the negotiations could be quickly realized, and that it would be important for Peres, when he met him "to know that Syria has always been eager to achieve peace as soon as possible."[10]

Within hours of the Sharaa-Rifkind news conference, Israel's economics and planning minister, Yossi Beilin, a close Peres ally, was responding on Israeli television. Beilin said it was terrible "to hear such talk about something good coming out of it. He does not even express regret about the murder." But the Israeli minister noted, "It was the late Prime Minister Yitzhak Rabin who said that the depth of withdrawal on the Golan Heights would be equal to the extent of peace. We are committed to the same formula. If the Syrians are prepared to accept this formula, which means that they will have the price of full normalization with Israel, *we are prepared to start negotiations even at this stage*. We have an entire year, I hope, in which we can make peace."[11] He warned the Syrians, meanwhile, that "if they think they are now dealing with a different government which is prepared to make concessions on vital issues that the previous government was not prepared to concede, then I can only say that they are mistaken."[12]

The signaling with Damascus was under way. Fewer than four full days had passed since Rabin's murder. When he was asked about the speed with which he reversed his predecessor's earlier decision to hold elections before proceeding any further on the Syrian track, Peres replied simply, "It fits my temperament to act rapidly."[13]

THE NEW APPROACH: "FLYING HIGH AND FAST"

If Beilin was one of Peres's aides who was urging him to engage actively and rapidly on the Syrian track, Uri Savir was clearly another.[14] Since 1992 Savir had been the director general in the foreign ministry, which Peres headed until he took over as prime minister. In that capacity, Savir had been Peres's main person overseeing, first, the clandestine talks with the PLO in Norway and, then, the negotiation and implementation of the Oslo I and Oslo II agreements. According to Savir, some six to twelve months before Rabin was assassinated, both he and Beilin had come to the conclusion that there was a good chance that Labor might lose the next general elections—and that it was therefore important to make the peace process as "irreversible" as possible before the elections were held. He recalled that

> I wrote a paper for Peres in 1994, urging him to try to get a Syrian agreement before an agreement on Jerusalem, because the Jerusalem issue might explode the whole process.
>
> Also, while Rabin was still alive, Peres had raised with him the link between the Syrian track of the talks and the idea of "comprehensiveness." That was in '94, too. Rabin gave him permission to raise this issue with Dennis Ross, but the idea died. After the assassination of Rabin, Peres and I thought we could make a link between our view of comprehensiveness and that of the Syrians. There was a strange convergence on this.[15]

At the conceptual level, Savir said, "There was a difference between the outlook that Peres and I shared, and that of Rabin and Rabinovich. We on our side believe that peace creates a dynamic that is less under the control of leaders than Israelis generally assume. But we think that peace can create good long-term dynamics."[16]

In 1998 Peres himself described the approach that he brought to the Syrian track after Rabin's killing as follows:

> The Syrians knew that Rabin had been ready to go down from the Golan Heights. I said that whatever Rabin agreed, I would be prepared to follow. I wanted to do the same thing he had been doing with some changes. I wanted to make the Syrian agreement the "last one in the Arab world"—that is, we would have a big ceremony for the peace agreement and all the Arab leaders would participate. President Assad, I understand, agreed to this. Also, I wanted to have an economic agreement. I thought we could be relatively open regarding timing [of the implementation phase], if we can answer the psychological need in Israel to develop trust in Syria's intentions. . . .

I thought putting economics into the negotiations would be attractive to the Syrians. There was the attraction of market-based economics and science-based development. The idea that markets are more important than countries, and so on. I'm not sure how specific this was in their [the Syrians'] eyes. But I think that economics change attitudes more than politics. . . .

I also thought the water question should be given more importance. We couldn't go down from the Golan Heights without ensuring that. I thought we could reach an agreement on water.

Could Rabin have gone faster than he did with Syria? No, he went very fast. There was a misunderstanding on security, though. President Assad thought our withdrawal would be to the border of 4 June 1967. But there is no such thing as a "border" of 4 June 1967. There was a 4 June "situation." What Rabin said was that the depth of our withdrawal would depend on the depth of peace.[17]

The decision that he came to so rapidly after Rabin's death, to revitalize the Syrian track in the hope of reaching a full peace agreement with Syria—or better still, an all-Arab peace agreement—meant, as Beilin and Savir had clearly indicated, that Peres was prepared to forgo the idea of calling early elections so that he would have enough time to get this ambitious diplomatic task completed. That decision was not popular with all Labor Party members. A number of Labor activists, Knesset members, and even ministers, felt at that time that their party would do well to profit relatively rapidly from the wave of outrage that swept most of Israeli society after Rabin's killing, in order to turn that outrage into a stronger electoral mandate.[18]

One U.S. official involved in the negotiations has recalled, "There was no way we could *not* respond to Peres's determination to achieve a breakthrough on the Syrian track, even though some argued that it would not work and attention was still needed for the Israeli-Palestinian relationship. . . . We were driven by Peres's agenda. We accepted far too uncritically many of the assumptions Peres made."[19] For his part, Ross has noted, "The assassination changed everything. For this administration, it changed what was meant by 'taking risks for peace.' Peres wanted to change the whole framework. After the assassination, our impulse was against telling any Israeli leader what to do!"[20]

Ross had been in Israel briefly for the funeral. Ten days later he traveled there again. He recalled: "We had what some referred to as fifty-five hours of discussions during that visit, about the Syrian track.

Peres wanted to know everything that had gone on. And every time his guys seemed cautious about it, he urged them to overcome their caution."[21] He explained that during those discussions, which took place over four days, the evolution on the Syrian track became evident, and there were "points of convergence that Peres and his people had not known about before."[22]

Peres described the sequence of events a little differently: "After Rabin was killed, I got a message from the Americans that the Syrians wanted us to finish the peace," he said in an interview. "I said I wanted to know that they were prepared to *finish* the process before our elections, because I did not want to go to the elections 'in the middle of an open-heart operation,' as it were."[23]

At the same time that Peres was bringing himself up to speed on the details of the Syrian negotiation, he was working on putting together his new government. On November 22, he presented the new cabinet list and its program to the Knesset. He followed Rabin in keeping the defense portfolio for himself. (He did not immediately appoint another cabinet member as deputy defense minister; on November 27, he announced that retired General Ori Or would fill that position.) Beilin was named "minister in the prime minister's office." The new foreign minister would be former chief of staff Ehud Barak.

In the speech in which he presented his new cabinet to the Knesset, Peres vowed, "We will continue bearing the flag carried by Yitzhak Rabin when he was gunned down, and others will bear it after us. No to violence; yes to peace." He stated that "Israel is in the midst of economic prosperity, social betterment, and political momentum," and attributed those achievements to "the resumption of the peace process —that is, the peace agreement with Jordan, the interim agreements with the Palestinians, the building of economic peace in conjunction with the political peace . . . and our aspirations for peace with Syria and Lebanon. All these have opened up a new world to us. Almost the entire world is now open to us." He also sent a clear message to President Assad:

> I would like to propose to the Syrian president that we make a real contribution to put an end to the era of war in the Middle East. Let me clarify that peace between Syria and Israel, a peace that will be submitted to the public for approval, will be capable of creating the historic opportunity for bringing comprehensive peace to the entire region.

The negotiations with Syria can come in the form of a comprehensive and regional agreement in all fields, whether political, strategic, or economic. The resolution of the conflict between our two countries can bring additional great benefits to the peoples of the region. Peace can bring a new standard of living to the peoples of the region, and a high standard of living is the best guarantee for stable peace. Political peace means an end to war. Economic peace means the beginning of growth.[24]

In his response to Peres's speech, opposition leader Netanyahu explained his approach to the peace process as follows: "We believe that only when two minimal conditions are met can there be true peace between us and our neighbors. The first condition is that the Arab side be sincere in its intentions toward peace, and the second is that there be appropriate security and deterrent measures in case these intentions change, those who stand behind them are replaced, or the intentions should be proven false." In the case of Syria, he said, "I am not at all sure—and that is an understatement—that he [Assad] wants peace with Israel, because whoever uses murderous Hezbollah terrorism against us in south Lebanon and whoever continues to use the Palestinian terrorist organizations in Damascus is not exactly showing signs of a genuine desire for peace." He also stated, "Peace is conditional on adequate security arrangements, which means remaining in our positions on the Golan Heights. Permit me to quote something with which I totally agree, something which Yitzhak Rabin said on the eve of the [1992] elections: Anybody who gives up the Golan Heights cedes Israel's security, and without security there cannot be peace."

"We believe," Netanyahu concluded, "that in order to prevent a future war with Syria and for the sake of a stable peace with Syria when the time comes, we must keep the Golan Heights. Not only has that debate not changed, but it apparently will face us all in the coming year."[25]

Peres and his peace team continued to watch Syria closely. Savir quickly shifted his focus from the extensive expertise he had acquired on matters Palestinian to matters Syrian. Among the preparations he undertook in this regard was a reading of "one hundred" previous speeches by President Assad.[26] On November 24, Savir told a mainly Arabic satellite television station based in London (in English) that "we have an interest to make peace with Syria, [and] in our view we can make it before the Israeli elections." He had been appointed by Peres, he told his viewers, to coordinate all aspects of the peace process—and this might include taking direct charge of the Syrian track as well.[27]

From their vantage point to the northeast, the Syrians were closely watching what was happening in Israel. A commentary published on November 25 by one of the government-controlled dailies in Damascus noted, "The musical chairs game played by Israeli prime minister Peres and his foreign minister, Barak, yesterday when they made statements on regional peace is reminiscent of an intriguing contradiction that marked the relationship between the late Prime Minister Rabin and his foreign minister, Peres." But for now, the commentary urged

> let us brush aside the contradiction between Peres and Rabin, and also the one seen between Peres and Barak. . . . What we would like to say is that the statement Peres made yesterday [that is, in his Knesset speech] is highly significant if it reflects a new stand he really believes in, although this statement is merely an acknowledgement of a fact. This fact is an objective one which people may overlook for some time, but never circumvent forever. His statement that "an agreement with Syria is highly significant, and would lead to true peace in the region" is an acknowledgement of an objective fact that cannot be denied any longer. The desperate attempts to sidestep Syria and its regional role have all failed. This is what prompted Peres to make this statement.

However, the writer added, "There are fears that Peres did not mean what he said, and that his statement does not reflect a change of heart that takes hard facts into account."[28]

By the end of November, quite a lot of evidence had accrued to the effect that there was indeed such a "musical chairs game," or perhaps a more serious difference of opinion, between Peres and Barak over Golan. In an interview published December 1, for example, Peres was asked his reaction "to the foreign minister's statement two days ago that from the purely military point of view, Israel should stay on the Golan Heights even in peacetime." "I say," Peres replied, "that there is no pure military consideration. Military considerations are prominent, but there are other considerations, such as political, financial, and economic ones."[29] Such a response seems appropriate from the political leadership of a democratic country to a person who, although nominally charged with running the country's diplomacy, nevertheless still seemed to be representing mostly military considerations. Peres's answer was also clearly in line with the new, multifaceted approach that he was hoping to bring to the talks with Damascus.

DEADLY SHADOW PLAY IN LEBANON

In his early weeks in office, while he was trying to formulate and push forward his "new approach" with Syria, Peres—who did not have a background of active military service—had to deal with some old familiar issues related to Israeli-Syrian relations that continued to be raised by Barak and other members of Israel's well-entrenched military establishment. The issues included not only those directly related to Golan, but also the continuing skirmishes between the IDF and Hezbollah in south Lebanon. A number of times in November 1995, the tensions inside south Lebanon spilled over into Israel in the form of small-scale Katyusha attacks launched by Hezbollah against sites in the north of the country. The Katyusha attacks were not militarily significant, compared with the huge ground-, air-, and sea-based firepower that Israel could bring to bear against Lebanon whenever it chose. But they did cause sporadic casualties in northern Israel—while also causing widespread disruptions in life there, as residents headed for their shelters whenever the sirens told them to. Thus, they faced Peres with some tough questions.

These were exactly the same questions that Rabin had been facing in Lebanon up until the day of his death. Throughout the first ten months of 1995, it was becoming increasingly clear that Hezbollah had refined the deadliness of the tactics it was able to employ against the IDF and its allies inside the security zone, and the number of Israeli soldiers killed in action there mounted inexorably throughout the year.

Back in May 1995, as we have seen, Rabin was starting to admit openly that his Operation Accountability had failed to suppress Hezbollah's activities. At a broader level, one evident weakness of the agreement that ended the 1993 fighting was that it established no monitoring or follow-up mechanism. In the absence of such a mechanism, fighters *on the ground* on both sides of the line were able to spark escalations with relative ease—including escalations that ended up hurting civilians and their property—simply by claiming that "the other side did it first." Thus, although there is some evidence throughout summer and fall 1995 that the Syrians and the Lebanese government were trying to rein in Hezbollah—still, it was clear that they were not always successful in that endeavor.

On the other side of the front line, meanwhile, some evidence suggests that the IDF commanders on the ground were not always tireless in their efforts to actively avoid civilian casualties in Lebanon. For example, in early July 1995, Israel's state radio reported that Prime Minister Rabin had criticized an IDF decision to authorize firing at the large south Lebanese city of Nabatiyeh that had resulted in the deaths of two young girls. A Northern Command debriefing into the shelling showed that it had been "a mistake," the radio reported. The IDF's own radio cited some anonymous ministers at the cabinet meeting as having described the firing, in addition, as "unnecessary."[30] Meanwhile, Hezbollah continued to follow what appeared to be one of its own "rules of engagement," that any casualties among civilians in the zone under its control would trigger shelling or Katyusha attacks against northern Israel: It responded to the girls' killing by lobbing "several Katyushas" into northern Israel. (These did not cause any casualties.)[31] A few days later, the well-informed daily *Ha'aretz* was reporting that Rabin had ordered the head of the Northern Command, General Amiram Levin, "to tone down his reactions and remarks against Hezbollah."[32]

By the beginning of November 1995, the tension in south Lebanon was mounting again. In a long interview with Israeli television (that too soon afterward would turn out to be his last), Rabin was pressed hard by interviewers Shim'on Schiffer and Ehud Ya'ari to spell out what kind of a military operation could put a stop to Hezbollah's activities in Lebanon. In his responses, Rabin repeatedly returned to the argument he had been reported as making the previous June, to the effect that there was no purely military solution for Israel's problems in Lebanon, and that these could be resolved only by reaching a peace agreement with Syria. Rabin's public statement of this argument was so important that the interview is worth quoting at some length here. "Terror," he told the viewers,

> has never been eradicated solely by military means, without supplementary political means. Mistakes must not be made.

SCHIFFER The regular killing of IDF soldiers every week—[RABIN, interrupting] Sir, mistakes must not be made. *People must know that in the absence of a political solution with Syria, we will have to pay a bloody toll in Lebanon.*

YA'ARI In the 1960s, Israel conducted air raids on training camps used by the terrorists near Damascus in al-Hama and al-Zabadani. Isn't this on the agenda today?

RABIN Whoever wants to get Katyusha salvos or to engage in a war with Syria—[pauses] The situation at that time does not resemble the one today. We are living a totally different reality. Whoever is prepared to go to war in Lebanon once again and pay a more painful price than we paid in 1982, 1983, 1984, until mid-1985, let him do so. I will not do it. I know that Israel faces tough enemies; *I know that without a political solution, we will not put an end to the pain of casualties in Lebanon.* Therefore, we must show our resistance and find solutions, seeing that certain incidents could have been avoided and need not have happened. This is a war we must wage and tackle. *We must know that without a political solution with Syria, there will be no solution to the terror from Lebanon.*[33]

Three days after that broadcast, Rabin was dead. The man who succeeded him lacked two key attributes in his response to the challenges that inevitably came to face him in Lebanon: first, the decades of experience that Rabin had accrued in directing military encounters on the "northern front," which gave him a keen understanding of the limitations on the effectiveness of the use of military force in Lebanon; and, second, the stature of a military man, which enabled Rabin to face down his military commanders when they displayed an excess of zeal inside Lebanon.

One early test of how Peres would deal with the challenges coming from the south Lebanese battlefields came at the end of November. The day that Peres appointed former military officer Ori Or to be his deputy defense minister, November 27, coincided with the eruption of yet another round of tension in south Lebanon. In the course of it, the IDF had demolished two houses in south Lebanon; Hezbollah launched Katyusha volleys against northern Israel, injuring eight Israelis. The IDF responded with what were described as "heavy retaliatory air attacks and artillery shelling on south Lebanon."[34]

On November 28, Peres and Or toured northern Israel. Or told the IDF Radio station that "perhaps the day is not far off when we are forced to react in such a way as to *make the residents of Lebanese villages,* in which Hezbollah men hide north of the security zone, *feel less secure than they do today.*"[35] Later that day, Peres seemed to be trying to calm the situation when he told IDF Radio listeners that "Israel is not interested either in verbal or other escalation."[36] But in a television interview later that evening, Or once again sounded threatening: "We may reach a situation wherein we will have to say, 'Gentlemen, the rules of the game are being changed; no more Operation Accountability or anything else, and the rules have to be reset.'" Once again, he threatened that Israel might escalate actions against Lebanese villagers.[37]

In an apparent attempt to justify his approach, Or claimed in this interview that "the late Prime Minister Yitzhak Rabin said that if there are six months of calm in Lebanon we will be ready for negotiations."[38] It may be true that, at an earlier point in his life, Rabin may have said something like this. But in June, and more forcefully in early November 1995, the late prime minister and military hero had clearly been expressing himself (as noted previously) as resigned to having to absorb some Israeli casualties along the Lebanese-Israeli border pending conclusion of a peace agreement with Syria.

On November 30, an editorial in the Damascus daily *Al-Ba'th* noted that it seemed strange that the escalations in Lebanon, which it attributed to the "Israeli rulers," was occurring at the same time that Peres was intensively sending out his peace feelers to Damascus. The writer speculated that,

> Some members of the new Israeli government might have cherished the negotiating tactic used by the Americans during their negotiations with the Vietnamese. For it is public knowledge that barbarous and devastating U.S. air raids preceded each and every round of negotiations with the Vietnamese. Nonetheless, it must be made clear that these aggressive acts did not soften the stands of the Vietnamese negotiators. . . . We are saying that these members of the Israeli government must recall this, because the use of intimidation and threats with Syria is useless.[39]

The editorial writer was probably correct to attribute the Machiavellian tendencies to "some members" of the Israeli government, rather than to Peres himself. For by late November, it seemed evident that there were serious differences of opinion between Peres and many of the former military men and others inside his cabinet—over both the strategic implications of a pullback from Golan and the best way to act in Lebanon.[40]

Differences over Lebanon were also evident between Peres and the professional military establishment. On November 30, *Ha'aretz* reported that Peres had received a request the previous day from Chief of Staff Shahak to launch an undisclosed "operations plan" for south Lebanon. Peres was reported as being mindful of the need to avoid an escalation there, and argued against launching the plan. "We do not need to impress anyone," Peres reportedly said. The newspaper noted that ministers who had participated in an informal "ministerial consultation" on the matter agreed to give Peres sole authority to determine the nature of the IDF's actions in Lebanon (now being described, once again, as "responses")—but that they had limited the duration of this authority to four days.[41] Clearly, the new prime minister was having some trouble making his authority felt on this issue.

PREPARING TO RESUME

In early December the diplomatic pace heated up. Dennis Ross returned to the Middle East and shuttled energetically between Israel and Syria, testing the intentions, plans, and concerns of both parties. He also helped Peres and his team prepare for the visit the new prime minister would make to Washington in the second week of the month.

After one of Ross's visits to Damascus, the usually well-informed Israeli Channel 1 television news reported that "Israel is seeking to obtain a political agreement in principle about the nature of the peace treaty with Syria before deciding on the security arrangements," and that "before he reveals Israel's proposals to President Clinton next week, Prime Minister Shimon Peres also wants to obtain a commitment on the part of President al-Assad to conduct uninterrupted and serious negotiations in order to reach a breakthrough within six months." Also that evening, Channel 2 quoted "a senior political source" as saying that "Israel would be prepared to forgo an early-warning station presence on the Golan and suffice with the presence of U.S. soldiers on Mount Hermon in exchange for a Syrian agreement to a deep demilitarization stretching all the way to the outskirts of Damascus." The same source noted that "such stations would be of no significance in peacetime when the Syrian Army is deployed near Damascus."[42] The issue of ground-based early-warning stations that had caused so much grief in July no longer seemed to be a sticking point for the Israeli side.[43] (Ambassador Moalem has confirmed that in the series of talks that resumed at the end of December, the Israelis made no further mention of keeping ground stations in Golan.)[44]

Before Peres left for the United States, Israeli television, apparently as well-informed as ever, reported that during the meeting with Clinton which would take place December 11, the two leaders would discuss a detailed proposal for resuming the negotiations with Syria. The proposal, this report stated, would have the following main components:

— Peres will propose immediately starting discussions on Israel's withdrawal from the Golan Heights and south Lebanon simultaneously with all the other issues.
— Israel is willing to pay the full price for full peace, which will include full normalization and include all Arab countries except for Sudan, Iraq, and Libya.
— Peres will ask the Americans to increase their involvement and will explain to Clinton that he expects a tripartite summit with al-Assad in the near future. Peres will propose holding the talks secretly, acknowledging only the fact they are being held.

President Clinton will talk with President al-Assad by telephone immediately after he meets Prime Minister Peres. U.S. secretary of state Warren Christopher will come to the region as early as next Thursday [December 14] in a bid to coordinate the opening of the negotiations.[45]

In an interview with IDF Radio before leaving, Peres was still as carefully coy as he had learned to become (after his graveside conversation with Rabinovich) in the way he referred to the idea of full withdrawal. "I have not yet spoken about a full withdrawal from the Golan Heights, and I do not know if I will do so in the future," he said. "If, however, you are asking me whether we are talking about full regional peace, then the answer is affirmative."[46]

During his meeting with Clinton, Peres focused heavily on the next steps he wanted to take in the Syrian track, and on the United States' role in helping to bring about its resumption. "Today," he told a White House news conference after the meeting,

we seek an opening of a new, maybe a final, chapter: the end of war in the Middle East in its totality. Peace between Syria and Israel and between Lebanon and Israel will leave no reason whatsoever for the continuation of belligerency. . . . President al-Assad and myself can, with the assistance of your leadership, Mr. President, and the assistance of your administration and Congress, build a new equation of genuine peace and security to end terror, to begin a market economy. I speak of boundaries of permanent peace; I speak of lands of new and great opportunity. Peace between us must indeed put an end to the conflict that has mired our region for so long.[47]

While in Washington, Peres also spoke to a joint session of Congress. He urged the American lawmakers—traditionally a group skeptical of

Syria's intentions—to give their support to his effort to conclude a peace agreement with Syria. For their part, people in the administration reportedly cautioned Peres that, while they could give some effort to supporting the Syrian track for the next six months, after that time "the president would find it difficult to devote time to international affairs"—presumably because of his own need to campaign for reelection in late 1996.[48] Political sources accompanying Peres in Washington were also reported as telling the media that "in the past few days, Saudi Arabia sent an unequivocal message to the United States that Riyadh is prepared to establish full diplomatic relations with Israel as soon as Damascus and Jerusalem sign a peace treaty."[49]

While Peres was still in Washington, Clinton did indeed pick up the phone to speak to President Assad, as the earlier Israeli television report had predicted. During this call, according to the well-informed British writer Patrick Seale, Clinton told Assad that he would be sending Secretary Christopher to Damascus "to convey what he termed the 'good news.'" By December 14, Christopher was in Damascus as part of a quick, multistage shuttle between Syria and Israel. According to Seale, Christopher told Assad of the "good meeting" that he and the president had with Peres. Christopher, Seale wrote, "quoted Peres as telling Clinton, 'I will stand by the commitment which Rabin put in your pocket.'"[50] This latter reference was, according to Syrians whom Seale had consulted, clearly to Rabin's earlier verbal undertaking to the Americans to withdraw to the June 4, 1967, line.

Ambassador Moalem has elaborated a bit more on Christopher's discussion with Assad. First, Moalem said, Christopher assured Assad that Peres wanted to resume the talks on the Syrian track. Then,

> Assad said, We are ready, if Peres is ready to re-commit Israel to firstly, the "Aims and Principles" document, and secondly, the full withdrawal. Assad asked Secretary Christopher why Peres did not go to early elections, because if we want to finish our talks, we can't have political surprises in the middle. So the Secretary went to Peres. Peres reassured him of the two commitments as requested, and Peres said that he preferred peace to elections, and that he hoped to achieve full peace on the Syrian and Lebanese tracks during 1996.[51]

Moalem has also said of this period that "President Assad asked Secretary Christopher: Since Labor has 85 percent support in Israel, isn't it better that Peres go for an early election? The answer came from Peres that he prefers peace to elections. We resumed [the talks] on the expectation that we could continue the negotiations until an election the next fall."[52]

On December 16, Christopher announced in Jerusalem that the talks would resume at a location near Washington on December 27. They would cover, he noted, "all issues related to peace between Syria and Israel." Washington's policy would be "to help the two sides make progress in the peace process."[53] A radical new formula was being tried. In the parlance that Uri Savir introduced, it became known as "flying high and fast."

PRE-RESUMPTION SIGNALING

After Peres acceded to the premiership, he took Israel's conduct of the peace diplomacy with Syria into several new and unexpected directions. The decision to change course on the sequencing between closing the deal with Syria and holding the Israeli elections was only the first of these new directions. In addition, in the talks that would now be speedily resumed, Peres would be abandoning Rabin's staid, longtime reliance on a carefully calibrated agenda that was designed to move sequentially through the list of agenda items one by one, not coming (for example) to the discussion of the "nature of peace" until after the "security arrangements" had all been thoroughly nailed down. At Peres's urging, everything would now be discussed in a multiplicity of parallel discussions that would cover all aspects of the negotiation in a linked, simultaneous manner. Yet another change was the Peres team's insistence that Syria bring with it to any future signing ceremony the leaders of Saudi Arabia and most other Arab states.

Before the planned talks got under way, however, there was some final signaling between the Syrian and Israeli leaderships, and some final steps on both sides to explain the new approach to the leaders' respective publics.

The signaling was conducted, as had so often been the case in the past, through actions taken (or not taken) in Lebanon. On December 19, Syrian foreign minister Sharaa traveled to the Lebanese presidential palace near Beirut, where he met with President Elias Hrawi, Foreign Minister Faris Buwayz, and House Speaker Nabih Berri. At a late-evening news conference with Buwayz afterwards, Sharaa referred to a ten-point

proposal regarding procedural issues that Christopher had brought to
Damascus, with Sharaa's understanding being that the proposal "ex-
pressed the viewpoint of . . . Israeli prime minister Shimon Peres."[54]
Among these points, Sharaa said, one referred to "an agreement on the
Syrian-Israeli track to be followed by an agreement on the Lebanese-
Israeli track." He also said,

> As for calm in south Lebanon, we are against escalation in south Leba-
> non. Syria's stance in this regard is known. We see that what takes place
> in south Lebanon sometimes goes beyond the reasonable limits. This is
> because of Israeli shelling of Lebanese villages and cities and grave
> human losses among Lebanese civilians as well as Lebanese Resistance
> retaliation for this provocation by firing Katyusha rockets on northern
> Israel. We do not support such escalation. We support calming things
> down in south Lebanon.[55]

Response to these remarks from inside Israel gave an indication of
possible continued differences in approach between the military establishment and the new prime minister. IDF Radio was quick off the
mark in its 7 A.M. broadcast the next day, announcing "the security
establishment" (without further definition) had noted that "there is still
no proof on the ground to back" the Syrian position, as stated by Sharaa.
However, the evidence adduced on the broadcast to counter Sharaa's
claims apparently dated from before the time of the Syrian minister's
announcement.[56] Within hours Peres was reported—also on IDF Radio
—as expressing his "satisfaction with Syrian activity aimed at calming
the situation in south Lebanon."[57] Later that evening, Savir, who now
also announced clearly that he, and not Rabinovich, would be heading
the new talks with Syria, expressed satisfaction that Sharaa's public
announcement of Syria's desire for calm in Lebanon "even went beyond
what was agreed in advance. It was supposed to be quiet: a tacit agreement or, at least, a tacit understanding."[58]

In that same television broadcast, Savir made a broad effort to explain
the nuance and advantages of the new approach to the Israeli public.
Again, because of the importance of this authorized, high-level effort
to reframe an issue that had long been of concern to the Israeli public,
much of this interview will be presented here.

Asked by interviewer Ehud Ya'ari how he would define "success"
at the end of the two planned rounds of talks, Savir responded: "I think
a success would be the definition of a joint objective regarding the

character and quality of peace; regarding how we plan to advance toward achieving this objective; and defining the format of negotiations, which will enable us to find a common language—a thing that was missing in the bilateral negotiations up to now."

Ya'ari compared the negotiations to a game of chess or poker and commented, "We have paid a heavy price for returning to the talks; we have given clear hints regarding our willingness to withdraw to the international border, evacuate settlements, and possibly drop our demand for early-warning stations. Do you feel comfortable with this?"

Savir replied with an impressive attempt to reframe the concept of the negotiations from one of a zero-sum contest to one of mutual advantage:

> I am not being sent to play games but rather to negotiate a new relationship with Syria in all respects and on all issues. You stressed the territorial issue, but we are also dealing with the quality of our relations: economic relations, regional relations, and the security arrangements. This is one big package, and when we achieve this end, Israel will emerge stronger and more secure.

Ya'ari then introduced a call-in viewer who asked about the security risks involved in any full withdrawal of Israeli troops from Golan. (The caller just happened to be Yehuda Harel, a leader of Golan's Third Way movement.) "If we think there are chances of another war, there will be no agreement under such conditions," Savir replied. He attempted to assure Harel that

> Israel will not make an agreement at all costs. Israel must compare two situations: 1. A situation in which there is no agreement. We must ask what is the probability of a war in such a situation and under what conditions would this war be fought. 2. A negotiations process in which we aim to neutralize the Syrian ability to conduct a war, its ability to surprise us, and its very desire to launch a war.

Ya'ari asked if Savir would be taking to the talks a map showing the western edge of the Golan Heights. Once again, Savir tried to reframe the issue—this time away from the until-then dominant obsession with geographical lines:

> We are not going with any maps. . . . We want to chart a map that deals with our relations with Syria; a map of the Middle East the day after peace; a map of our economic relations with Syria; a map of our security arrangements with Syria; and a map of Israel's and Syria's international relations vis-à-vis the United States. When we finally have

answers to these questions, we will chart the geographic territorial map. Incidentally, I believe that during these stages, the negotiations will involve a much higher level of decision makers.

"Our objective," the negotiator underlined later, "is to create a dependency on peace and to make cooperation advantageous."

Regarding the Peres team's regionwide aspirations in its pursuit of the agreement with Syria, Savir said, "After we conclude the talks with Syria and Lebanon in a full and true peace, we will, in fact, be closing the circle of peace. . . . We believe that countries such as Saudi Arabia and the North African states will join this circle when the peace accord is signed, even if the negotiations with the Palestinians are still going on." But he noted at the same time that "We have no intention of avoiding the negotiations on the permanent arrangement with the Palestinians."

Ya'ari countered by introducing another example of the incrementalist "old-think": "In that case, you may be asked: Why not let the Syrians cool off?" "What good would it do to us," Savir replied,

> to let the Syrians cool off or even freeze? After all, it is a matter of political wisdom. No one is racing to the negotiations. The decision to aspire to an agreement was a carefully considered choice. I do not understand all the questions about our rushing to negotiate. Isn't fifty years of conflict enough? Five years have passed since the Madrid conference. Isn't that enough? Today, al-Assad is speaking about peace, and Syria is speaking in positive terms. There is still more ground for Syria to cover: It must think about a Syrian Embassy in Israel and an Israeli Embassy in Syria, and it is beginning to speak in such terms. Yesterday, the Syrian foreign minister even spoke for the first time about calm in Lebanon.

It was at this point that Savir noted that Sharaa had gone beyond what had been agreed to in this regard. "So, now that we have all these signs," he argued,

> why not take advantage of this? We have been punished for doing nothing many times in the past. If you do nothing, you take the greatest risk. I believe that with the strategy the prime minister is formulating, with the backing of the foreign minister and the entire cabinet, we will create new rules of the game based, I believe, on one thing: the desire of the Arab world to get closer to the West through us. Please note how important it is for the Syrians that the Americans be in the room, as you asked before. Americans in the room means Americans in the region. In the past, the USSR was in the region. The USSR supplied arms; today, the United States supplies food. That is the big difference.

"It is not a matter of trust," he told Ya'ari at another point; "we have this tendency to look for hugs from the Arabs. It must be an Arab interest —Palestinian in this case and Syrian in the future—to maintain good-neighborly relations with Israel, and this is getting stronger through these processes in terms of security, economy, and peace." (Regarding the question that Savir raised here about the value of seeking "hugs from Arabs," Moalem has said: "Israel believed that you can push a button to make peace warm, to direct Syrian popular attitudes from a state of war to a state of peace. This is not logical, especially since it is rare to find a household in Syria that has not lost someone on the battlefield. . . . An agreement, which is signed by our leadership, tells what is required from our side, but we cannot be obliged to make the peace warm.")[59]

At the end of Savir's television appearance before the resumption of the Syrian talks, the interviewer drew the new chief negotiator's attention to the fact that people who were busy conducting lengthy discussions with the Syrians would have little time to concern themselves with the upcoming party primary elections. "That is good," Savir replied.[60]

Two days later, Peres underlined just how far he and his team were prepared to go in the redesign of Israel's longtime security concept, alongside their attempt to reframe the diplomatic questions of war and peace. "Give me peace and we will give up the atom," stated the Israeli prime minister (who, when he was working for Prime Minister David Ben-Gurion in the mid-1950s, had conducted the negotiations with France that inaugurated Israel's impressive nuclear weapons program). "That's the whole story. If we achieve regional peace, I think we can make the Middle East free of any nuclear threat."[61] In making this statement—also to Ya'ari's television program—Peres was doing two unprecedented things. He was giving the first recognition ever to come from an Israeli head of government that Israel did indeed have "the atom," and that it did contribute to the "nuclear threat" in the region. (For how can a government give up what it does not have?) At the same time, he was adding these high stakes to those that he was prepared to play in the event of success in the negotiation.

From the Syrian side, the news was less dramatic, but also encouraging. On December 23, President Assad was in Cairo for one of the periodic consultations he held with President Mubarak throughout his participation in the peace talks. He told a joint news conference held after his talks there that during his meetings with Secretary Christopher "an atmosphere of openness was emphasized that was better than previously. No one discussed any specific issue with me. There is nothing specific, but general ideas and views characterized by openness and a desire to advance the peace process." He added that "Syria supports this."[62]

Assad may well have felt that he had some explaining to do to the Syrian and broader Arab public on the "comprehensiveness" issue in light of both what might have appeared to be a departure from his previous insistence on maintaining a comprehensive approach to peacemaking, and also all the talk now coming out of Israel to the effect that Syria would bring all the other major Arab states with it to the final peace agreement. "Since the Oslo agreement," he recalled,

> we have engaged in no specific activity to help or hinder the Palestinians —I mean the PLO, of course. The PLO took this thing upon itself. At the time, I told the PLO chairman that we were not happy with that. Nevertheless, we would not do things to hinder the agreement; that is, we did not want to create a problem with our Palestinian brothers; we have enough problems in the Arab world. Things are happening, as we and you hear.
>
> But anyway, they have now signed an agreement, which is a peace agreement. In our view, comprehensiveness now means Syria and Lebanon. Syria has not changed its expression about a just and comprehensive solution since before the Madrid conference was launched. This was discussed with the Americans, and we stipulated it as a basic principle.
>
> By a comprehensive solution we mean [including] the people around Israel, in general, who are directly concerned with the peace. Of course, peace is a peace for all the Arabs; all the Arabs are involved in it. But things have always started from the surrounding, or the cordon states, as they have recently been called. Of the cordon states, only Syria and Lebanon have not concluded agreements with Israel. Comprehensive peace will be achieved when Syria and Lebanon sign a peace agreement. Naturally, I never mean that an Arab will abandon the other Arabs. The issues of the Arabs, no matter how they look and how some of the Arabs view them, will remain Arab issues. Assistance and feelings of pan-Arab responsibility will remain the basis. At certain times in the past we used to try to impose particular methods or views. Now we have discovered that this is no longer useful, especially, as you know, since some people have adopted the cry of "end the custodianship" and things like that. We back the ending of custodianship.[63]

In sum, Assad was indicating that he was ready to deal with the Peres team's open-ended format, and that he was prepared to engage in negotiations that would result, at this point, in peace agreements only on the Syrian and Lebanese fronts. On the issue of bringing in the other Arab states, he appeared guarded, to say the least. Nevertheless, his position was probably the best that the Israelis could hope to hear him express in public at this time.

Yossi Beilin gave voice to the Peres group's satisfaction with Assad's statements;[64] and the two delegations made their way to the United States for talks that, as both sides had already agreed, would be very different from anything Rabin had ever envisioned. Only fifty days had passed since his death.

6

The Wye Plantation Talks:
A Hopeful New Experiment
Interrupted

THE NEW FORMULA

The talks that opened at the Aspen Institute's Wye Plantation on Maryland's eastern shore on December 27, 1995, were very different from all the Syrian-Israeli encounters that had preceded them. No longer would the two teams be encountering each other in the fusty first-floor meeting rooms of the State Department megalith in the American capital, retreating each evening to hotel rooms and besieged by the constant demands of the world (especially Israeli) media. The new setting was, by design, more like a team-building corporate retreat. Each new round of the talks was broken into two three-day portions, with a long weekend in between for consultations with the sides' respective leaderships. During the three-day half-sessions, members of the Syrian, Israeli, and American teams would live and work together in the Wye Plantation's small though well-equipped residential conference center. The December weather would not allow use of the many outdoor recreation facilities at Wye, but there were still ping-pong and pool tables, and roaring fireplaces to provide ambience for the leisure hours.

In many stages of his negotiations with the Palestinians, from the earliest contacts in Norway onwards, Savir had come to see the advantages of such an informal, secluded physical environment, and one can surmise that it was largely at his urging that the Wye Plantation formula was designed the way it was. But one large difference between his encounters with the Palestinians and those at Wye with the Syrians was that at Wye, presumably at the Syrians' strong urging, there was an active presence of the third-party sponsors as well: the U.S. delegation, led by Dennis Ross, took part at Wye as a "full partner" in the negotiating venture.

On the Israeli side, leadership of the negotiating team had now moved away from the ambassador in Washington to Savir, while on the Syrian side, leadership had moved away from Allaf (who suffered a rapidly progressing physical debility) to the ambassador in Washington who had been an important part of the talks all along, Walid Moalem.

The structuring and content of the agenda at Wye differed greatly from all the Syrian-Israeli talks that had already taken place. While Rabin was still alive, the talks had moved slowly and systematically under the agenda developed at the very beginning of his premiership: first, the question of withdrawal; then, the various items under the rubric of security arrangements, which was where they had gotten stuck back in July. Under Rabin, the issues of the nature of peace, and the question of how all the moves would be phased and implemented barely got onto the table at all. (There had been some slow but noticeable movement in the long background negotiation, conducted mainly through the U.S. intermediaries, over the total length of the implementation period and the number of stages in it.) At Wye, by contrast, all these topics were on the agenda, and openly discussed between the Syrian and Israeli negotiators in parallel but joined subnegotiations in which separate groups of negotiators simultaneously discussed different aspects of the nature of peace, the security arrangements, and a resolution of the tricky water issue, even while legal representatives were starting to design the different phases of implementation and draft the outlines of the resulting agreement.

Joel Singer was an international law specialist who had worked a lot with Savir in his conduct of the negotiations with the Palestinians. (Prior to that, as legal advisor to the IDF, Singer had been involved behind the scenes in the negotiating of all agreements concluded between Israel and its neighbors since 1973.) Now, he came to Wye as the legal specialist in Savir's team. He has recalled that "Peres said he needed us to conclude a framework agreement before the elections. Therefore, we could not concentrate on just one aspect at a time—from the timing point of view. Also, tactically within the negotiation, they are all connected: there are tradeoffs among them. That was why we started negotiations on all aspects at once—but without committing on any one until the whole package would be complete."[1] According to one State Department official associated with the talks, this last important part of the ground rules at Wye had been established "at the Syrians' insistence."[2]

This official surmised that the Syrians seemed to like the overall Wye formula. "They liked to be away from Washington, D.C., and all the pressures of the press. They liked the egalitarian nature of it, and the fact that no one was running off between sessions to meet folks in the Congress. They liked the informality. They liked the way we introduced our military figures into the negotiations."[3]

The Syrians were also happy that at the opening of the Wye talks, responding to a request from Moalem, Dennis Ross read out the whole text of the "Aims and Principles" document, as agreed on the previous May, "so that it could serve as the guideline for our discussion of security arrangements."[4]

For Uri Savir, the encounter at Wye was his first direct contact with officials from Syria. He has written that,

> From our standpoint, the [Syrian] negotiations were a more difficult intellectual challenge than the talks with the Palestinians, because we had to adjust to dealing with a mindset radically different from our own. On the emotional level, however, the negotiations with the Syrians were easier because, far from feeling that we were dealing with life-and-death issues of coexistence in the same land, there was a sense among both delegations that, *if necessary, we could go on living without peace.*
>
> . . . In each set of negotiations, we faced one key player. The difference between them was that Assad was more focused than Arafat and imposed his authority on his negotiators far more stringently. Moreover, none of us had ever been able to take the measure of the man in direct, personal contacts, so he remained something of an enigma in our eyes, though his spirit was ever present in the talks.[5]

Regarding the U.S. role within the negotiations, Singer recalled, "I realized that the Syrians always wanted to have Americans at the meetings. . . . But the State Department had not brought a lawyer to the meetings, at my suggestion, so the legal group was the only group without an American in it." The Syrian legal specialist at Wye was law professor Riad Daoudi. According to Singer, the two of them were given the tasks of dealing with normalization and starting work on the treaty.[6]

The ground rule that nothing was agreed on until everything was agreed on allowed a considerable degree of progress on points previously untouched. Normalization of relations was a key example of this.

Under Rabin, the Israeli strategy had been to defer discussion of normalization issues until *after* satisfactory agreement had been reached on security arrangements. That strategy was one that the Syrian leadership, which traditionally has been very wary of attempts to normalize Israeli-Arab relations, was probably comfortable with. Earlier in the talks, the Syrians had found an acceptable way in which they could refer to the idea of normalization—as an agenda item for the future—without using words associated with the Arab *tatbi'* (normalization): they used the phrase "normal (or ordinary) peaceful relations," and let it go at that.

Now, in Wye, the issue was front and center on the negotiating table. In a notable and unprecedented shift, the Syrian negotiators expressed their readiness to discuss the content of "normalization" under three headings: the exchange of embassies, the transport of goods across the border, and the movement of people across the border (though in the first Syrian definition of this, according to Singer, this would involve only the transit of Israelis through Syria on their way to Turkey). Singer recalled that his counter to this Syrian opening offer was to produce a list of eighteen points on which he wanted to discuss normalization measures—"and they said 'impossible!' This was at the first meeting."

At a subsequent meeting, Singer suggested that he and Daoudi work together in trying to assign the Israelis' eighteen points into one or another of each of Daoudi's accepted categories. "I managed to put twelve of mine in under his three points," he recalled. "Then, together, we presented the results of this to the others at Wye."[7] According to Savir, these twelve areas of normalization included termination of the economic boycott of Israel and establishment of telephone, fax, postal, rail, and maritime links.[8]

Regarding economic cooperation, meanwhile, Savir had come up with an approach that combined discussion of possible joint ventures, some plans for Syria's foreign creditors to cancel its debts, and the development of "a network of private-sector groups in the United States, Israel, Saudi Arabia, and Syria (with the European Union and Japan to join at a later stage)."[9] For his part, Ambassador Moalem was expressing a wariness on this subject that was widespread in Syria when he later told an interviewer about the Israeli economic proposals at Wye:

> They wanted open borders, open markets for their goods, and so on. This would have an obvious effect on our own economy. Our economic regulations are not against them; we do not open our markets to any country. And how can you integrate two economies when one has a per capita income of $900 per year and the other has a per capita income of $15,000 per year? Such integration is not possible, so we discussed a transitional period during which we could raise our economy to the level where there can be competition without undue hardship on our society.[10]

In fact, Savir seems to have had some sensitivity to these concerns, and it was partly to help meet them that he proposed the creation of the business groups. "We knew President Assad was intrigued by this idea," he said:

> We knew this in two ways. Firstly, through Warren Christopher. At the beginning, he tried to disillusion us about the whole idea. But then during his January shuttle he came and said, "I don't believe it! President Assad talked 70 percent of the time about economics!" Secondly, I knew this through the back-channel that existed between Moalem, Dennis Ross and myself.[11]

When Christopher himself was asked by David Makovsky whether he considered Assad ready for "real normalization" with Israel, he replied,

> We talked about that in considerable detail, the content of peace. I think that if they get back to that track they'll find there's lots of work that's been done on that. There are certain areas where he [Assad] was resistant because he felt he couldn't compel private transactions or commercial transactions. . . . But nevertheless within the bounds of those conversations was an acceptance of the idea of real normalization.

Christopher confirmed, too, that Assad was willing, in the context of the envisaged peace agreement, to allow Israeli tourists to visit Damascus. "I think he recognized the importance of opening his country but he was protective of doing it [in] a way that didn't dash or dismantle its economy," he said.[12]

The first round of Wye took place December 27–29, 1995, and January 3–5, 1996. After that, the negotiating teams returned home. On January 10, Secretary Christopher arrived in Israel to conduct some shuttle diplomacy with Damascus (and also to oversee final arrangements for the Palestinian elections in the West Bank and Gaza, which would take place January 20). The second round of Wye occurred January 24–26 and January 29–31, 1996. Christopher then conducted another Israel-Syria shuttle in the days from February 4 onward. The third round of Wye ran February 27–29, and was supposed to resume the following week, but it was suspended by the Israeli side on March 4.

By the end of the first full round under the new formula, all the participants seemed to agree that it was working well. Chief U.S. negotiator Dennis Ross expressed his delight that more had been achieved in their six days of talks so far than during the four years of Israeli-Syrian negotiations that had gone before. Uri Savir told Israeli television that "I am less doubtful than in the past about the Syrian determination to attain peace—real peace, as the Syrians call it," and added, "We heard the Syrians also saying that an Israeli-Syrian peace agreement will put an end to the Middle East conflict, which is definitely a step forward."[13]

From their side, the Syrians were also careful to provide up-to-date status reports for their public at home. The evening news on Syrian television on January 5 contained a report that Ambassador Moalem "described the talks that were concluded this evening as serious and useful." Moalem reportedly noted that the talks dealt with "many issues, chief of which is the Israeli withdrawal from the occupied Syrian Golan Heights to the 4 June 1967 line, ordinary peace relations, security arrangements, and the implementation timetable," and with "the broader framework, given that Syria is the key to a just and comprehensive peace in the region." He was quoted as having concluded: "The results of the talks show that it is possible to achieve substantive progress on the main issues despite the existence of difficulties and gaps between the positions of the two sides on some basic elements of peace."[14]

For a Syrian official to admit to the Syrian public that his government was now actively discussing the establishment of "ordinary peace relations" with Israel was unprecedented. Israeli officials were still careful not to reveal to their public any details about the depth of the withdrawal from Golan that remained their sole, but generally unstated, working hypothesis in the talks.

The Israeli negotiators' taboo on spelling out the depth of the envisioned withdrawal was broken only once during this period, and that occurred inside the negotiating room at Wye. According to Moalem, during one of the January sessions, he remarked in a plenary session that he had found Rabin, "like a soldier, very cautious, and always sitting in the hall with his hand on his gun, whereas Peres wants us to fly high and fast." Moalem recalled that Rabinovich then "became provoked and said, 'Under Rabin we agreed to withdraw to the line of 4 June 1967!'" Moalem recalled that he turned to Ross at that point and asked him to put into the minutes what Rabinovich had just said. Savir, meanwhile, immediately left the room with Rabinovich, and Moalem heard them outside, shouting at each other.[15] The Israelis' intention was still clearly to avoid spelling out directly to the Syrians the "hypothesis" on which they were basing their participation in the talks, but still having this important clarification conveyed only as a less-than-explicit "understanding" through the Americans.

Another incident that marred the generally peaceable and constructive atmosphere at Wye occurred during the second round, after Israeli Major-General Uzi Dayan, a nephew of Syria's nemesis, Moshe Dayan, and now the head of the IDF planning branch, joined the talks in January. According to one of the American participants, Dayan was giving a presentation in which he was explaining Israel's demand that Syria drastically scale back the size of the forces that it kept deployed behind Golan. Laying out a map of the region, he then reportedly laid his hand on it to indicate the area he had in mind—and it fell right onto the Syrian capital, Damascus. For Moalem, this was too much. As he later confessed, this was one point at which he lost the cool and constructive demeanor for which all the other participants otherwise gave him credit. (Dennis Ross has noted, however, that at a later session Dayan —who had just received another posting that would take him away from the talks at Wye—made a short farewell speech in which he talked about how much his participation there had meant to him. "People on both sides of the table were really moved by what he said," Ross recalled.)[16]

In his memoir, Savir summed up the achievements of Wye in eight broad fields. In addition to the nature of peaceful relations, and economic relations, as noted above, these were comprehensive peace, security arrangements, the depth of the withdrawal from the Golan Heights, water, the United States' role in the negotiations, and methodology for future progress.[17]

Moalem has described the account of the talks that Savir gave in his book as essentially accurate, "except that it did not mention what happened between me and Itamar, or anything about the issue of withdrawal." He judged that during the two-and-a-half rounds of the Wye talks,

> We completed 75 percent of the work of negotiating an agreement. We agreed that there would be a complete Israeli withdrawal, to be implemented in two stages—though there was still a gap on the total implementation time, with them requiring three years, and us offering sixteen months.
>
> Regarding security arrangements, we agreed there would be early warning from air and space; zones of demilitarization and zones of limited forces in the area from Quneitra to Safad, that is, the "relevant areas" —though we still disagreed on the types and precise locations of these deployments. We even agreed on some confidence-building measures.
>
> Regarding normalization, I agreed on nine of the fifteen elements that were on the table.[18]

GATHERING STORM CLOUDS

If the ambience within the carefully structured environment of the Wye Plantation was generally amicable and constructive, outside its closely guarded gates during the early weeks of 1996 heavy storm clouds were once again starting to gather. Increasingly, forces external to the negotiation started to make their impact felt within it as well.

Among the most potent of these external forces was the pressure building up on Peres to abandon the decision he had made so rapidly in early November to keep the date for Israel's elections as late as possible to give the negotiators the maximum chance of achieving the hoped-for breakthrough with the Syrians. As had been the case with the political constraints mounting against Rabin the previous July, on this occasion, too, the pressure was mounting within his own party and his own cabinet, as well as in the ranks of the political opposition.

In his memoir, Savir dated a watershed in this regard to January 1996, and named a couple of the most prominent Labor politicians involved in raising criticisms of Peres's Syrian policy. "Ehud Barak," he wrote,

> the former chief of staff and now foreign minister, who was very creative and constructive in helping to forge a model for the future peace

with Syria, and with whom I consulted by phone for several hours each night during the talks, suddenly began to express views very critical of the Syrians. Other Labor contenders for Knesset seats tried to gain popularity by criticizing the negotiating team itself. Micha Goldman, the deputy minister of education, called for me to be replaced because of my "ill-founded optimism."[19]

On January 11, while Christopher was in Israel, Barak told IDF Radio that he considered "it is too early to determine whether we have a partner for extensive, substantive, and thorough negotiations of the issues." The radio's reporter noted, "There definitely seems to be a contradiction here. Speaking after the last round of talks, Uri Savir said we have a partner for negotiations, while Barak said today he is not yet convinced of this."[20]

By the time the second round of Wye opened at the end of the month, Barak had arranged his schedule to be not far away, in Washington, D.C. and New York. While on that trip, he was reported as deriding, in notably tasteless terms for someone charged with conduct of his nation's diplomacy, one of the key aspects of the Syrian negotiation that the prime minister and his chief negotiator placed a high value on. "We want and say that the peace may include twenty Arab leaders," Israeli television quoted him as saying. "So, twenty men wearing yellow jellabas will show up. Will this influence jellaba-owners? No, but it creates great expectations in the Israeli public." The broadcasters also played a tape of Barak saying, "I do not expect these talks to solve all the problems between us and Syria. Therefore, it does not stand to reason that these talks will end in an agreement."[21] (In one U.S. official's view, Barak's main motivation in that period, which explained much of what he said about the negotiations with Syria, was to push for earlier, rather than later, elections.)[22]

For an Israeli prime minister to have a foreign minister who was a bit of a loose cannon was not unprecedented. But the degree to which Barak, as foreign minister, was able to undercut Peres's efforts to conduct a central portion of his diplomacy was without precedent—and undercut it he undoubtedly did. On January 27, a signed column by the editor-in-chief of the Damascus daily *Al-Thawra* called on Peres to "correct Barak's statements and prevent him from making more, especially since Barak is pushing the talks and the peace process toward a tunnel. His statements constitute a rejection of the bases of the peace

process."[23] The next day, a commentary by Muhammad 'Ali Buzah in
Al-Thawra noted the following:

> Israeli positions, which were expressed in one way or another and
> which preceded the talks and accompanied them moment by moment,
> have . . . shown signs and data which make it impossible to assume that
> the Israeli side came to the talks in good faith and that it is negotiating
> with a real desire for peace. . . .
>
> The wave of optimism has been dissipated by the recent Israeli state-
> ments and by Israeli foreign minister Ehud Barak's provocative
> remarks, whether those made to the Israeli Army's radio or to the con-
> ference of the Jewish organization heads in New York regarding peace
> with Syria.[24]

Relayed back to Israel, meanwhile, Barak's comments gave further permission to members of the political elite from all parties who were critical of Peres's Syrian initiative, to work to undercut his efforts.

Some voices of criticism regarding Peres's broad strategy in the negotiations were heard even from within the Israeli negotiating team itself.
Joel Singer knew it was bad practice in a negotiation to tell the other
side that you want something very strongly: "I said at the time that it
was impossible to meet the deadline Peres had set [of completing the
negotiation before the Israeli campaign season began]—and bad strategy to declare this. . . . Yes, there was major progress at Wye. But we
could not have done it all in eight months."[25]

Outside the negotiating room, and outside Israel, additional tension
was also brewing in south Lebanon, where some sporadic incidents
had continued even after the (relative) calm that had followed Sharaa's
December 19 statement. On the opening day of the Wye talks' first
round, the deputy secretary general of Hezbollah was quoted as defi-
antly stating, "We are a resistance directed against the invaders and not
a party to the negotiating process. The resistance does not constitute
a card in the negotiations. It is an act of struggle for the liberation of
the land."[26]

On the ground in south Lebanon, the fighting continued. On December 29, the IDF shelled the village of Qabriha (this was done "by mistake," it was later reported). The next day Hezbollah responded by firing
two salvoes of Katyusha rockets into northern Israel. Secretary Christopher reportedly woke Minister Sharaa immediately after the rockets had
landed, even though it was 1 A.M. in Damascus, and extracted from him

a promise that "he would take steps to prevent an exacerbation of the situation along Israel's northern border."[27]

By January 15, in the wake of Christopher's visit to Damascus that month, Israeli television was reporting that Assad had once again promised Christopher that he would "see about toning down Hezbollah's activities in south Lebanon." What were described as "Israeli sources" had reportedly confirmed that, "Syria has imposed new restrictions on attacks on the security zone."[28] (The next day, Hezbollah, defiant as ever, claimed that it was now able to develop its own Katyusha rockets.)[29] A planned visit to Syria by the vice president of Hezbollah's principal state backer, Iran, ended up being "postponed."[30]

The continuance of some clashes in south Lebanon during the period of the Wye talks—with escalatory pressures apparently being exerted by fighters on both sides of the front line there—undoubtedly contributed to a lessening of confidence in the negotiation from important parts of the political elite in both Israel and Syria. On the Syrian side, in addition, one key action taken by Israel in another Arab arena caused significant public questioning of Peres's good faith. This was the Mossad's early January assassination of Yahya Ayyash, technical chief for the hard-line Palestinian group, Hamas.

Back in late October, one of Prime Minister Rabin's last acts before his own violent death had been to authorize a Mossad assassination, in Malta, of the leader of Islamic Jihad, Fathi al-Shaqaqi. (That move was described by an Israeli commentator at the time as "the first assassination of the 1996 election campaign.")[31] Now, it was Peres's turn to authorize an action with a similar end, this time inside the nominally Palestinian-controlled area of Gaza.

Because Ayyash's killing was carried out in a very high-tech and coordinated fashion, it was quickly (and unrefutedly) attributed to Israel's inventive secret service. One well-connected Syrian intellectual has reported that in Damascus news of the assassination caused Syrians seriously to reconsider a general attitude towards Peres that earlier had welcomed him (with some degree of comparison with his predecessor) as a "man of peace." This was particularly the case, the Syrian informant said, because Hamas was committed at that time to an informal cease-fire with Israel that had been negotiated with Yasser Arafat in order to allow a calm atmosphere for the upcoming Palestinian elections —but still, the general success of that cease-fire had not prevented

Peres from authorizing the assassination.[32] (In his memoir, Uri Savir wrote of Ayyash's killing, "I believed that such activities were seldom advantageous.")[33]

Other storm clouds were rumbling to the north of Syria, in Turkey. During January, these may not have provided much pause for thought on either side of the Syrian-Israeli negotiating table, but later Turkish-related factors were to make their own contribution to a general questioning in Syria regarding the Israeli leadership's true intentions in the region.

Inside the Wye negotiations, Turkey's relevance to the talks was felt in two main areas. In the discussions on water, Turkey was seen as a party that could help provide Syria with additional water that would, in effect, compensate it for the loss of control over Golan's water sources which Israel insisted on retaining.[34] Additionally, in the discussions on security arrangements, Turkey's sometimes seemingly hostile presence north of Syria had an undeniable effect on Syria's perceived security needs regarding the size and deployment of its armed forces.

In mid-January, a writer in *Nokta*, an Istanbul periodical considered generally close to the Turkish military, noted that "Syria, with which we share the longest border, is among our most problematic neighbors."[35] Turkey's military-dominated leadership had long-standing disputes with Damascus over three main issues: Syria's claim to sovereignty over the province allocated to Turkey as Hatay; Turkish claims that Syria gave help to the Kurdish Workers' Party (PKK), which was waging a fierce (and fiercely countered) battle for secession of the Kurdish-populated regions of eastern Turkey; and Syria's demand that Turkey reach a formal agreement over allocation of the waters of the Euphrates River. "Turkey believes that Syria is creating a confrontation over water," the *Nokta* commentator wrote. He also noted that a report published the previous September, "with the permission of the Office of the Chief of the General Staff," had stated that "relations between the two countries are marked by a crisis of confidence."[36] *Le Monde* correspondent Alain Gresh has written that it was at the start of 1996 that Turkey's undersecretary of state for foreign affairs asked an Israeli diplomat, "How can you negotiate with Syria? Have you gone mad. . . ? You must stop at once. That's my government's official position."[37]

For Peres, clearly, the pressures coming from inside his country, and from inside his own party and cabinet, were more important than any of these other, external factors. At some stage at the end of January, he seems to have reached a decision to reverse course, and go for early elections. Savir has written:

> The Israeli political arena impressed the Syrians as chaotic, and they felt that Peres was unable to discipline the Knesset deputies. All this led Peres to conclude that, rather than wait until November [for elections], he must ask the country for a clear mandate to pursue his peace policy as soon as possible—and a number of optimistic pollsters encouraged him in that direction.
>
> My own recommendation was different.[38]

Moalem recalled that at the end of the second round of the Wye talks, Secretary Christopher joined the Syrian negotiators for an *iftar,* the evening meal with which Muslims break the Ramadan fast,

> and then he asked to meet me alone. He informed me of the sad decision of Peres to go for early elections. I was astonished. I told the Secretary it would kill our talks. He insisted that I should tell President Assad that he [Christopher] and President Clinton were eager that the talks should proceed. I told him I could not convince President Assad of this, and that he should try. He did, on his next visit to Damascus, and he succeeded.[39]

Soon after that, Moalem had one of the periodic meetings he held alone, with Ross and Savir, during which the three men worked together to help to plan the future course of their negotiation. "Uri explained why Peres had decided on an early election, but I saw that he considered it was a mistake."[40]

Peres had one final gambit he was hoping to try. He had still not informed his own public that he was going for early elections. (Indeed, on January 31, the same day that Round Two of the talks was winding up in Wye, he was still assuring Israeli television viewers that his decision on the timing of the elections had not yet been made, though it soon would be.)[41] Then, on February 4, Christopher arrived in Israel to start another round of Israel-Syria shuttling. As one official has recalled what happened:

> Peres asked us to convey to Assad that he would be ready to forgo early elections but he needed a summit meeting with Assad. "We can fly high and fast together, or low and slow," as he put it. This was not necessarily popular in Israel. Everyone in Labor was pressing him to go to early elections. We were not keen on early elections. We said to Peres: What happens if you call early elections and there are a couple of bombs during

the campaign? Also, the history of Labor calling early elections is not good: they lost them back in 1977. Also, Peres had finally succeeded in projecting himself to the public as a real statesman. If he went to early elections, would he lose this?[42]

Savir has recalled of this episode, "The discussions were going too slowly, we wanted to speed them up. Unlike Rabin, Peres was ready to reduce the implementation period for the treaty. We thought that it required a summit between Peres and Assad to reach a quick conclusion."[43]

It is possible to conjecture that Assad himself felt somewhat pressured by this quick succession of signals from Peres. (Rabinovich described the Syrian leader—presumably based on a later report from the Americans—as having been in a "foul mood.")[44] In any event, Assad refused to accede to the request for a speedy summit. In an interview Moalem would grant to the *Journal of Palestine Studies* later that year, he explained:

> We have repeatedly stated that this type of meeting requires careful preparation: If a meeting at the summit level is a failure, all further opportunities will be closed. You need to define beforehand precisely what points the summit should solve: The gaps between the two positions must be narrow, and you need to know that this meeting is truly the final stage of the agreement. For these reasons, when President Assad was informed of Prime Minister Peres's wish to meet, he said it was premature.
>
> So the Israelis knew beforehand what President Assad's response would be, because this was an ongoing request on their part. This could not have been the reason for their calling early elections. . . . Peres's decision to call early elections must have depended on pressures from within his own party, because the margin between Labor and Likud had started to narrow in the polls.[45]

The Syrian envoy has also confirmed that neither the Israelis nor the Americans attempted to make any preparation, through the diplomatic channel that he himself provided, for Peres's request for the summit. "It was never mentioned in our talks," he said. "It wasn't part of our agenda."[46]

Although Assad deflected Peres's request for a speedy summit, he did accede to the request (as conveyed to him in a letter from President Clinton, as well as at Peres's and Christopher's urging) to keep the Wye talks ticking over at some level for the duration of the Israeli election campaign. On February 6, while Christopher was still in Damascus he

announced that the next round of the Wye talks would open on February 28. The secretary then returned to Israel and gave Peres Assad's
response on the request for a summit. As Peres recalled it, the answer
he got back through Christopher was that Assad "said he was ready to
meet, but he could not agree to a date."[47]

On the evening of February 11, Peres finally laid to rest the rumors
that had been swirling around Israel for the preceding weeks, and
announced to Israeli television viewers that he had decided to go for
early elections. (Under Israeli law, these could be held no fewer than
three months after this announcement.) "I propose that we hold a
short, inexpensive, and fair campaign," he told the viewers. "We must
not repeat the terrible accusations of treason, murder, and such words.
We must explain to the people the differences of opinion—to the extent
that they exist—in a civilized manner. We will act with restraint; it is my
hope that the opposition will do likewise." Regarding Syria, he said:

> The Syrian track has been opened, and it has been shown that there is a
> chance for progress toward a comprehensive Middle East peace and an
> end to violence in Lebanon. We also learned, however, that several
> issues—two in particular: security arrangements and assuring the sup-
> ply of water—require a great deal of time. Therefore, we decided that the
> negotiations with Syria must not be conducted under the pressure of
> elections. Christopher's successful visit to Damascus determined that the
> negotiations can continue to be conducted independent of the elections.

In addition, he reiterated the long-standing commitment that the agreement with Syria would be brought to a national referendum, regardless of the decision on early elections.[48]

NEGOTIATING UNDER THE SHADOW OF ELECTIONS

On February 27, the negotiating teams came together at Wye to start
the third round of their talks. According to Savir, there was some discussion of security arrangements, though it did not show much
progress.[49] General Shaul Mufaz had replaced Uzi Dayan on the Israeli
team; the Syrian military specialists were General Ibrahim al-Omar,
the head of the Syrian Reconnaissance Office, and General Hassan al-
Khalil, the deputy head of Syrian military intelligence.[50] According to
one of the American participants, one idea that was actively explored
to resolve the complex of problems regarding early warning was the

use of tethered balloons. The broader challenge of transforming the decades-long relationship of hostility into one of cooperation over war-prevention continued to be explored.[51]

In addition, the delegation heads were able to start mapping out how the work would be continued after the Israeli elections had been conducted in May. As Savir recalled it, they were planning to have three working groups: one on security arrangements and border delineation; one on all aspects of normalization, including diplomatic and economic relations, and the broader regional aspects of peace; and a drafting committee under Singer and Daoudi.[52]

But already, before the participants reached Wye for this third round, the atmosphere on the ground in the Middle East was becoming noticeably more tense.

Inside Israel, the official launching of the election campaign had added a strong charge of partisan polarization to the tenor of public discourse: The stakes in all disputes were now seen as much higher, since each of the issues in dispute might prove decisive in determining which party (and in a very real sense, which vision of Israel's role in the Middle East) would dominate for the next four years. In addition, these would be the first polls in which a direct election for Israel's new prime minister would be held alongside, but separate from, the elections for the Knesset. Many of the old, party-dominated rules of the game had been jettisoned. Almost inevitably, this presidential-style election became the most highly personalized of any ever held in the country.

The opposition's contender for prime minister, Binyamin Netanyahu, had lived a long time in the United States, and seemed to have a strong knack for how to campaign under the new system. In a television interview conducted a few days before Peres's announcement on the elections, Netanyahu gave a preview of how he was planning to run his campaign. Though he was lagging seriously in opinion polls, he expressed his confidence that he could win the election: "I will lead because I am convinced of my way and [because] of the backing we will gain for a comprehensive program to safeguard Jerusalem and the Golan, which is the right path to bring peace." He spoke derisively of "Shimon Peres's path, which will bring us down from the Golan Heights to the banks of Lake Tiberias. . . ."[53] He must have realized that Golan was a potentially valuable wedge issue that could split traditional Labor voters away from their leadership and bring them over either to

Likud or at least to Third Way, which was planning to field its own list of candidates in the elections.

Regional tensions continued to rise. The day after Peres's announcement, veteran Israeli commentator Nahum Barnea wrote of his performance that "Peres . . . stands in splendid isolation. He has no one to beat in his party and no one to lose to. Only his own mistakes (or external terrorism) might steal the show from him."[54] Less than two weeks later, on February 25, a Palestinian suicide bomber blew himself up on a bus in a Jewish-populated portion of Jerusalem, killing twenty-four people; one of them was Barnea's son. Savir was a friend of the Barnea family. He left for Washington later that same day for Round Three of the Wye talks, which opened two days later. When he met Moalem, he told him about the Barneas' tragedy. As Savir later recalled his Syrian counterpart's response, Moalem "mumbled that it was regrettable, but, like his fellow Syrians, he could not bring himself to forthrightly denounce violence against Israelis."[55]

Moalem has reminded interlocutors that, though he was actively engaged in peace talks, his country still—pending the conclusion of the envisaged peace agreement—remained in a state of war with Israel. In addition, as a government representative, he has always been careful not to transgress his government's officially sanctioned point of view on any matter. President Assad's formulation on terrorism, repeated in the Syrian media and by all Syrian officials, was that "we call the criminal a terrorist, but we cannot call the citizen who defends his homeland a terrorist. Some people use glamorous slogans, such as democracy, human rights, and liberties to extort others and pressure them. Syria cannot be subjugated by the word terrorism, nor can it be intimidated by charges of terrorism."[56] The Syrians had recently been angered by being placed, yet again, on the U.S. State Department's list of states that sponsored terrorism.

On February 26, another suicide bomber blew himself up at a hitchhiking post for Israeli soldiers in southern Israel. A female soldier was killed. Two days later, a signed article by the chief editor of the government-owned English-language daily, *Syria Times*, condemned the two attacks "and the recent acts of violence," describing them as "an ordeal to many Israelis."[57] (A pro-Hamas radio station based in a Syrian-controlled area of Lebanon would later state, with regard to those two bombings and two more that followed them a week later, that "All this is done in revenge for the blood of the martyrs murdered by the Zionists, including . . . Yahya Ayyash.")[58]

On February 27, the same day that the negotiators launched their third round at Wye, Iranian vice president Habibi was making his rescheduled visit to Syria. Assad, it seems, was starting to hedge bets which up until Peres's announcement of the elections had been placed primarily on the success of the accelerated peace talks with Israel.

An announcement on Iran's state radio noted that, while in Syria, Habibi would co-chair a meeting of the two countries' bilateral commission with Syrian vice president Khaddam. The commentary noted:

> While it seemed that after the start of talks between Damascus and Tel Aviv, a split had occurred in relations between the two allies, the contacts between the two countries . . . showed that Tehran and Damascus continue to need each other. . . .
>
> Following the break in the talks between Syria and the Zionist regime, and after Damascus insisted on its just demands that Israeli forces should withdraw from the Golan Heights, Israel and America began to exert extensive propaganda pressure against Syria. America announced that it would keep Syria's name on the black list as a terrorist-breeding country. The Zionist regime, on its part, and in spite of the fact that it is itself the agent of tension and war in the Middle East region, made peace-seeking gestures and presented Syria as the side that caused a break in the talks.
>
> Under these circumstances, coordination between Iran and Syria, while strengthening their positions vis-à-vis common enemies, will also fortify Syria's stance in the face of pressures brought on it to make it give way to the concessions that the Zionist regime wants.[59]

While in Damascus, Habibi received a briefing on the situation in south Lebanon from a high-ranking delegation from Lebanese Hezbollah, headed by Shaykh Hasan Nasrallah and Husayn al-Musawi. He also had a meeting with a group of ten leaders of Palestinian factions opposed to the Oslo accords. These included a representative of Hamas and the secretary general of Islamic Jihad.[60]

If, during February, Assad was strengthening his fallback position in the event that the talks with Israel should fail, then so too was Peres. For it was sometime in February that the Israeli premier gave the go-ahead for the signing of a secret defense-cooperation agreement with Turkey that reportedly had been negotiated earlier—but not signed—by Rabin.[61] In late 1997 Ori Or, who in February 1996 was Peres's deputy as defense minister, would tell French interviewer Alain Gresh that, "although Turkey has never taken part in a war alongside us, it is a positive factor for Israel that Syria has an enemy on its northern frontiers. Syria will never attack Turkey, but it can't exclude the reverse. Turkey has a long experience of fighting outside its borders, in particular in the north of Iraq."[62]

In his account of Peres's decision to sign the pact, Rabinovich tried to be more diplomatic: "In an earlier decade Israel might well have seen a security pact with Turkey as having an anti-Syrian edge. This was not the case in 1996, but there was no persuading the Syrians that this was so." However, Rabinovich admitted that the Israelis never attempted to "initiate any discussion" with their Syrian negotiating partners on this topic and, indeed, that Israel had been willing to keep the pact under wraps.[63]

In February 1996, therefore, the leaders in both Syria and Israel seemed to be taking actions to strengthen their fallback positions. Back at the Wye Plantation, however, the third round of talks opened without any glitches on February 27, and seemed to get off to a good start. According to Ambassador Moalem, "We had very productive talks about the 'relevant areas.'"[64] At the end of the first week of the round, on Saturday, March 3, Savir, Moalem, and Ross met at Ross's house, as had become their custom, to evaluate what their teams had achieved in the first half of the new round, and to plan for the upcoming days of talks. According to Savir, during this meeting, "Ross expressed to Moalem his administration's concern that the Iranians were using Syria as a conduit for passing on instructions to Hamas to escalate its terror attacks on Israel. Moalem asked for evidence."[65]

The following day, the terror bombers struck again in Israel: In two separate blasts, a total of thirty-one Israelis, most of them civilians, were killed. The Israeli team that had been preparing to complete the round of Wye talks summarily flew home. Before they left, Ross met Moalem and told him that the Israelis had received instructions to return home. Ross then told Savir that Moalem had sent him "his personal wishes" and had expressed the hope that the talks would resume soon.[66]

CONCLUSION: LESSONS FROM WYE

Peres's March 4 decision to suspend his team's participation in the Wye talks brought to an end the bold experiment in Syrian-Israeli peacemaking whose launching he and his team had decided on just four months earlier. It also—though this was not his intention at the time—brought to an abrupt halt the four-and-a-half years of direct Israeli-Syrian talks that had been launched at the Madrid conference in 1991.

After Peres's suspension of the talks, things rapidly went from bad to worse in the Israeli-Syrian relationship (see chapter 7). Then, over the three years that followed March 1996, a certain bitterness against the whole experience of the fifty-two months of talks seemed to set in on both sides of the dividing line. Among the political elites in both countries, some variant of the view that "what happened in those talks just *proves* the other side is impossible to deal with" enjoyed considerable support in the spring of 1998.[67]

In spite of those worrying trends in broad popular attitudes, however, there remained among the participants in the Wye talks a strong sense that the discussions had broken considerable and very fruitful new ground. Indeed, if the talks are resumed, the work that was done at Wye in fleshing out and starting to link together all the different dimensions of what a peace agreement between these two countries would look like will provide an excellent launching point for those who decide to complete the task. For their part, throughout the forty months that followed the suspension of the talks, the Syrians continued to stress that the leaving-off point at Wye was the only starting point they would consider for any resumption of talks.

What were the aspects of the Wye formula that seemed to prove most valuable? These can be summarized as follows:

1. The seriousness with which both national leaderships committed themselves in December 1995 to reaching a final resolution of the long-standing hostilities and to building "normal peaceful relations" between them. On both sides this involved a commitment to radically changing existing norms and public attitudes in key areas. In Israel, Peres showed that he was prepared, even more actively than Rabin before him, to explore the possibility of effecting a total Israeli pullback from Golan. In Syria, Assad showed that he was prepared actively to explore not only fairly stringent limitations on Syria's deployment of its armed forces, but also the upending of previously held taboos on creating normal peaceful links with Israel.

2. The active engagement of the U.S. administration in the venture. The Americans provided the location—and obviously much more—for the talks. Once Peres had brought home to President Clinton the urgency with which he wanted to approach—and complete—this venture, U.S. diplomacy swung into full gear. From early November onward, Secretary Christopher spent a considerable amount of time planning and implementing the Wye talks; and then, between each round, he contributed his own shuttle diplomacy between the two leaders. Without his personal ability to reassure each leader regarding the intentions and plans of the other, the Wye talks could never have gotten off the ground. Inside the negotiating rooms, the U.S. negotiators, led by Dennis Ross, played an active "bridging" role; and alongside the formal negotiating encounters, Ross fostered the development of the three-person team leaders' planning group.

3. The regional comprehensiveness of the peacemaking vision. Savir was probably right in having identified that this could be an important point of overlap between the two leaderships. The Syrians were undoubtedly pleased to receive the recognition of the regionwide role that Peres's approach implied. Given the poor state of their relations with Yasser Arafat, the Syrians' pleasure on this score was probably further increased by some sense that their gaining this recognition, from both Israel and the United States, meant that it would no longer be only Arafat who would gain political credit in the West for allowing Israel to develop relations with other Arab parties.

4. The ambience and comprehensive, multitopic structure of the Wye talks. Some mention of the contribution made by the informal, secluded ambience of the Wye setting has been made. In addition, the demanding new intensity with which the talks were being scheduled, and the parallel structure of the various sets of talks signaled to decision makers on both sides that this time the intention really was to work toward completion in the shortest possible time. It was also in this context that the negotiators discovered important new areas of potential convergence regarding economic issues, which until then generally had been presumed to be something the Assad leadership considered to be more of an Israeli imposition than a potential benefit.[68]

5. Development of the team leaders' group. In connection with some previous rounds of the talks on this track, there had been some consultations in which only the two team leaders had participated, along with Dennis Ross. But now, given the pace at which the talks were proceeding, the leadership forum saw rapid development as the three men worked long and hard as a team to keep the various proliferating strands of the negotiation together. In the course of that interaction, trade-offs started to be explored whose implications were considerably more than merely procedural. Both Savir and Ross have expressed the judgment that the development of this group made a significant contribution to the success of the Wye formula. According to Savir, President Assad told Christopher and Ross that he agreed to use of the team leaders' group as an authorized back-channel where "potential flexibilities and real sensitivities could be informally tested."[69]

If all these factors were helping to bring about the notable successes that were witnessed during the Wye talks, how then can we explain the deterioration of relations that began after Peres announced his decision to hold May elections and would gather speed so rapidly after the Israeli side suspended its participation? The greater part of this analysis will await the next chapter. At this point it is probably enough to note that the very boldness with which the two sides had agreed to adopt an approach to peacemaking in late 1995 that was so radically different from what had gone before increased the stakes in the negotiation. The Wye formula was intended by its Israeli authors to be a "go-for-broke" kind of venture; and it was evidently on this basis that Syria's traditionally cautious leadership signed onto it. When Peres abruptly switched signals with his decision to hold elections before completion of the negotiation, it was not only the Americans who felt confused and slightly uneasy at this shift: They—and Peres—probably underestimated or ignored the degree to which President Assad felt betrayed by this move. (One of Assad's reactions at that point had, after all, been to tell Iran that Vice President Habibi would now be welcome in Damascus.)

After Peres pulled his negotiators home from Wye, however, Israeli-Syrian relations would rapidly deteriorate even further.

7
Disintegration

THE DYNAMICS OF PEACEMAKING GO INTO REVERSE

At a formal level, a study of the Syrian-Israeli bilateral talks that flowed from the Madrid conference might stop at March 4, 1996, the day on which the government of Israel suspended its participation in the talks. After that day, there were no bilateral peace talks between these two countries for at least the forty months that followed. The only direct contact between them in that period occurred in a much more limited context: that of the five-country committee established in mid-1996 to monitor compliance with a new agreement concerning south Lebanon.

However, for a broader look at how the experience of the bilateral talks affected the tenor of relations between the two national leaderships and the two peoples, and to assess the prospects for any success in future peace efforts on this track, it is useful to examine in some detail the dramatic breakdown in relations that occurred in the aftermath of Israel's suspension of its participation in the Wye talks. The three months that followed March 4, 1996, were marked by a head-spinning succession of major events in the Middle East. Practically all of these events contributed to an ever-worsening breakdown in trust and relations between the two sides.

On March 6, IDF Radio reported that Rabinovich was "disappointed —although not surprised—yesterday when Syrian Foreign Minister Farouq al-Sharaa refused to accede to Secretary of State Christopher's request that Syria operate against the terror organizations [judged to have been responsible for the bombings of the preceding days], or at least denounce the attacks."[1] By then, the Israeli team had already pulled out of the Wye talks. Two years later, Sharaa would explain his government's position as follows:

> We asked what does Syria have to do with it? We're not responsible for what happened. And we're not in a state of peace. We're still in a state of war, though negotiating for peace. . . . When there is peace, things will be different. Take into consideration that fifty years is not enough for the Israelis to forget and forgive [what Nazi Germany did to European Jews]. But here we are, still in a state of war, with our lands still occupied, and we have lost tens of thousands in this war. How can we send a message or statement of condolence?[2]

On the question of resuming the suspended peace talks, Rabinovich had told IDF Radio: "At this point, none of us are speaking about a precise date in the near future for the resumption of the talks. There have already been breaks in these negotiations that went on for months, and when they were resumed, it was usually possible to pick them up from the point where they left off rather than regress in the talks." The reporter noted that "Rabinovich believes that it is preferable to maintain what he terms constructive ambiguity rather than committing ourselves to a precise date for the resumption of the negotiations with Syria."[3] It was not until March 22, and in the context of efforts to prevent a complete breakdown in Lebanon, that a senior Israeli figure—in this case, Savir's close ally, Minister Yossi Beilin—would publicly state, "We will certainly be able to [resume the peace talks with Syria] after the elections."[4] However, as Ambassador Moalem recalled it, after Ross had told him on March 4 of the Israelis' decision to suspend, he received the impression from Ross that "the talks would be resumed in the next two or three weeks."[5]

One well-placed observer then in Damascus has noted that he was surprised by the intensity of the disappointment evinced by Syrians connected with the peace talks when they learned that the Israelis had suspended their participation.[6] On March 6, Syria's government television station announced the suspension in a short and matter-of-fact way. The announcement said that Dennis Ross had informed the Syrian delegation that the Israelis had decided to suspend the talks, "so the Israeli delegation members may take part in the funeral ceremony for the victims of the recent bombings in Israel." It added, "The Syrian delegation told the U.S. sponsor that Syria remains committed to the peace process to achieve a just and comprehensive peace in the region."[7]

In Israel, one of the government's immediate responses to the bombings of early March was to tighten even further the noose of "closure" around Palestinian-populated areas in the West Bank and Gaza that it had imposed after the first two bombs. Then, Prime Minister Peres joined President Clinton in planning a massive diplomatic-political response to the suicide bombers in the form of a hastily convened international meeting entitled "Summit of the Peacemakers." The summit was hosted March 13 by Egypt's president Hosni Mubarak in the Sinai resort town of Sharm al-Sheikh.

Dozens of government leaders and foreign ministers from around the world came to the summit, which was seen by many as an attempt by the Clinton administration and others to stem the hemorrhaging of support that had been inflicted on Peres's election campaign by the four explosions. From the Arab world, the Palestinian Authority's Yasser Arafat, Jordan's King Hussein, and Morocco's King Hassan all attended, as did the foreign ministers of Saudi Arabia, Algeria, Tunisia, and seven other Arab states. Syria, though invited, notably did not attend.

The joint statement issued by the summiteers spelled out that the gathering had "three fundamental objectives: to enhance the peace process; to promote security; and to combat terror." The participants emphasized "their strong condemnation of all acts of terror . . . whatever its motivation and whoever its perpetrator, including recent attacks in Israel."[8]

In remarks made after the conference, Peres stressed not only the antiterrorism provisions that the conferees had agreed on, but also the presence of thirteen high-level Arab delegations there. "I do not recall any [previous] Arab declarations either so unequivocal or so cautious about not harming the peace process," he said, adding:

> In fact, there was not even one anti-Israeli pronouncement. . . . This also shows that the dream about a comprehensive peace in the Middle East is possible. Israel today maintains relations with seven Arab states, but this time thirteen turned up. . . . For thirteen Arab countries to arise and loudly express their pain over the victims fallen in Israel—and reference is to Israel only—is noteworthy![9]

Although the summit seemed to be a huge success, there simmered within its halls and even between its two co-chairs, the United States and Egypt, a degree of tension regarding the extent to which the primary focus of the effort should be on fighting terrorism or on supporting peace efforts. By and large the United States and Israel wanted to put the emphasis on fighting terrorism; the Arab delegations wanted the focus placed on supporting peace efforts; and the positions of other delegations were somewhere between these two poles.

For Syria's part, though it had been invited to the summit, it had not been consulted at all in its planning; and the Syrian leadership remained extremely wary about the whole venture. In a news conference shortly after the gathering concluded, Foreign Minister Sharaa said, "If we had been certain that there was enough time for in-depth discussion and an objective exchange of views to reiterate our well-known stand on terrorism and the differentiation between what is and is not terrorism— that is, the struggle to resist occupation—we would not have hesitated to participate."[10] From his vantage point, Moalem has recalled that both the United States and Israel seemed "happy" that the Syrians did not attend the gathering.[11]

For the Syrian leadership, the issue of terrorism had long been a sensitive point in its relationship with Washington. During the Reagan years, much of the official American hostility to Syria was focused on American accusations that Syria supported terrorism in Lebanon. Syria's view on that point had always been that it was providing legitimate support inside "sisterly" Lebanon to Lebanese nationals who were fighting an Israeli force presence there that had no legitimacy under international law.[12] In the mid-1990s, many in the United States still tended to follow the Israelis' lead in categorizing as "terrorism" the actions of Lebanese nationals resisting the IDF's continued presence in their country, while the Syrian authorities—like the Lebanese authorities— considered such activities to be those of a legitimate national-liberation movement. In the Palestinian arena meanwhile, Washington and Damascus disagreed strongly about the support that Syria gave to Palestinian factions critical of the Oslo Accords. Some of these factions were associated with acts like the suicide bombs that indeed seemed aimed primarily at sowing terror among Israeli civilians.

In February 1996, in the aftermath of Peres's announcement of the elections, the Clinton administration had once again confirmed that it considered Syria to be, according to the designation required by Congress, a state that supported terrorism.[13] That action, along with the abruptness with which the Peres government had suspended its participation in the peace talks, also probably helped to account for the sensitivity with which Damascus responded to the convening of the Sharm al-Sheikh summit.

On March 12, as the summiteers gathered in Egypt, an announcer on Syrian television read a long, impassioned criticism of what it described as the "selectivity" of the conference. The commentary asked why the massacre of twenty-nine Palestinian worshippers at the Ibrahimi Mosque in Hebron two years earlier was not mentioned in the summit's joint statement, and accused summit organizers of keeping silent on a long list of Israeli government actions which it dubbed as terrorist. It quoted (yet again) the comments President Assad had made about terrorism three years earlier (see chapter 6). The commentary also accused Israel of having obstructed the peace process, and argued explicitly that "the continuation of the occupation is responsible for violence and counter-violence."[14]

Four days later, Syria's English-language daily defended the presence of the anti-Oslo Palestinian organizations in Damascus with the following argument:

> Israel and the entire world should be reminded that a half million Palestinian refugees who were expelled from their homeland and houses by Israel came to Syria. It is natural for them to have their own organizations in Damascus and to abide by the international resolutions that guarantee their right to repatriation, unless Israel is plotting to liquidate them and to close their file on the pretext of peace.[15]

Over the weeks that followed the four Palestinian bombs, it became clear that the bombers had succeeded in heightening tensions in Israel's relationships with all its neighbors. In the case of the Egyptian and Jordanian governments and the Palestinian Authority, those parties had by then reached significant (if not, in the case of the Palestinians, final) peace agreements with Israel that they valued. After the bombings, those leaders thus felt obliged to defend their relationship with the Israeli government by taking bold steps to reassure Israeli public opinion of their sympathy and the depth of their antiterrorist commitment—even if, in doing so, they should incur quite significant criticisms of one-sidedness from their own publics. The Syrian and Lebanese authorities, on the other hand, had no such agreements with Israel to defend. In addition, the government of Israel had demonstrated the seemingly low value it placed on its relationship with Syria by abruptly pulling out of the talks on the Syrian track, even before making any attempt to establish whether there was any direct relationship between Damascus and the perpetrators of the bombings (who were, after all, Palestinians, not Syrians).

Tension between Syria and Israel thus continued to rise quickly throughout the days and weeks following the Sharm al-Sheikh summit. As had so often happened under such circumstances in the past—and as also tended to happen in the run-up to Israeli elections—the first place to feel the effects was Lebanon.

BACKDROP TO A NEW CONFRONTATION IN LEBANON

While the Wye talks were being held, the tensions in south Lebanon never came close to escalating out of the control of the political leaderships in Israel and Syria. After Peres's announcement of early elections, however, and even more so after his suspension of the peace talks on March 4, the calculation in Damascus regarding the need to limit escalation in Lebanon clearly shifted.[16] Evidently, the parallel calculation on that score inside Israel's political leadership was shifting during those weeks, too.

Throughout March, and especially in the wake of the Sharm al-Sheikh summit (with its heavy doses of antiterrorism rhetoric), tensions in south Lebanon and along the Lebanese-Israeli border rose rapidly toward a boiling point. By March 20, Peres seems to have become convinced of the need to project himself as taking tough action against Hezbollah: "We must give them a beating; we have no choice," he told IDF Radio that day.[17] (In his recollections two years later, Peres still seemed to conflate the crisis he had experienced from the Palestinian bombs and the concurrent rise in tensions in south Lebanon. "We had Hamas in the south and Hezbollah in the north," he said.)[18]

At the same time that Peres was talking tough about the need to "give Hezbollah a beating," however, he was still continuing his efforts —conducted through the United States—to request the Syrians to rein in Hezbollah.[19] Yet this time around, Assad was not inclined to be helpful: "I asked President Assad to restrain Hezbollah, but his reaction was lukewarm," Peres later recalled.[20]

In Washington, the Clinton administration seemed to identify a clear interest (albeit a little belatedly) in trying to avoid the escalation it now saw threatening in Lebanon. Any such escalation could, after all, throw in question the support that many Arab and other countries had pledged to the worldwide counterterrorism efforts launched at the Sharm al-Sheikh summit. On March 18, U.S. ambassador to Israel Martin Indyk reportedly relayed to Peres what was described as "a U.S. demand to avoid a military operation in south Lebanon." Indyk reportedly said that the United States "wants to exhaust all the political moves with Syria in a bid to calm tempers down in the region." This communication was reportedly accompanied by U.S. demands that Assad also do what he could to restore calm.[21]

For a couple of weeks, these diplomatic efforts seemed to have a chance at succeeding: The Syrian leadership was neither merely sitting back and awaiting further developments, nor (as many in Israel seemed to think) throwing itself wholeheartedly into the embrace of the Iranians. Instead, it was conducting an active effort to explain its case to governments, especially Arab and European governments, that could be expected to be somewhat sympathetic to it. Amidst all the high-level hoopla of the Sharm al-Sheikh summit, Syria's position as a nonattender may have left it somewhat diplomatically isolated, but Syria's general political standing within the Arab world in March 1996 was by no means weak. Indeed, in the speech that Saudi foreign minister Prince Saud Al Faisal gave at the summit, he was clearly signaling his support for Syria's position on many issues.[22]

On April 2, President Mubarak traveled to Damascus for the latest in his continuing series of bilateral summits with Assad. In the news conference after their meeting, Assad assessed the status of the peace talks with Israel in the following, cautious terms:

> We all can see that Israel is hampering, obstructing, delaying, and slowing moves and suspending talks. In my opinion, the Israelis have not made up their minds on the peace process. They have not done so. If we view the talks or the negotiations as a gateway to peace, this gateway has started to narrow. *I am not saying it has been closed, but it has gotten significantly narrower.*[23]

Asked specifically whether Syria was complying with the U.S. request to try to ease tensions in Lebanon, Assad did not give a direct response. Instead, he accused Israel of committing repeated infractions of the 1993 understanding.[24] (Two days earlier, Lebanon's government radio station reported that the Israelis had killed two construction workers working on a water tower in the village of Yater. Hezbollah then threatened a retaliation against northern Israel.)[25]

Within days of the Assad-Mubarak summit, a significant new factor entered the regionwide balance when Turkey's defense minister Oltan Sungurlu publicly revealed the existence (and many of the terms) of the defense-cooperation agreement concluded with Israel the month before. Sungurlu made reference to Syria's having recently agreed to provide similar support to Turkey's old nemesis, Greece—although this allegation was immediately denied by the Turkish foreign minister.[26] Other Turkish government representatives later attempted to point out that the military agreements with Israel were "not directed against anybody." To the Syrian leadership, however, the nature and timing of Sungurlu's disclosures seemed sinister in the extreme. From Damascus it seemed that Israel, having already concluded a strategic cooperation agreement with Jordan, was now also putting itself in a position to put additional military pressure on Syria from the north.[27] An April 9 editorial in *Al-Thawra* stated, "It is clear that Israel, which obstructed the peace efforts, does not seek peace, but claims to do so—out of its hypocrisy—in order to conceal its aggressive intentions." Israel's real role had been exposed, the paper added, "with the disclosure of its military alliance with Jordan and Turkey to surround and besiege Syria."[28]

The disclosure of the Israeli-Turkish military arrangement may well also have caused the Syrians some sense of betrayal by Turkey. Savir has written that in some of the Thursday night dinners he shared with Moalem at the time of the Wye talks, the Syrian envoy "hinted at an improved relationship between Syria and Turkey." He attributed to Moalem the judgment that, "Turkey would essentially become . . . a partner in the comprehensive regional peace," and noted that at that time Dennis Ross "was planning to hold discussions with the Turkish government on these ideas."[29] It cannot have helped to calm Damascus's fears to learn that a joint American-Jordanian military exercise was scheduled to take place in Jordan on April 12.

By April 10, the balance of opinion inside the Israeli cabinet had already reached a turning point. That evening, Israel's Channel 2 television reported "The feeling today is that the era of self-restraint has ended. . . . As far as Peres is concerned, an operation should press the Lebanese government. *We can hit important Lebanese targets, for example. Such pressure will force the Beirut government to press Hezbollah.*"[30]

Clearly, Peres and his ministers were planning something like a repeat of the July 1993 operation. Deputy Defense Minister Or also signaled that the deliberate application of pressure against civilians would be a major part of the upcoming campaign when he told television viewers: "We should and will take a series of actions . . . that will make Hezbollah, and mainly the Lebanese government, *assume responsibility for the lives of the Lebanese citizens who live north of the security zone.*" On the same broadcast, correspondent Ehud Ya'ari reported, "Official U.S. administration reactions have not called for restraint. This means that there is a feeling that the United States is currently clearing the way for *whatever means Israel chooses to use and has not yet pursued.*"[31]

The next day, the IDF launched the large-scale action in Lebanon to which it gave the name Operation Grapes of Wrath.

AN EXPLOSION OF WRATH

The nature of the campaign that Israel waged between April 11 and April 26, 1996, was dominated by the following pair of facts which had applied to all of Israel's engagements in Lebanon since the mid-1980s:

1. The Israeli government and public were not prepared to send any significant ground units into Lebanon and risk a repeat of the draining attrition it had suffered between 1982 and 1985: 600 soldiers lost during the 1982 invasion, and 699 during the three subsequent years during which it extricated itself back to the security zone.

2. Without such a deployment of ground forces, it was clear to everyone in Israel's political and military leadership that they could not succeed in destroying Hezbollah's infrastructure in Lebanon merely through use of their own standoff forces, however lethal. (It is also hard to see how they could have achieved it even with ground force deployments.)

The line of strategy that had developed inside the military establishment to deal with these uncomfortable facts—and used to only short-lived effect in July 1993—was to employ the massively lethal capabilities of Israel's standoff forces to apply pressure on Lebanese civilian and civilian interests in the areas of Hezbollah influence so that these civilians would then pressure their government into taking steps to crack down on Hezbollah.

The Israeli campaign failed to maintain essential distinctions between combatants and noncombatants in Lebanon. Indeed, as in 1993, the 1996 campaign relied on the forced evacuation of hundreds of thousands of civilians—with all the attendant hardships, deaths, and casualties that this would necessarily involve—as an integral part of the broader strategic plan, and not as a mere by-product of it. During Operation Grapes of Wrath, the IDF threatened the entire populations of ninety-six villages, towns, and cities inside Lebanon, warning that they should evacuate their communities according to impossibly rigid deadlines, or they would "bear the consequences." Once evacuated, the IDF considered these locations "free-fire zones," where they could use their standoff weapons at will. On April 19, the International Committee of the Red Cross issued a strong appeal against this tactic, noting in a rare public statement: "The orders to evacuate an entire region [were] in this case contrary to international humanitarian law," and moreover that these orders "do not exempt Israel from the obligation to respect civilians still on the spot."[32]

On April 18, Israeli artillery commanders who were apparently involved in an exchange of fire with Hezbollah guerrillas operating from near a United Nations base at Qana ended up firing on the UN base itself, killing more than one hundred civilians of all ages who had sought shelter there.

The evening after the tragedy, Peres went on Israeli television to explain to viewers: "I do not believe that the IDF knew that refugees were concentrated there or else the soldiers would not have shelled the location. . . . What we did not know was that approximately five hundred or six hundred villagers who had fled their homes were massed there in unbelievably crowded conditions."[33] However, eight days later, in an extensive military review that he and General Shahak gave of the conduct of the war, IDF intelligence chief Moshe Ya'alon noted, "Several days before the incident, UNIFIL [the UN Interim Force in Lebanon] reported to us that approximately five thousand to six thousand people were living around their camps. When we asked what camps, their response was that they could not go into details and could provide us only with general information." Ya'alon admitted in the review that on April 18, the IDF had received no specific information regarding the presence or absence of refugees at the Qana camp since the result of an aerial survey that had been conducted "several days" before the incident.[34] On

April 15, however, the nearby town of Qana had been one of sixteen towns and villages whose residents the IDF had given two hours' notice over the SLA radio station that they should evacuate their communities completely: "Everyone who remains in his home after this time will expose himself to the danger of death at his own risk," they were told.[35] So it should have seemed quite likely, to say the least, that the Qana base would be one of the UN locations where evacuees had sought shelter. In his review, Ya'alon claimed that the decision to shell had been justified, and that "the hits were mostly accurate. . . . To our regret, however, a small number of shells *overshot their mark*. Even had we photographed the camp several hours earlier, we would not have spotted the refugees because they were in two covered sheds."[36]

In an interview two years later, Peres explained Operation Grapes of Wrath in the following terms:

> Our basic strategy was not to shoot anyone or kill anyone, but to put pressure on Hezbollah. This would be created by shooting outside the villages. No one was killed except at Kafr Qana. This was tragic. We wanted to hit a Hezbollah unit next to the camp, but our eighteen-man unit came under attack and asked for artillery support. But six shells went out of orbit. No one knew there were refugees in the camp. I took full responsibility.[37]

In the judgment of the veteran Israeli military analyst Ze'ev Schiff, "If it had not been for Qana, the IDF would have bombed much more."[38] Even before that incident it should have become evident to Peres and his advisers that the strategy they had articulated for the war—to use force and threats of force to pressure Lebanese civilians to, in turn, pressure their government to crack down on Hezbollah—was not proceeding as planned. In fact, in the political environment of April 1996, the sheer scale of the IDF's assault on the south—and on important civilian installations in and around Beirut—had exactly the opposite political effect. On April 16, Lebanese prime minister Rafiq al-Hariri, a person by no means inclined to be a Hezbollah apologist, was telling a news conference in Saudi Arabia, "Today Israel is striking at Lebanon, not Hezbollah. Look for yourself at what has happened to Hezbollah. We have said that these operations will strengthen Hezbollah. *It is as if Israel has been assigned to strengthen Hezbollah.*"[39]

For the first few days after the launching of Grapes of Wrath, the Clinton administration notably abstained from denouncing this massive new escalation in Lebanon; it also blocked all attempts to have the UN Security Council issue a condemnatory resolution. It was only on April 15 that the first hints emerged of a U.S. effort to explore possibilities for ending the fighting. By then, other mediators were well on their way in their own, separate attempts to mediate a cease-fire for Lebanon.[40] In the aftermath of the Qana incident, Clinton repeated his call for "all parties to agree to an immediate cease-fire," and announced he would send Secretary Christopher to the Middle East to help to negotiate it. Nevertheless, he still declined to criticize Israel, limiting his remarks regarding Qana to an expression of sympathy for those who had died there.[41]

Hezbollah and the Syrians both quickly became aware that the Israeli assault was tipping the political scales in Lebanon and throughout the Arab world against the Israeli government. They were in little hurry to let Israel off the hook with a quick cease-fire.

Nor was Peres eager for a quick cease-fire. In a piece penned from Israel on April 17, British correspondent Patrick Cockburn noted that Grapes of Wrath was wildly popular among Jewish Israelis. It served, he wrote, as an exuberant reassertion of Israeli power after a period (in the aftermath of the four Palestinian bombs) in which many Israelis had felt notably threatened and powerless, and had blamed Peres for that powerlessness. "Even members of the Labor Party who are not overjoyed by what is happening in Lebanon can see its political advantages. Likud has lost its best card, which was to attack Peres as soft on security," Cockburn wrote. In a warning that seemed eerily prescient, he noted, "The danger for Israel is that the use of excessive force in Lebanon will ultimately be counterproductive."[42]

After Qana, Peres apparently had second thoughts about the wisdom of continuing the operation as originally planned. On April 23, a report in *Yedi'ot Aharonot* noted that several hours after the scope of the killing in Qana became known,

> under orders from Shimon Peres . . . the IDF significantly reduced its aerial activities and artillery fire in south Lebanon. The deviation from the operation plan caused significant unrest among Northern Command officers. On April 21, Lieutenant General Amnon Shahak, chief of staff, summoned top Northern Command brass and admonished them for remarks attributed to them in the media according to which the officers criticized the decision to lower the profile of the operation.

On April 22, however, and once again under orders from Peres, "the IDF went back to the original plan for Operation Grapes of Wrath."[43]

Throughout this crisis it became increasingly evident that in the absence of the kind of political effects the Israeli military had hoped for inside Lebanon, the only way that Grapes of Wrath could be brought to an end would be, as in 1993, by enrolling the diplomatic good offices of President Assad. A veritable Who's Who of high-level envoys made their way to Damascus; but still, Assad played hard to get.

On April 24, a commentary on Syrian television stated tartly "Yesterday, Israeli prime minister Shimon Peres said he alone shoulders the responsibility for the Qana massacre. With this announcement, Peres deserves the title of killer of children. This title might help him take a large step toward success in the elections that will be held in Israel late next month."[44] The personal nature of this attack against Peres was a rare new theme in Syrian rhetoric, and was an expression of the deep resentment and betrayal with which nearly all Syrians and other Arabs were reacting to Peres's launching and continuation of Grapes of Wrath. Many in the Arab political elite, including in Syria, previously had been intrigued by Peres's reputation as "Mr. Peace," and by the boldness of his overtures towards the PLO while such contacts were still subject to broadly supported taboos in Israeli society. For those in the Syrian leadership, the sense of betrayal in April 1996 was particularly intense, since just weeks earlier the Assad regime had come close to concluding a peace treaty and inaugurating a normalization of relations with the government led by this man. "Before it started its latest invasion of southern Lebanon on 11 April," the April 24 commentary noted, "Israel withdrew its negotiating delegation from Maryland. Before that, Peres reneged on his announcement that peace is more important to him than the elections by saying that security is more important to him than peace. All these steps were, in fact, part of a plan to abandon and abort the peace process. . . ."[45]

If the beginning of this commentary had provided a chance to vent deeply felt feelings (and also to reassure the Syrian public that its leadership remained sensitive to their concerns), its ending was vintage Assad diplomacy, and revealed to his people the real thrust of what he was working for: "The current efforts should focus on ending the savage invasion and preventing it from achieving its goals, which Israel will never be able to achieve. Failure to work out a political solution

will escalate tension and increase the danger. . . . It is very important
to return to the foundations of the peace process, as stipulated in the
Madrid conference of 1991, and not to boast of perpetrating bloody
massacres. . . ."[46]

On April 26, the diplomatic efforts thus signaled bore fruit. In an
agreement negotiated by the Americans and the French, these two governments and those of Lebanon, Israel, and Syria all finally announced
their agreement to the terms for a cease-fire:

1. Armed groups in Lebanon will not carry out attacks by Katyusha
   rockets or by any kind of weapon into Israel.
2. Israel and those cooperating with it will not fire any kind of weapon
   at civilians or civilian targets in Lebanon.
3. Beyond this, the two parties commit to ensuring that under no circumstances will civilians be the target of attack and that civilian pop-
   ulated areas and industrial and electrical installations will not be
   used as launching grounds for attacks.
4. Without violating this understanding, nothing herein shall preclude
   any party from exercising the right of self-defense.[47]

The terms of this agreement were announced simultaneously in
Beirut, Damascus, and Jerusalem. In Beirut, French foreign minister
Hervé de Charette accompanied Lebanese prime minister Rafiq al-Hariri
at the announcement. In Jerusalem, Secretary Christopher accompanied Peres.[48] In a rare display of anger toward the United States,
Assad had made known to Christopher during this round of diplomacy
that he would not be welcome in Damascus.

The new agreement had a number of features that distinguished it
from the understandings agreed to in 1993. First, the new agreement
was written down, in English terms agreed to by all the parties mentioned
in it. Second, it established a monitoring mechanism to be supervised
by a committee in which France, Syria, and the United States, along
with Lebanon and Israel, would all be represented. Finally, it spelled out
the explicit understanding of all parties that a cease-fire in Lebanon was
no substitute for a "comprehensive peace," and that peace talks on the
Syrian and Lebanese tracks should be resumed, although it attached
no deadline to this move.

In a notable blow to Israel's original war aims, this agreement, like
that of 1993, made no mention of placing any restrictions on the actions
of Lebanese organizations combating Israel's troop presence in Lebanon,

except for the humanitarian restrictions referred to above, which were not new, and were (as before) supposed to apply equally to the activities of the IDF and its allies in Lebanon. That evening, an interviewer from Israeli television began an interview with Peres by asking up-front whether the agreement would "prevent Hezbollah from continuing to operate." Peres gave no direct answer. Instead, his response seemed to underline the importance that he (unlike many in Israel) accorded to the word of the Syrians: "First, we have excellent experience with Syria. They signed a Golan Heights agreement in 1974 and since then not a single shot or Katyusha has been fired on the Golan Heights. I see two achievements at the outset: One, this is a written agreement; two, the fact that Syria is part of it. It is difficult to get a Syrian commitment, but when it is obtained, they uphold it."[49]

From the opposition benches, Netanyahu lost no time in slamming the agreement. He told television viewers: "First, Hezbollah is there and is capable of firing Katyushas at any time. Second, it has Israel's permission under this accord to fire at, kill, and maim IDF soldiers in the security zone. Third, it has a safe haven. It is not allowed to fire from inside these safe havens, but it can move one hundred meters from the south Lebanese villages where it is located and trains, hit IDF soldiers, and then return to the safe havens—but we are prevented from harming these bases." His interviewer asked him what he would have done if he had been prime minister: "I would have acted differently. I would have disbanded Hezbollah's infrastructure in south Lebanon." How? "In a military action."[50]

AFTER GRAPES OF WRATH

In Lebanon the conclusion of the April 26 cease-fire allowed the four hundred thousand civilians who had been forced out of their homes and communities in the south to return. The infrastructural damage they found—along the roads and in their towns, villages, and workplaces—was enormous. South of the border, meanwhile, the conclusion of the cease-fire allowed Israelis to return to their major preoccupation of those weeks: the campaign for their first-ever presidential-style election on May 30.

Peace issues dominated this election, which was seen by most participants as constituting a broad national referendum on the way that

Labor had conducted the peace talks over the past four years. Though the Palestinian track of the talks was probably more important to most Israeli voters than the Syrian track, the latter was a key issue for a number of Israelis, notably those living in Golan and their supporters, along with everyone in northern Israel and elsewhere who had been affected by the recent hostilities in Lebanon.

On May 15, the political parties issued their platforms. Labor's pledged that "Israel will continue negotiations on a permanent peace with the Palestinian Authority, Syria and Lebanon." Regarding Golan, the platform came up with a noncommittal new description of the region as "a nationally important region to the State of Israel." The peace talks with Syria would, it promised, "continue on the basis of the Security Council Resolutions 242 and 338. The agreement we are seeking will be based on secure borders and dependable security arrangements, guaranteed water sources essential to Israel, and the establishment of full, normal relations between the two countries, emphasizing economic cooperation." The agreement with Syria would "accompany agreements with most of the other Arab states." Any agreement reached would still be brought to a referendum, as promised by Rabin back in 1994, after negotiations on it were complete.[51]

Likud's platform paid little attention to the possibility of negotiations with Syria. After listing nine conditions it pledged to implement on the Palestinian track, there was only the following brief reference to matters related to Syria: "The Tenth Knesset [in 1981] passed a resolution proposed by the Likud government to apply Israeli law, jurisdiction, and administration on the Golan Heights, thus setting Israeli sovereignty over the area."[52] The Third Way Party, by contrast, placed much greater focus on Syrian-related issues. Fielding its first-ever list in a national election, Third Way's platform argued (however inaccurately) that "Israel is entitled to retain territories captured in a war of defense." The platform focused on the importance of a geographic concept it described as the "eastern backbone" of Israel, "from the Golan Heights to Elat," and declared all of this backbone to be "vital to Israel's future in times of peace as well as war." Therefore, it pledged, Third Way would seek to make "the development and population of the entire eastern sector a central national project, to which extensive resources will be directed. The accelerated population of the eastern sector will counterbalance the dangerously exclusive settlement of the coastal area."[53]

Of the majority-Jewish parties, only the left-wingers of Meretz had a platform that was unequivocally (though not unconditionally) in favor of peace with Syria: "Despite Syria's hard-line position, peace with Syria has strategic importance," it stated.

> Peace with Syria will eliminate the danger of a sudden war, will afford quiet on the northern border, and will pave the way for a full regional peace. Thus, in return for a full peace with Syria, a peace anchored in exacting security arrangements, Israel must agree to a gradual withdrawal to the international border. The security arrangements must be comprehensive and diverse, based on demilitarization, extensive force reduction, sophisticated monitoring techniques and international guarantees.[54]

If Peres's standing in the opinion polls, and that of Labor in its parallel elections to the Knesset, had been badly dented by the Palestinian bombs of late winter, by early May they appeared to have made up that deficit—at least among Jewish voters. But around 16 percent of Israel's voters were Palestinian-Israelis (as they describe themselves), or Israeli Arabs, as the Israeli government describes them. Ever since Labor's election in 1992, the government had been able to count on the support of the Arab community in its pursuit of successive peace moves, including votes on key issues from Knesset members from the Arab parties. But Grapes of Wrath caused a crisis in Peres's relationship with the Israeli Arabs—one which, as he admitted in an interview with an Israeli-Arab interviewer in mid-May, had taken him by surprise.[55] Arab community leaders were not about to urge their constituencies to vote for Netanyahu or Likud—but in a crucial move which they only partially rescinded, they did urge followers *not to vote for Peres* in the prime ministerial race. When the returns came in during the early morning following the election, it became evident that these forgone votes from Israeli Arabs had helped tip the scales against Peres. Netanyahu won a victory that surprised nearly all the opinion pollsters—by a margin of somewhere under fifty thousand.[56]

LIKUD'S RETURN

Netanyahu's victory at the polls shocked nearly everyone who had been involved in the peace process up to that time, including, apparently, the Syrians. But had some in Damascus been secretly rooting for a Likud victory? Or, had Likud's leaders been sending messages to Damascus implying that, if elected, they would be eager to deal with Damascus? The latter possibility had been discussed by various parties a number of times in 1995. Certainly in the early 1990s, a number of Likud personalities had shown themselves decidedly more eager to deal with Arab states (including Syria) than with the Palestinians. These individuals included Dore Gold, who was Netanyahu's key advisor on peace-process affairs during the 1996 elections and later was named Israel's ambassador to the United Nations.[57]

The traditional point of view in Damascus regarding Israel's domestic politics had been that there was "no difference" between Likud and Labor; and that they were "all Zionists, anyway, so what's the difference?" Farouq Sharaa had been sounding a new variation on that theme when he told a Spanish interviewer in May 1995: "We are simply optimistic about the future. We will fully recover our land, whoever governs in Israel." His reasoning:

> Israel's higher interest is to make peace with Syria. Moreover, the entire international community will exert considerable pressure on a Likud government if it tries to abort the peace process. Last, Likud does not include the Golan Heights among its expansionary aims. The same thing happened with Sinai, which Menachem Begin returned to Egypt. The settlements on the Golan Heights belong to the Labor Party, which encouraged the annexation of that territory.

Intriguingly, Sharaa then added: "We have received hints over the past few months that, if it wins, Likud will show considerable enthusiasm to sign a peace agreement with Syria, and they know that peace with us cannot be attained without a complete withdrawal from the Golan Heights."[58]

In early November 1995, Prime Minister Rabin told interviewers that he had "additional proof . . . regarding messages Netanyahu sent to the Syrians to the effect that they would do better to wait until after the elections." These messages, he said, "most certainly" included something different from what Netanyahu was saying in public at the time.[59] It is not clear whether this claim regarding "proof" was a pre-electoral ploy to sully Netanyahu's name, or if the Likud leader indeed had been sending messages of that nature to Damascus. But three days after that interview, Rabin was dead; and over the seven months that followed, the Syrian leadership was forced to deal with a rapid succession of changes of pace and expectation regarding the peace talks, as detailed previously. When Netanyahu's victory was finally announced at the end of May, it is quite possible that President Assad did not know at all what to expect from him. His first reaction was to fly to Cairo for another quick huddle with President Mubarak.

At the customary news conference with which the two presidents concluded their summit, Mubarak articulated a cautious reaction to Netanyahu's accession to Israel's premiership: "Although the speech made yesterday by the prime minister–elect did not inspire optimism, we found it wise to wait and see what the actual policy of the new government will be. We will act in the light of this policy." Assad, though also guarded, was slightly more negative:

> We are not really talking about the resumption of negotiations now. First we would like to understand the situation properly. We think that we understand much from the statements that have been made, although sometimes we receive information that conflicts with the statements. For this reason, we will seek to get more information. We do not feel that matters are moving in a positive direction.[60]

The Arab leaders did not have long to wait. By June 17, when Netanyahu presented the final draft of his government's guidelines to the Knesset, the only reference to Syrian-related issues stated, "The Government of Israel will conduct negotiations with Syria without preconditions."[61] On the basis of these painstakingly negotiated guidelines he formed a right-wing–dominated government containing a large contingent of religious parties—and Avigdor Kahalani, representing the four members that Third Way had been able to place in the Knesset.

Talk of "negotiations without preconditions," or—another old Likud formula favored by Netanyahu—"peace for peace" (instead of "land for peace"), was extremely disappointing to the Syrian leaders. So was another old failed Likud trial balloon that Netanyahu and Dore Gold tried to relaunch: "Lebanon first."

Syria was by no means the only Arab party whose previous hopes in the peace talks received a major pummeling as a result of Netanyahu's election. In late June, Assad joined other Arab leaders at a summit hastily convened in Egypt to assess the situation.

On July 12, Dore Gold was Netanyahu's representative in meetings that were convened in Washington to set up the south Lebanon monitoring mechanism.[62] While in Washington, he reportedly held a ten-minute tête-à-tête with Moalem, who was representing Syria in the monitoring talks. Gold used the time to relay to the Syrian authorities a message from Netanyahu to Assad, calling for "the resumption of the negotiations without preconditions." Moalem reportedly informed him that no talks were possible before Israel committed itself to a complete withdrawal from Golan.[63]

And that was it in terms of new developments in Israeli-Syrian peace-making. Peres may well have intended, after a victory at the polls, to resume the talks with Syria where he had left off three months earlier. Yet he was not reelected, and the fact that it was he who had suspended the talks made it that much easier for Netanyahu not to resume them. Instead of actively re-engaging in the peace talks, the new government set in motion an accelerated program of strengthening Israel's demographic and administrative hold on Golan.

During the three years of Likud government that followed, there was no meaningful movement on the Israel-Syrian track at all. In late May 1999, as Netanyahu prepared to hand over the reins of government to his successor—Labor's Ehud Barak—he tried to claim that he had inaugurated a number of promising and productive proposals to Assad through various third parties, including the Omani foreign minister, American business executive and former ambassador Ronald Lauder, and European Union emissary Miguel Moratinos.[64] But no one involved in the peace talks on the American or Syrian sides gave any credence to the claims of a man widely viewed, by that point, as being endowed with only a limp sense of integrity.

During Netanyahu's premiership, meanwhile, there had been a number of other developments in the region, and further afield, which would affect the future of the Syrian-Israeli track. In brief, these included:

▪ A significant escalation of military tensions between the two powers later in 1996, and then in late 1997 the disclosure that Yehuda Gil, the Mossad agent in charge of making assessments regarding Syria's intentions for at least three years previously, had been fabricating many of his alleged "human-intelligence" reports to the effect that Assad's true intentions toward Israel were belligerent.[65]

▪ The continuation of Israeli (and SLA) losses in south Lebanon, with the volume of opinion in Israel that favored any quick withdrawal from Lebanon, even one conducted unilaterally, rising throughout Netanyahu's term.[66]

▪ Prolonged periods of paralysis on the Palestinian track, a total freeze on the Lebanese track, and other deep-seated problems on the Jordanian and "multilateral" tracks, leading to increased frustrations with Likud from nearly all Arab leaders and publics.

▪ The apparent consolidation of prospects that President Assad's younger son, Bashar, might one day succeed him.

▪ A relatively speedy (though not necessarily irreversible) decline in the political fortunes of Likud's first "new generation" leader, Binyamin Netanyahu, as allies from inside and outside his party deserted him throughout his premiership, forcing him to call an early—and for him, disastrous—election in May 1999.

▪ The rise in the political fortunes of former chief of staff Ehud Barak, who had taken over the Labor leadership from Peres after the latter's electoral defeat in 1996, culminating in Barak's strong showing in the 1999 election.

▪ Continued transformation of Israel's party system, with the elimination of the four-seat mandate that the (Golan-focused) Third Way Party had enjoyed in the 1996–99 Knesset,[67] a continued decline in the number of parliamentary seats held by Israel's traditional "big two" parties, Labor and Likud, and the strengthening of sizeable new power blocs, including from the Sephardi religious party, Shas, and the Russian-immigrant parties.

ANATOMY OF A DISINTEGRATION

The impact that developments such as these may have on the prospects for a breakthrough on the Syrian track in the Barak era will be examined in more detail in the next chapter. Here it is worth summing up some of the lessons of the rapid deterioration in relations that occurred during those crucial twelve weeks between March 4 and May 30, 1996.

Emotions on both sides of the Israeli-Syria divide were running extremely high during those weeks. At the level of the two countries' respective policymakers, during the heady early weeks of the Wye talks, there had been a sense of real excitement that this time, finally, they were about to put an end to the state of war between them. But in the wake of the Palestinian bombs and the Israeli responses to them, that sense of positive intensity seemed on both sides to become transformed or deflected into a correspondingly strong sense of *negative* emotion: of bitterness, anger, betrayal, and recrimination against the party which until recently had seemed like a fully plausible peace partner.

Even two years afterward, much of the bitterness engendered during those weeks still remained. Among Israelis who had participated in the talks with Syria, there was a strong sense that, at the very least, Assad had willfully missed an opportunity for peace that had been presented to him under Labor; that he could have reined in Hezbollah (and even, with less plausibility, the Palestinian extremists), but had chosen not to; that he could have helped Peres win the 1996 election, but did not do so. "To hell with Assad," one Israeli formerly very supportive of the peace talks remarked in spring 1998. "If he finds himself under pressure from Turkey now, so be it!"[68]

On the Syrian side, meanwhile, after Peres's announcement of early elections in early February 1996 there had been some significant disappointment caused by the perception that he had gone back on his earlier avowals that he considered "peace more important than elections." At that point, the Syrians saw Peres abruptly shifting the negotiation in which they felt they had invested so much time and energy onto the back burner, and their own role transformed from that of partners in the important venture of building a regionwide peace into subsidiary stage-props for Peres's reelection campaign. That disappointment hardened into a feeling of anti-Peres (and more broadly anti-Israeli) bitterness in the aftermath of Peres's March 4 suspension of Israel's participation in the talks; the holding of the Sharm al-Sheikh summit; and, finally, Peres's launching of Operation Grapes of Wrath. For many Syrians, this bitterness was tempered by a sense of relief that, although Peres may have turned out to be either a weak or a duplicitous partner in the peace venture, at least Assad had been smart enough not to get trapped, as the Palestinians seemingly had been, into concluding with Peres an agreement that would have to be implemented under the untrustworthy Netanyahu.

In March 1998, Foreign Minister Sharaa would struggle to find a way to express, in English, a very complex view of Peres:

My view was that he was a Utopian man: definitely a man of peace, but because he was Utopian he could definitely damage that—especially when he went into Lebanon and attacked Hezbollah two months before the Israeli election. He was easily provoked to show that he was a man of "security," of "confrontation." It's not that he's naïve, but his genuine search for peace is taken lightly by him sometimes. He overreacted in Lebanon![69]

8

The Past as Prelude

PEACEMAKING AS LEARNING

On May 17, 1999, Labor leader Ehud Barak was elected prime minister of Israel, winning 56 percent of the vote in a two-way race against Netanyahu. The parliamentary elections that were also held that day brought a decrease in the number of Knesset seats given to Likud (from thirty-two down to nineteen), and the elimination of all four seats that Third Way had had in the preceding Knesset. Those elections also brought about a decrease in Labor's seats (from thirty-four to twenty-seven) as well as a large rise in seats going to Shas, Russian-immigrant parties, and other parties outside the two-party mainstream of an earlier political era. Nevertheless, the net effect seems to be to give Barak a significantly stronger mandate in the Knesset on many peace-related issues than the one Rabin had struggled with in the mid-1990s.

The 1999 elections brought to the premiership a man who, like his mentor Yitzhak Rabin, had made his first career in the IDF, ending up as its chief of staff. Barak was also the first of Israel's premiers who had personally taken part in peace talks with the Syrians—though, as noted in chapters 3 through 6, the record of that participation, and of the impact that Barak had on the negotiation during his short term in the foreign ministry, seemed somewhat mixed.

Samuel Lewis, who had known Barak since the late 1970s, has judged him to be a person willing to "think outside the box" and explore new ideas. "He is like Rabin, but more creative," Lewis said. "Also, he won a much stronger political basis for his premiership than the one Rabin had. Don't forget that Rabin's slowness in the talks with Syrians . . . was also due to his weak political position."[1] For his part, Ambassador Moalem judged that Barak had around 70 votes in the Knesset that would support a "land-for-peace" deal with Syria. "Now he has no excuse not to start where Labor [under Peres] left off," the Syrian envoy concluded.[2]

At its core, making peace is a learning experience, as two (or more) parties previously hostile to each other come to view their relationship as one that first permits, and then perhaps mandates, an increasing degree of cooperation. To be successful, this reframing needs to be applied not only to each party's view of "the other," but also to its own self-image. This is particularly the case in long-standing conflicts such as the fifty-year state of war between Israel and Syria, where the self-definition of the ruling elite on either side of the dividing line has been formed, in some part at least, by the very fact of the existence and continuation of the conflict.

Members of the Israeli elite have a strong image of their country as a state "surrounded by enemies," and members of the Syrian elite have a strong sense of their country as "the last Arab state to stand up to the Israelis and hold up the banner of Arab and Palestinian rights." In both cases, the armed forces also play a role in national life, the national economy, and national sentiment that goes considerably beyond their role in security affairs. When members of the political elites in such countries start to engage seriously in the business of crafting a peace agreement between them—as the leaders of both Syria and Israel did after June 1992—that meant they had to start rethinking not only their views of each other but also their views of themselves, and the roles that their *own* states might play in building a future region at peace.

Ample evidence (as presented throughout this study) suggests that this was not an easy, or linear, process for the leadership on either side of the line. Yet there is also ample evidence showing that by early 1996 both leaderships had made considerable strides in *learning* more about the requirements of a future, cooperative peace than they had demonstrated in earlier years. On the Israeli side, the two outstanding pieces of public evidence in this regard are the interviews that first Rabin, and then Uri Savir, gave to the media in November and December 1995, respectively, as described in chapter 5. The most outstanding pieces of evidence in the more shrouded Israeli diplomatic record are the commitments that Rabin offered *conditionally* in August 1993 and July 1994, to the effect that if his conditions regarding the other three legs of the table could be met, then he would be prepared to promise a full Israeli withdrawal from the Golan Heights to the June 4, 1967, line.

On the Syrian side, meanwhile, the most outstanding bundle of evidence attesting to President Assad's understanding of Israel's wide-ranging conditions for a peace accord, and his readiness to give active and often positive consideration to them, is that offered by the speed with which he took the decision to engage in the accelerated, multi-issue negotiation at Wye, and then the generally constructive record of his emissaries' participation there.

That readiness to start thinking actively about a future in which their two states would have a cooperative rather than belligerent relationship, as evinced in late 1995 and early 1996 by both the Rabin/Peres leadership in Israel and the Assad leadership in Syria, did not come from nowhere. It was the result of a painfully drawn-out learning process which along the way continued unnecessarily to claim the lives of scores of civilians, primarily in Lebanon but also in Israel, and of combatants from all sides. The continuation of the state of war between Israel and Syria also kept the military spending of both states considerably higher than it need otherwise have been, locking up resources that both states (but particularly Syria, which receives little foreign aid) needed desperately for their economic and social development. The analysis that follows will chart some aspects of the learning process between the two leaderships, in the hope that those years of costly learning will not have to be repeated.

PRE-MADRID LEARNING

When the Israeli and Syrian delegations met in Madrid, the leaderships and political elites that they represented had already learned some valuable lessons about the limits of the power each was able to exert over the other. In particular, the outcome of the October War of 1973 had shown that *neither side could impose its will wholly on the other through the use of force.* After 1973, that conclusion hardened into a long-lasting (though not necessarily unchangeable over the longer term) strategic

fact. The conclusion of the disengagement agreement of 1974 represented, at one level, the concretizing of that fact on the ground. The interactions, contests, and signaling that the two sides conducted inside
Lebanon in the years after 1974 also underlined the centrality of the
grand strategic standoff: In Lebanon, as in Golan, the two sides learned
once again that they could not impose their respective wills on the other.

From the 1970s on, the relationship between Syria and Israel at the
military level could be described as one of highly asymmetrical "mutually assured devastation." With its sophisticated arsenal of weapons of
mass destruction, Israel could threaten considerable devastation inside
Syria as a deterrent to any sizeable Syrian offensive. Until 1987 or so,
Syria could rely somewhat on a counterdeterrent threat from the Soviet
Union. After the credibility of that counterdeterrent eroded to near zero
with the collapse of Soviet power, Syria still retained its own, relatively
unsophisticated arsenal of standoff, mass-destruction weapons to use as
a counterdeterrent.[3]

The 1982–85 interactions in Lebanon had a particular relevance in
the evolution of this strategic balance. It was in the conduct of the
ground campaign in Lebanon in those years that the Israeli public as a
whole first came to appreciate (in lessons analogous to those imposed
on the American public by the Vietnam encounter) that not even military superiority at every level of the escalation ladder could compensate
for a gross imbalance in the levels of hard political interest associated
with Lebanon by the parties concerned, or for the resulting lack of a
workable Israeli political strategy there. In Lebanon, the Syrians also
learned (if they had not known this before) that not even their alliance
with Moscow and their total political-military victory within the Lebanese body politic could force Israeli compliance with UN Resolution
425, so long as Israel continued to receive effective backing for its continued presence in the security zone from Washington.

After the collapse of Soviet power in the early 1990s, global strategic
geography shifted from the competition of the Cold War to the (sometimes uncertain) leadership of Washington. Still, the essential strategic
standoff in the Middle East between Israel and Syria continued.
Throughout the 1990s, Israel continued to enjoy an ever-closer relationship with the world's sole remaining superpower, while Syria failed in
nearly all its attempts to win anything from Washington that was much
warmer than distantly correct diplomatic relations. However, even that

increasing disparity in global strategic relationships was still not sufficient to enable Israel to impose its will on Syria regarding central peace-process issues.

As we have seen, neither side came into the post-Madrid negotiating room alone. Each came in diplomatically armed with a whole network of relationships (positive and negative), obligations, expectations, and insecurities regarding other powers. For Israel, its relationship with the United States was always the most significant of these. Yet Israel also had significant links with Europe; as the 1990s progressed (and even more so, after the signing of the Oslo Accords) it built webs of valuable new relationships with scores of additional governments, including many that had previously been cool to Israel, some of them in the heart of the Middle East.

Syria also entered the negotiating room armed with valuable alliances. These links never compensated for the advantage Israel enjoyed by virtue of its ties to Washington, but they meant that Syria's position was never as diplomatically isolated as some in the United States imagined (or, perhaps, hoped) it to be. The first tier of such ties included those with Egypt, Saudi Arabia, and the non-Saudi Gulf Cooperation Council countries. It was Syria's decision to join Egypt in entering the Desert Storm coalition on the GCC (and U.S.) side that gave Damascus the entry ticket to the post–Desert Storm round of peace diplomacy. The relationships with Egypt and the GCC states thereafter formed a valuable part of what Syria brought into the negotiating room. In particular, the role of Egypt as a general facilitator, interpreter, and hand-holder in the Israeli-Syrian talks is one that merits further recognition and exploration. The Syrians also brought into the room their relationships with Lebanon, several European powers, and Iran.

FALLBACK POSITIONS

As in the 1993 or 1995 diplomacy over Lebanon, President Assad could offer to trade on aspects of his relationship with Iran to demonstrate Syrian helpfulness in areas of concern to Israel. The general effect of the Syrian-Iranian link on the Israeli-Syrian negotiations of the mid-1990s can be viewed in a number of different (and not mutually incompatible) ways. It can be seen as helping to give Syria a degree of political-strategic self-confidence, without which it might have been far harder for Assad to have engaged in real peacemaking. It can be seen as a potential asset that the Syrians might bring into the broader peace process, given the persistent interest with which some in both Israel and Iran have viewed the prospect of a better relationship in the future. It also can be seen as helping to strengthen the fallback position Syria could enjoy in the event that the diplomacy with Israel should fail. (Syria's close and long-standing ties with Saudi Arabia were also an important part of its fallback position.)[4]

All along, Israel had what probably seemed to most Israelis to be a workable fallback position—namely, to let the diplomacy with Syria fail, and not to withdraw from Golan at all. Certainly, it never seemed to most Israelis, throughout the period studied, that they would have to pay any significant cost at all (to the United States or any other outside power) if their leaders should choose that option.

Uri Savir was therefore quite correct when he surmised that in the negotiations with Syria, "there was a sense among both delegations that, if necessary, we could go on living without peace."[5] This sense, on each side of the table, that reaching a successful conclusion in the negotiations was *optional,* and that the party concerned had what it viewed as a viable fallback position, was another defining characteristic of the negotiation.

TESTING

When Rabin came into office in 1992, some members of his entourage seemed generally intrigued by the idea that after so many decades there might be a real opening for peace with Syria. But they continued to seek reassurance on what seemed to be a fundamental question: Was President Assad's participation in the peace talks from Madrid onward the result of a "strategic" decision in Damascus, or only a "tactical" decision (designed, one assumes, to lure an unsuspecting Israel into lowering its defenses prior to a surprise military attack from Syria)? This question did not permit an easy answer. The rhetoric coming from Damascus was still coy: It still made frequent reference to peace being *"khiyar istrateeji"* (a strategic option), but not *"al-khiyar al-istrateeji"* (the strategic option).[6]

From Syria's viewpoint, Rabin's true intentions appeared equally untested. Between the two crusty, ultracautious leaders there ensued a classic Alphonse and Gaston situation in which neither wanted to be the first to tip his hand openly to the other regarding the strength of his desire for peace. Each might well have feared that in doing so, he would somehow weaken his own negotiating position. Indeed, absent any such clear signal coming from the other party, it is entirely possible to posit that neither of the two men really knew completely what he himself could or should seek in this relatively new process of diplomacy.

One way of testing the intentions of an actual or potential Arab interlocutor that Israeli leaders traditionally had used was to engage in some form of back-channel or "track-two" diplomacy.[7] In Israel's peace diplomacy with Egypt, Jordan, and the PLO, assurances provided by quiet back-channel contacts with those other interlocutors had played, or came to play, an important part in paving the way for breakthroughs at the public, formal level.

However, Assad was different. As Moalem explained in late 1996,

> There is no need for a back channel: Both sides can go through the American mediator with any new ideas, and in our view secret talks are eventually bound to cause mistrust and misunderstanding. We may not reveal the details but we always tell our public the general direction of our talks, where we are meeting, when we start, when we finish. That is why you find support for the Syrian position in the Arab world.[8]

In that interview, Moalem stated that "we never had back-channel negotiations or 'testing' meetings; everything takes place in the negotiating room." During the period under study, however, there was one instance of the Assad regime allowing some form of (totally authorized) back-channel communication. This channel was provided by the participation of a handful of designated Syrian nationals in discussions with Israelis under the auspices of the Washington-based Initiative for Peace and Cooperation in the Middle East. However, the venture proved to be a bad experience for all the Syrians involved: Though the Initiative had set ground rules mandating discretion by the participants, one of the Israelis, the pro-Likud figure Yossi Olmert, almost immediately leaked information about sensitive security discussions—to CNN![9] The other, much more important, channel that allowed for some signaling and informal testing of new ideas that emerged during the peace talks was that provided by the informal planning meetings that developed in conjunction with the formal talks, which allowed Allaf and Moalem to explore some ideas with Rabinovich, and then with Savir—though always with Ross, and sometimes also Secretary Christopher or another American official present. Those discussions proved considerably more constructive in helping to build understanding and dispel mistrust between the two sides as the formal talks progressed.

As for "track-two" diplomacy, the idea of any kind of involvement by nongovernmental actors in the affairs of state was one that to all officials of the Assad regime in Syria would have seemed anarchic, unpredictable, and uncontrollably democratic.

Even in the absence of informal contacts, however, there was still much that an Israeli government actively committed to pushing the peace process forward could and should have done through formal diplomatic channels to test Syrian intentions. The transmission of a series of questions through formal channels could have helped to push the testing exercise forward (as could, perhaps, the establishment of ways of signaling on the ground). For example, after Rabin first received the news from Secretary Baker in July 1992, to the effect that Baker had found Assad "ready to make peace with Israel,"[10] he could have engaged in the active *testing* of Assad's intentions by transmitting to him a set of questions seeking further clarification on specific points: Did this mean that Assad was prepared to do X in the realm of security arrangements, or Y in the realm of normalization of relations, and so forth? In August 1993, after Assad received Rabin's intriguing message regarding his readiness to consider a full withdrawal, he came back almost immediately with a set of further clarifications that he required in this regard, in the expectation—as Moalem said—that Rabin's communication signaled the start of the real negotiation. And in a real sense, it was, although it proved much slower than the Syrians had expected.

In July 1992, Rabin was faced with what must have been a comparably intriguing opening move from Assad, but he chose not to test Assad's intentions in a similar way. Instead, as Rabinovich has recalled, the Israeli leader chose to sit back for a further year and let the Arab parties compete to make the next move. Thus, it took a full year before the interactive testing of intentions began in earnest. When it did—both through diplomatic exchanges and through the important signaling on the ground in Lebanon—the talks finally started to gather some momentum.

POST-MADRID REFRAMING

The fact that the Israel-Syria negotiation seemed more or less optional to policymakers on both sides (as noted above) meant that the broad reevaluation of their relationship that would be needed to budge it from the forty-five-year legacy of military competitiveness to one of broad, peaceful cooperation also assumed an "optional" character. Neither side had been forced to the table by the kind of existential political-military crisis that can force a rapid rethinking. Rather, they had been cajoled, maneuvered, and politicked into starting their talks through the skillful wiles of Secretary of State Baker. It is probably fair to say that when the negotiators from the two countries first met in Madrid, neither of their political elites had yet engaged very much in the kind of broad conceptual reframing that would be needed to find a common, cooperative vision. Nor is there any evidence from the Shamir era that during or after his time in office the old Likud stalwart and his allies ever even started to engage in such rethinking.

A certain amount of peace-oriented reframing does seem to have occurred on the Syrian side in those early post-Madrid months. For by the time the Rabin-Rabinovich team entered the talks in summer 1992, the Syrians were ready with an agenda which indicated—along with their traditional demand for full Israeli withdrawal—a new willingness to discuss security arrangements, the details of a peaceful relationship, and some degree of gradualism in the implementation of the agreement. Additional indicators of Syria's increasing readiness for peace with Israel during the period from Madrid through January 1996 came from the slow but steady evolution in the references made to Israel and its leaders by Syria's government-controlled media in their increasingly sophisticated analysis of Israel's internal politics that was evinced in those media—and then, as noted above, from the rapidity with which Assad decided to engage in Peres's "flying high and fast" venture at peacemaking. Indeed, Rabin's assassination can be seen as the kind of catastrophic event that can force those connected with it suddenly to reveal their true interests—or at least something closer to their true interests. From that standpoint, the readiness that the Assad leadership showed then to accelerate and broaden his emissaries' engagement in the diplomacy with Israel was a very welcome sign.

In his memoir, Itamar Rabinovich was generally dismissive of the ability of Syria's leadership to understand the Israeli political scene. Yet commentaries such as those that appeared in the Syrian media at the time of Peres's accession to power indicated that Syria's leaders had access to analysis with an unprecedentedly strong ability to discern even fine distinctions between the positions espoused by different figures in the Israeli political scene. At a more personal level, Ambassador Moalem has attested to the fact that he learned a lot about Israeli sensitivities through his fifty-two-month engagement in the peace talks. "Mostly, I came to understand more about how deeply they feel about being rejected by the region where they live," he said. "That's why I thought it was important to talk with them, for example, about the old days in [pre-1492] Andalusia, when there was a wonderful Arab-Jewish coexistence."[11]

Regarding the Israeli Labor leaders (given that Likud never showed much capacity for peace-oriented learning), Rabin seems to have taken a fairly long time to start thinking seriously about the prospect of having a cooperative, rather than competitive, relationship with Syria. He wasted many crucial months early in his premiership before he showed himself ready to start committing heavily to success on the Syrian track. Once he did so, however, he demonstrated an impressive willingness to start doing things, both inside and outside the negotiating room, that showed he had at last embarked on the kind of far-reaching reconceptualization of the issues in Syria and Lebanon that would be needed to start building a long-term peace.

Rabin was a leader of unrivaled credibility within the Israeli political system on all questions regarding war and peace. Once he started talking in public about the need for (and potential benefits of) a peace agreement with Syria, he showed himself well positioned to start changing the long-held views of the majority of the Israeli public on this issue. But the change in his rhetoric that became increasingly evident through the summer and especially the early fall of 1995 came relatively late. By the time it did start to become evident, those people and parties inside Israel that still clung to the old zero-sum view of unending conflict or competition with Syria had already had a long time to mobilize public support. As Ze'ev Schiff has noted, delay can be fatal in the search for a viable Middle East peace, "because the only thing you can be sure of in this region is that round the corner will be a surprise."[12]

If Rabin had survived into 1996, it is possible that he could have succeeded in that year in bringing about peace agreements with Syria (and Lebanon) that would have ended Israel's situation of being in a state of war with neighboring states, transforming the strategic geography of the entire Middle East (as well as the determinants of the Palestine issue). But he was killed, a martyr to his impressive commitment to rethinking the tough issues of his country's relations with its neighbors.

When Peres took over the reins of government, he and his negotiators showed from the very start an impressive ability to engage in constructive reframing of the relationship with Syria—along with an impressive commitment to bringing the peace talks to a timely and successful conclusion. Yet Peres lacked the political credibility within the Israeli system that had been Rabin's strongest asset. He also, apparently, lacked the understanding of the enduring political realities in Lebanon which, by 1995, had allowed Rabin to avoid becoming too damagingly entangled in the imbroglio there.

TIMING

If the above analysis places more emphasis on Rabin's time-wasting in the negotiations than on Assad's, there are two reasons for doing so. First, the Israeli party was always the stronger party within this negotiation: It was nearly always able to dominate decisions about the pace, scope, agenda, and shape of the talks. Second, the record of Israeli procrastination in the early Rabin years is more strongly established—and admitted to by key Rabin aides—than any record of deliberate Syrian procrastination. What one may criticize of Assad's record in this regard is that he suspended his participation in the talks between December 1992 and May 1993 (though the pressures on him to do so, in response to Rabin's blunder on the expulsions, was every bit as strong as the pressure on Peres to suspend Israel's participation three years later); that he did not object strongly enough to Rabin's successive decisions to "back-burner" his track; and that he did not agree to Peres's request for a summit.

Most analysts in Israel and the West until now have put the onus squarely on Assad for having "miscalculated" or "missed the opportunity" to make peace with the Rabin-Peres administration in Israel.[13] For his part, Ze'ev Schiff has said that both Assad and Rabin contributed to the missing of opportunities in that era.[14] However, the analysis in the present study strongly suggests that it was mainly Rabin's procrastination throughout most of his first three years in office that gave the antiwithdrawal forces the time they needed to mobilize against his efforts.

THE ARCHITECTURE OF PEACE

The question of Rabin's "wasting time" in his early months in office was closely linked (as Rabinovich has admitted) to the tactics he adopted in order to maneuver between the different tracks of the peace process. This way of seeing the different tracks as competing—as opposed to complementing—one another can perhaps be understood as a hold-over from decades of dealing with the hostility emanating from Israel's neighbors through a classic divide-and-rule approach. That approach had given Israel a valuable advantage in the decades when its relations with neighbors were predominantly those of war; but Rabin seems to have given little thought to the question of whether it might still be helpful in a time of building a regionwide peace. Indeed, in a region at peace, as the European and numerous other examples have shown, each nation gains a strong interest in the development of harmonious relations among *all* members of the regional system.

A damaging corollary to the effort at divide and rule was the argument Rabin resorted to over and over again that Israel "could not digest" progress in more than one track at a time. The counterargument—that simultaneous successes won on a multiplicity of tracks would be likely to strengthen one another and thus make the whole process even more attractive to Israelis than partial treaties concluded seriatim on each track separately—was seldom even heard in Israel before Peres's arrival (with the major exception to this rule being Deputy Foreign Minister Yossi Beilin).

From the other side of the table, when Syria and the other Arab participants entered the post-Madrid diplomacy, their own relations were still largely dominated by a paradigm of competition with one another. In the early years of the peace talks, the Syrian leadership may well have placed as much theoretical value as ever on the value of inter-Arab "coordination." At the practical level, though, it remained largely locked into long-standing relationships of hostility and mutual mistrust with both the PLO leadership and Jordan. Assad did, however, try on significant occasions to restructure those relationships in a way helpful to the peace process—as, for example, when he helped persuade Arafat to resume the talks with Israel in the spring of 1993.

Both the PLO and Jordan then made their separate deals with Israel "behind Assad's back," which seemed to discourage the Syrian president from repeating such efforts at coordination. Indeed, by June 1999 Moalem was stating, "If the opportunity comes for Syria and Lebanon to make peace with Israel, we won't wait for a solution of the Palestinian problem—though we would continue to support the Palestinians, as the Egyptians and Jordanians have done."[15]

With both Egypt and Lebanon, Assad *was* able throughout the 1990s to maintain a level of coordination that was generally helpful to the peace process. With Egypt, the relationship had become more or less one of a younger brother facing the passage of peace with Israel taking advice and help from an elder brother who had already gone through that passage. With Lebanon, the relationship was very different: It probably would be more accurate to say that Assad acted like the stern parent of the bunch of (often fratricidal) children who made up the Lebanese body politic.[16]

ON PUBLIC DIPLOMACY

Starting to view peacemaking as a cooperative venture rather than a continuation of the old competitive zero-sum thinking by other means requires that the peacemakers pay increased attention to the broad political context of their efforts—in this case, on both sides of the national divide. This is one very specific version of the concept loosely called "public diplomacy," though this term often had a range of other meanings for different participants in the Israeli-Syrian negotiations.

For Rabinovich, for example, as evidenced throughout his memoir, his calls for public diplomacy were essentially appeals to the Syrian leadership to take highly visible actions that could help reassure *the Israeli public* that peace was a good idea. "Could we persuade the Syrians from Assad down that without public diplomacy and without reaching out to the Israeli public no agreement with Syria would be feasible?" he asked—though nowhere there did he express any recognition that there might be a need for reciprocal gestures on the part of Israeli leaders and officials to reach out to the Syrian public.[17]

Sharaa and Moalem (and most likely President Assad) have a very different view of the public dimension of diplomacy: It is the job of Syrian leaders to educate the Syrian public for peace, and of Israeli leaders to similarly educate the Israeli public. "We always felt that the Israelis wanted Syria to do their work for them," Moalem has said. "They wanted *us* to convince *their* public that peace was in their interests. We prepared our public for peace with Israel."[18] For his part, Sharaa decried "the mentality of Israeli leaders who find it very difficult to educate their own people that peace is good for them. If you exclude one or two speeches from Rabin, you find the rest of his statements very tough. . . . While President Assad made so many statements on his need and desire for peace—even before the Madrid conference!"[19] (Rabin's view of public diplomacy may well have been closer to the Syrian view than it was to Rabinovich's.)

Once Uri Savir became involved in the Syrian track, he brought to it a version of public diplomacy that promised to display a much more interactive and reciprocal view of peacemaking than that shown in either of the above two versions. Though his memoir of the post-Madrid negotiations says little about public diplomacy with respect to Syria, it does portray a view of the peacemaking venture he led with the Palestinians in which the negotiators on both sides of the table became attentive to the political context of their actions on both their own *and the other side* of the national divide. For Savir and his Palestinian interlocutors, peacemaking really did seem to become something like a cooperative undertaking, and the chapter or so that he devoted to the Wye talks with the Syrians—taken along with the way that conference itself had been structured, mostly at his suggestion—revealed largely the same, essentially cooperative vision of the task of negotiation.

From Damascus, the dean of Syrian philosophers, Professor Sadeq al-Azem, has given a poignant picture of the emotional pulls and pushes associated with the venture of peacemaking that could have been voiced on either side of the line. In spring 1998 (when the prospects for peace seemed far away), Azem noted that the failure of Prime Minister Netanyahu to re-engage in the peace talks with Syria

> made us relieved and disappointed at the same time. There is relief because we know we don't have to face the hard decisions that an imminent peace would have confronted us with—plus, the failure of the talks is not our fault. There is disappointment because we had seen the light

at the end of the tunnel, but then it disappeared. We had started to make changes in our thinking. . . . Since Madrid, it became possible to discuss many things! But then, it came to nothing.[20]

HIGH-LEVEL VISITS

Another part of public diplomacy on which many in Israel had always placed considerable focus was the idea of high-level visits and other highly visible gestures of reassurance by Arab leaders. President Sadat's bold step in visiting Jerusalem in 1977 had been, of course, the most evident paradigm here, although that step came in the wake of many decades that Peres and others had already spent engaging in leadership-level contacts with King Hussein of Jordan. Once again, Assad broke what Peres and those around him considered as the desired Arab mold. As in the cases of back-channel communications and engagement in an Israel-focused public diplomacy, so too in this case the Syrian leader was not inclined to follow Sadat's example, as noted in chapter 6.

It is true that in Israel not all members of the policy elite placed the same high value as the Peres group on gestures of reassurance from Arab leaders. Rabin never seemed to make such an issue of the idea of Assad visiting Israel. Many in Israel (and especially, though highly predictably, those in the media) did continue to press for photo opportunities with high-level Syrians, such as the interview that television journalist Ehud Ya'ari was able to win from Minister Sharaa, or David Makovsky's participation in the Clinton-Assad joint press conference of October 1994. But some Israeli advocates of the peace process were more wary of such encounters. They noted that, given the huge cultural differences between the two countries—which included the prevalence in Israel of a view of the role of journalists that was far more irreverent and confrontational than most Syrians had ever become used to—some of these journalistic coups ran the risk of harming the cause of the peacemaking process far more than they helped it.

THE RISK OF FRUSTRATED HOPES

Given the very different view of the nature of the peacemaking venture held by the two leaderships, it is not surprising that (especially during the slow early years of the talks) both sides on occasion unwittingly committed acts that served as a cause for increased mistrust by the other side. It is all the more noteworthy, therefore, that between May 1995 and early March 1996 Rabin, Assad, and Peres all in their own way worked so hard to overcome this mistrust.

The most serious testing of President Assad's intentions came in late 1995, when Shimon Peres unexpectedly came to power and decided so rapidly to reach for a final agreement with Syria within a handful of months. The Peres team made clear to Assad from the very beginning that the only way they could win the public support that a peace agreement required would be if it offered Israelis a broad-reaching vision of a thorough, comprehensive, and multileveled peace. Assad responded positively. He threw his negotiators into an unprecedentedly rapid, broad, and detailed negotiation. Yet the momentum for this negotiation was too soon lost. Then, in a rapid sequence of events, it seemed to be thrown into a reverse gear that led to a rapid upswing of mistrust on both sides. Israeli voters then returned a Likud government which brought stasis to this negotiation for the whole of the next three years.

The dynamic of these developments is worthy of considerable further study. In late December 1995, the leaderships on both sides seemed to have wholly committed themselves to "going for broke" in their talks. When Peres then shifted course and judged that this would be impossible without the additional factor of a speedy summit with Assad (which he had no good reason to believe might be forthcoming prior to the endgame of the negotiation), the easiest explanation is probably to say that he had started to panic. Certainly, he seemed incapable of facing down the pressures coming from Barak and others in his party who were urging him toward a speedy election. But that panic (or weakness, or indecision) had serious consequences over the months that followed: for the people of south Lebanon; for the trust that various Arab interlocutors, including the Syrians and Lebanese, had in his true intentions toward them; and then, at the ballot box, for the political balance in Israel itself.

The rise in tensions and mistrust that occurred during those months —in both Israel and Syria—was very real, and had very real political consequences, especially in Israel. It showed the degree to which the hopes associated with the promise of a big breakthrough in peacemaking should not be taken lightly by leaders. For when grand hopes that are associated with the sense of risk in trying something bold and new are dashed, they can easily turn into their own destructive opposite.

Despite the bitterness that Peres's actions in March and April 1996 engendered among the Syrians, it is still entirely probable that if he had won reelection that year and sent his negotiators back to Wye, they would have found Moalem and his team there ready (after, perhaps, a short period of lecturing) to complete the negotiation of a peace treaty. Certainly, throughout the three years that followed Peres's defeat at the ballot box, the Assad leadership remained steadfast in its expressions of readiness to resume the talks with Israel, "where they had left off." The fact that the Syrians stuck steadfastly to this position in spite of all the disappointment associated with Peres's treatment of them, the bitterness associated with the actions he launched in Lebanon, and the frustration associated with the Netanyahu years, provided a significant resource for the resumption of the diplomacy in the following period.

In Israel, too, the anti-Syrian and generally anti-Arab bitterness of March and April 1996 took a while to dissipate. But when Israeli voters returned to the ballot box in May 1999, it turned out that the strength of the Golani antiwithdrawal forces had (for the moment, at least) virtually collapsed, and public attitudes toward a land-for-peace deal with Syria seemed considerably more positive than they had been in 1995. Those developments also provided a significant resource for a resumed negotiation.

THE ROLE OF THE UNITED STATES

A remarkable feature of the analysis provided above is that it makes almost no mention of the role of the U.S. cosponsor of the peace talks. That it should be possible to present a very full record of the Israeli-Syrian peace talks, like that above, in which the United States plays such an incidental role speaks volumes about the change that had occurred in the U.S. role since, for example, the Kissinger shuttles of 1973–74, or the Camp David peace talks of 1978.

As noted above, right up until the diplomatic rubber started to hit the road in 1995, there were valid questions still to be asked—of the leaderships in both Israel and Syria—regarding whether, and how strongly, they really wanted to bring about an Israeli-Syrian peace. The same questions can also be directed at the successive administrations in Washington in the period under study.

In the case of the Bush administration, the answer seems to be that during the buildup to Desert Storm and in the aftermath of it, President Bush and Secretary Baker became convinced both that an Israeli-Syrian peace was possible, and that it would make a significant contribution to the furtherance of U.S. interests in the region. Yet they seemed determined, at least initially, to avoid provoking an open confrontation on this issue with the Israeli government or Israel's many supporters in Congress. As part of that effort, the administration continued the practice inaugurated by President Reagan of consistently downplaying the idea that (as Kissinger had always forthrightly stated) the United States might have any particular interests of its own in helping to bring about Arab-Israeli peace. Nor did the Bush team ever present its own ideas, except in extremely broad-brush format, of what a final peace agreement should look like—on this front, or on any of Israel's other front lines with its neighbors. Instead, Bush and Baker relied on behind-the-scenes cajoling and the provision of widely differing letters of assurance to different parties to bring them to the Madrid peace table, while in the Palestinian arena it pursued a dogged campaign to link financial incentives to Israel with a cutback in settlements—a campaign that ended up, whether intended or not, helping a more pro-peace government come to power.

Bush and Baker did then make a significant contribution to opening up the way for talks on the Syrian track when Baker made the shuttle from Syria to Israel in late July 1992 and transmitted to Rabin the significant information about Assad's willingness to engage, and the Bush administration's willingness to commit to pushing the process forward. When Rabinovich had his first encounter with the Syrians at the negotiating table, they then represented two governments which both professed a strong commitment to the peace process, but which also deeply distrusted the intentions of the other side. In short, this was an ideal situation in which an actively involved mediator could ask the right probing questions to test intentions and move the process along, while encouraging each side to start looking at the larger goal of a region at peace and helping it to understand the concerns and foibles of the other better than before.

Instead, from Washington in August 1992: nothing. President Bush, then fighting for his political life, may well have had it in mind that after his hoped-for re-election he would step up and meet the challenge of this negotiation, but he was defeated at the polls. And the president who followed him into office came with no experience of conducting a Middle East policy, except for the deep sensitivity he always evinced to the need to avoid antagonizing Israel's supporters in the American elite. In addition, Clinton, along with many of those charged with running his Middle East policy, had a view of Yitzhak Rabin that bordered on hero worship. There is almost no evidence, from any part of the Clinton administration's record so long as Labor was in office, that either the president or those under him ever took any step in Arab-Israeli peace diplomacy that had not been cleared in advance with the Israelis. One mantra frequently heard from administration officials with regard to the various tracks of the peace diplomacy in those years was, "We cannot want peace more than the parties concerned." This argument— strange as it would have sounded in the era of Henry Kissinger—met with far too little challenge from within the American elite. For why, indeed, should the United States *not* have a range of its own interests in the Middle East from which derives a strong U.S. national interest in seeing the Arab-Israeli arena at peace?

If there is little evidence that Clinton and Christopher ever took any steps that would reveal to outsiders that they had differences with the government of Israel, this does not mean that *within* the intimacy of the U.S.-Israeli relationship there were not, on a number of occasions, fairly strong disagreements over the strategy and above all the *speed* of Israel's engagement in the diplomacy with Syria. Signs of such disagreements can be found at various points throughout Rabinovich's memoir, particularly with regard to Rabin's decisions in the summers of 1994 and 1995 to return the Syrian track to the back burner. Dennis Ross has said that on a number of occasions, as noted in chapter 2, Clinton might sympathetically challenge some of the assumptions on which Rabin was basing his diplomacy. Having done this however, as Ross has confirmed and the evidence from the public record strongly suggests, Clinton would generally then defer to Rabin's judgment on the matter. That tendency to defer to the Israeli leaders' views on questions of strategy and timing became, as Ross has noted, reinforced after the

Rabin-Peres camp's coup of securing the Oslo Accords, and then even more so after Rabin's assassination.

If, in the 1970s, the American role in Arab-Israeli negotiations had been that of an active and involved mediator, by the mid-1990s Clinton had publicly reconceptualized his administration's role into that of a facilitator. (Although, in truth, during the Labor years, he was less a disinterested facilitator of the peacemaking venture, as such, than he was a facilitator of the Israeli government's diplomatic agenda.) Talented and committed in that role he may well have been. The commitment that he and Christopher showed in this regard was shown by the thousands of hours that Christopher spent traveling to and within the Middle East to shuttle messages between Israel and Syria. Still, by restricting his administration almost wholly to the facilitator role, Clinton foreswore countless opportunities to challenge both the Syrians and the Israelis to move forward more rapidly and more effectively toward the sought-for peace. Thus he, too, must share with the parties much of the responsibility for the time that was—with such sad consequence—lost to the negotiations during those years.

During the Netanyahu years, the Clinton administration took no steps at all that indicated to Netanyahu that there might be any political or other costs associated with his stonewalling on the Syrian negotiation. Indeed, four months after Netanyahu's election, the administration gave him a gratuitous political boost when Secretary Christopher sent him a letter confirming that the "Aims and Principles" document that had been concluded after such hard diplomatic preparation just eighteen months earlier was not binding from the standpoint of international law—though the United States reserved the right to raise once again the issues covered in it.[21] Of course, that text had never been intended to be a complete, stand-alone document, though it was an important part of the security "leg" of the table of peace that the parties had worked to construct. (Ambassador Moalem subsequently expressed his bafflement over why Christopher had gone out of his way to disavow the text in 1996, "since at the time it had been completed, no one was happier than he was!")[22]

In his second term, Clinton took some steps to try to nudge Netanyahu into implementing what the preceding Labor government had promised to the Palestinians in their track (and the outcome there was meager, at best). On Syria, though, there was no such action.

Instead, an embattled president and a broadly pro-Likud Congress sent a strong message to the parties on both sides of the dividing line that this was not an issue that particularly mattered to them during the Netanyahu years.

In the post-Netanyahu period, new possibilities have opened up. If Prime Minister Barak should choose to re-engage in the diplomacy with Syria, there is every reason to suppose that he would find a willing and creative partner in Washington. Yet the feeling in the relevant parts of the State Department early on in the Barak premiership was still that it was *mainly up to him to decide.*

THE PAST AS PRELUDE

"Our objective must be clear and straightforward," President Bush said at the opening of the Madrid conference. "It is not simply to end the state of war in the Middle East and replace it with a state of non-belligerency. . . . Rather, we seek peace, real peace. And by real peace I mean treaties. Security. Diplomatic relations. Economic relations. Trade. Investment. Cultural exchange. Even tourism."

At the Wye Plantation talks held between December 1995 and March 1996, all the issues that Bush listed were actively and productively discussed by Syrian and Israeli officials. Ambassador Moalem has said that "75 percent" of the work of achieving a final peace treaty was completed there. Other participants may have different assessments, but what was clear was that the whole, very cautious period of learning that the two nations' leaders underwent in the years that preceded Wye, and then the creative activism of the early weeks of Peres's premiership, had brought the Israeli and Syrian governments considerably closer to defining the terms of a workable peace agreement than they had ever been before.

The analysis of the present chapter indicates that there were many differences in the approach the two national leaderships brought to the venture of peacemaking in the Rabin/Peres era (as there were, too, between Rabin's and Peres's approaches). By the time the two sides got to Wye, they did both seem fully committed to the speedy, creative, multitrack venture in cooperative peacemaking that was undertaken there. Thirty-nine months after the breakup of those talks, the Syrian side seemed essentially ready to resume. This time around, would a new, stronger political leadership in Israel be ready to take up that challenge? Could both sides indeed muster the political will to bring their negotiations to a close with enough speed to avoid other untoward developments in the region from intervening?

To ask these questions is not to downgrade the importance of what has been happening in the Palestinian-Israeli track meanwhile. There, too, one could easily argue that the hesitancy of Labor during its years in power in the mid-1990s helped to prepare the ground for a return of Likud's intransigence, that there were things the Palestinian leadership could have done to push the process forward that they did not do, and that a more forceful and visionary intervention from Washington could have brought about a considerably better outcome.

Both these major strands of the outstanding business of Arab-Israeli peacemaking share some attributes, but the Syrian track stands alone in carrying within it the prospect of major military confrontations in the years to come. It is thus in the interests of the survival and well-being of all in the region, including Israelis, Syrians, Lebanese, Palestinians, and others, that the lessons of what worked and what did not work in the Syrian-Israeli talks of 1991–96 should be well studied.

Notes

INTRODUCTION

1. In 1997, and again in summer 1998, Netanyahu sent a number of secret feelers to Damascus through third parties to probe the possibility of restarting the talks on some different basis. The Syrians appeared somewhat interested in those overtures, though none of them led to anything concrete. However, some potentially constructive ideas were explored.

2. Text as received from *Middle East Mirror* (London) and published by it and *Al-Hayat* (London) in English on June 23, 1999. Seale also wrote that Barak had told him other things that he was "not . . . at liberty to report fully."

3. Ibid. Assad's wording here would seem to allow his negotiators to return to the talks at a slightly different point from where they had left them, provided the record of what had already been achieved would be the "basis" of the resumed talks.

4. Ibid. Ze'ev Schiff has written that one of these Netanyahu-era intermediaries, Omani foreign minister Yusuf Ben Alawi, won the verbal agreement of both sides to a fifteen-point document, but that "The Syrians say Israel refused to supply written commitments, so the talks came to a halt." See Ze'ev Schiff, "Syria Agreed To Foreign Troops On Hermon," *Ha'aretz* (Tel Aviv), May 28, 1999. See also David Makovsky, "Syrians Had Promised A Deal With Lebanon," *Ha'aretz*, May 31, 1999.

5. The well-informed Israeli writer Aluf Ben has written that Barak learned an important lesson from what he considered to be Rabin's mistakes: "not to fear the [Israeli] public and to tell it straight from the outset that the objective is to reach peace." Ben added his own judgment that Barak would have to "begin preparing the Israeli public for a quick separation from the Golan Heights and from most of the West Bank." Aluf Ben, "Long Is The Day, Tender Is The Night, And The Time Is Very Short," *Ha'aretz*, July 20, 1999.

6. Text of press conference by President Clinton and Prime Minister Barak, *New York Times*, July 19, 1999.

7. Itamar Rabinovich, *The Brink of Peace: The Israeli-Syrian Negotiations* (Princeton, N.J.: Princeton University Press, 1998); and Uri Savir, *The Process: 1,100 Days That Changed The Middle East* (New York: Random House, 1998). Most of Savir's book relates his leadership of the Oslo peace talks with the PLO, but chapter 9 and the latter part of chapter 8 cover his leadership of the talks on the Syrian track during Peres's short tenure as premier. The third head of the Israeli team on this track was Yossi Ben-Aharon, who had preceded the other two.

8. "Fresh Light on the Syrian-Israeli Negotiations: An Interview with Ambassador Walid Al-Moualem," *Journal of Palestine Studies* 26, no. 2 (Winter 1997): 401–412.

9. Most of those interviews were conducted in early 1998. However, some of the early ones with Ambassador Moalem were conducted in late 1996, and the author was also able to conduct some valuable supplementary interviews in Washington, D.C. in June 1999.

10. After Peres had done considerable preparatory work on the Oslo agreement with the Palestinians, Rabin gave it his endorsement in August 1993. On that track, he showed himself increasingly capable of engaging in considerable reframing of old conflicts.

11. More details of this landmark interview are given in chapter 5.

1. THE MADRID CONFERENCE AND THE ISRAELI-SYRIAN TRACK

1. *New York Times*, October 31, 1991, A16–17. The *Times'* Thomas L. Friedman noted that Bush's remarks "were greeted with enthusiasm by Israelis and private anger by the Arabs, who complained bitterly . . . that the President seemed to emphasize what was important to Israel—the content of peace—while ignoring symbolic issues important to the Arabs—like Israeli settlements, the future of Jerusalem, and the formula of 'land for peace.'"

2. *New York Times*, November 1, 1991, A10.

3. Ibid., A11.

4. R. W. Apple, Jr., "Mideast Foes List Demands," *New York Times*, November 1, 1991, A1.

5. R. W. Apple, Jr., "How Sweet a Victory?" *New York Times*, October 31, 1991, A16.

6. The argument was aptly summed up for me by Samuel Lewis, a former ambassador to Israel who would become head of the U.S. State Department's policy planning staff in the first Clinton administration.

7. Author's interview, Damascus, March 1998.

8. In that year, a system of direct elections for prime minister was introduced, parallel to the votes for Knesset seats. See chapter 8.

9. Marvin Feuerwerger, "Israel, the Gulf War, and its Aftermath," in *The Middle East After Iraq's Invasion of Kuwait*, ed. Robert O. Freedman (Gainesville, Fla.: University Press of Florida, 1993), 238.

10. Leah Rabin, *Rabin: Our Life, His Legacy* (New York: G. P. Putnam's Sons, 1997), 253. In her memoir, Leah Rabin recalled that "over the years" prior to 1993, a professional mediator named Giora Eini had been needed to resolve disputes between the two men.

11. The most masterly and best-informed biography of the Syrian leader is Patrick Seale's *Asad: The Struggle for the Middle East* (Berkeley: University of California Press, 1988).

12. Many members of this strand, as of the previous one, happened also to be Alawis. For further helpful analyses of Syria's political leadership, see *Syria: Society, Culture, and Polity*, ed. Richard T. Antoun and Donald Quataert (Albany, N.Y.: SUNY Press, 1991); Alasdair Drysdale and Raymond A. Hinnebusch, *Syria and the Middle East Peace Process* (New York: Council on Foreign Relations Press, 1991); and Malik Mufti, *Sovereign Creations: Pan-Arabism and Political Order in Syria and Iraq* (Cornell, N.Y.: Cornell University Press, 1996).

13. "A Believer in the Road Already Traveled" (interview with Warren Christopher), *Ha'aretz* (English Internet edition), October 24, 1997.

14. The vast majority of those who perished or were left disabled from these assaults were Lebanese and Palestinians, most of whom were noncombatants. However, the casualties also included nonnegligible numbers of military personnel from both Israel and Syria. For more details, see Helena Cobban, *The Superpowers and the Syrian-Israeli Conflict* (New York: Praeger, 1991).

15. See Helena Cobban, *The Making of Modern Lebanon* (Boulder, Colo.: Westview Press, 1985).

16. Bush also noted in this speech that "geography cannot guarantee security and security does not come from military power alone." See "Transcript of President Bush's Address on End of the Gulf War," *New York Times*, March 7, 1991, A8.

17. James A. Baker III, *The Politics of Diplomacy: Revolution, War and Peace, 1989–1992* (New York: G. W. Putnam's Sons, 1995), 414–15, passim. When Baker was putting together the anti-Iraq coalition, prominent among those to whom he had promised a regional Mideast peace conference once Iraq had been forced out of Kuwait were the Soviets. This was also a reason why the Soviets, despite their declining power, were given a role as "cosponsors" of the Madrid conference (p. 294).

18. Ibid., 416. The interests of Arab-state nationals in a viable resolution of the Palestinian issue stemmed in varying parts from the broad public sympathy toward the Palestinian cause, a feeling that the Arab states had already suffered enough for the sake of the Palestinians, and the continued presence of hundreds of thousands of Palestinian refugees within each of the three Arab states in the process, even forty-three years after those individuals had fled the fighting in Palestine.

19. Ibid., 424.

20. Ibid., 295–96. Baker also writes (p. 296) that he had earlier dropped Damascus from the itinerary for his September 1990 trip, but that Bush told him, "I think you should go to Syria. I don't want to miss the boat again."

21. Ibid., 553. Baker also noted, "A month later, Israel opened another settlement—this one on the Golan Heights."

22. Syrian negotiator Ambassador Walid Moalem has said, "Before Madrid there were letters of assurance, and the Americans promised us that these would be published. But they never were. They were different [for each party]. There was no clear basis for the peace process. Each side participated on its basis." Author's interview, Washington, D.C., May 1998.

23. Baker, *The Politics of Diplomacy* 505–7, passim.

24. Ibid., 511.

25. Ibid., 508.

26. Syria specialist Patrick Seale has dubbed this engagement "The Six Day Walkover."

27. Some have argued that this Israeli measure, which was couched in terms of "extending Israeli jurisdiction to" Golan, somehow fell short of outright annexation. If such a distinction exists, it is hard to comprehend and, indeed, it is ignored in practice or openly dismissed as meaningless by most Israelis.

28. Arye Shalev, *Israel and Syria: Peace and Security on the Golan* (Boulder, Colo.: Westview Press, 1994), 45. General Shalev's study contains a wealth of detailed topographic and historical detail as well as numerous clear and informative maps.

29. For more details on this point, and some excellent maps, see Avner Yaniv, "Syria and Israel: The Politics of Escalation," in *Syria Under Assad,* ed. Moshe Ma'oz and Avner Yaniv (New York: St. Martin's Press, 1986), as well as Shalev, *Israel and Syria.*

30. One should also be aware of the not-inconsequential argument that the continuation of Israel's military occupation of the Golan was itself a major factor, or *the* major factor, in the Syrian leadership's decision to go to war in 1973.

31. In Egypt's case, at least, the intention was to use the war primarily as a catalyst for a negotiated return of its occupied land. The Syrians apparently hoped to regain their land in Golan through a greater reliance on military means. The difference in strategies between them led to many years of differences.

32. See Mark Tessler, *A History of the Israeli-Palestinian Conflict* (Bloomington, Ind.: Indiana University Press, 1994), 363–64.

33. The most comprehensive of these was the Johnston Plan of 1955, proposed by a personal representative of President Eisenhower. It called for the construction of dams, canals, and so forth, to optimize the yield from the Jordan Basin, bringing it to about one billion cubic meters of water per year, with almost 40 percent of this going to Israel, and 10 percent going to Syria. Israel accepted the plan, but Syria and other Arab states did not. See ibid., 362.

34. Estimates given by Adel Abdes-Salam of Damascus University, Department of Geography. Author's interview, Damascus, March 1998.

35. Author's interview with Yigal Kipnis (spokesman for The Way to Peace), Maale Gamla (Golan), March 1998.

36. In 1999, Shamir would tell Patrick Seale that "Syria is the boss in Lebanon, and has been for many years. It's not a normal situation." See Patrick Seale, "Shamir: 'The Golan is More Important to Us than to Syria,'" *Mideast Mirror* and *Al-Hayat* (London), June 28, 1999.

37. Murhaf Jouejati drew attention to this point in the presentation he made at the Middle East Institute in January 1998. Perhaps some parallelism can be seen here in the way that a form of pan-Jewishness is, for most Jewish Israelis, a core component of "Israeliness."

38. Author's interview, Tel Aviv, March 1998.

39. "Rabin on Peace Process, U.S. Involvement," *Ha'aretz*, April 14, 1995, B3; translated in *Foreign Broadcast Information Service/Daily Report: Near East and South Asia* (hereafter FBIS-NES) 95-073.

40. See, for example, Ze'ev Schiff, *Peace with Security: Israel's Minimal Security Requirements in Negotiations with Syria* (Washington, D.C.: Washington Institute for Near East Policy, 1993).

2. FROM SHAMIR TO RABIN

1. See the account in Thomas L. Friedman, "U.S. Now Expects the Mideast Talks to Take Time Out," *New York Times*, November 5, 1991, A8.

2. Ibid.

3. See reports in *New York Times*, November 4, 1991, A8, and November 5, 1991, A13. The Syrians were not reported at this point as taking any steps to help calm the situation in south Lebanon.

4. Between October 1952 and May 1953, unofficial envoys of the two governments explored the possibility of partitioning the DMZ. In most of those meetings, the Israeli team was headed by Major-General Moshe Dayan, and the Syrian side by Colonel Ghassan Jadid (whose brother Salah Jadid was to become president of Syria in the late 1960s). See Shalev, *Israel and Syria*, 36–37.

5. Seale, "Shamir: The Golan is More Important." Regarding the Palestinian track of the talks, Shamir told an Israeli interviewer in 1992, "I would have carried on autonomy talks for ten years, and meanwhile we would have reached half a million [Jewish] people in Judea and Samaria"; Yosef Harif, interview with Yitzhak Shamir, *Ma'ariv* (Tel Aviv), June 26, 1992.

6. Urit Galili, interview with Yossi Olmert, *Ha'aretz*, August 7 and 28, 1992; as cited in Avi Shlaim, *The Iron Wall: Israel and the Arab World since 1948* (New York: W. W. Norton, 1999), 470.

7. Moshe Ma'oz, *Syria and Israel: From War to Peacemaking* (New York: Oxford University Press, 1995), 217.

8. Author's interview, Washington, D.C., November 1996.

9. Baker, *The Politics of Diplomacy*, 554.

10. Ibid., 554–555.

11. For more information on the election results, see Appendix 1 in Freedman, ed., *The Middle East*, 217.

12. Baker, *The Politics of Diplomacy*, 555.

13. Rabin's ability to bring Shas into his government was significant, since for the first time it gave him a solid base of support within Israel's Sephardi (eastern Jewish) community, which had long been a bastion of support for Likud.

14. Rabinovich's account of how Rabin recruited him is fairly amusing. See *The Brink of Peace*, 54.

15. As cited in William B. Quandt, *Peace Process: American Diplomacy and the Arab-Israeli Conflict since 1967* (Washington, D.C.: Brookings Institution, 1993), 242.

16. "Rabin on Syria Talks, Dismantling Settlement," Israel Television Channel 1 (in Hebrew), May 26, 1995; as translated in FBIS-NES-95-103.

17. Ilan Shehori, "Labor Platform Vows Compromise 'in all sectors,'" *Ha'aretz* (Tel Aviv), May 31, 1992, A1, 10; as translated in FBIS-NES-92-105. This wording indicates that the Labor leadership had hardened its attitude toward Syrian-related issues since the previous November, when the party platform had stated, "Territorial compromise is also possible on the Golan Heights. Territories from which Israel will withdraw will be demilitarized." See David Makovsky, *Making Peace with the PLO: The Rabin Government's Road to the Oslo Accord* (Boulder, Colo.: Westview Press, 1996), 193.

18. Author's interview, Tel Aviv, March 1998.

19. Author's interview, Tel Aviv, March 1998. For a third evaluation of Rabin's attitude, see page 366 of Yoram Peri's "Afterword" in Yitzhak Rabin, *The Rabin Memoirs,* expanded ed. (Berkeley: University of California Press, 1996).

20. Author's interview, Tel Aviv, March 1998. See also Rabinovich, *The Brink of Peace*, 54–55.

21. Rabinovich, *The Brink of Peace*, 55.

22. Author's interview, Tel Aviv, March 1998. Haber also offered the judgment, which I understood to be one that he felt Rabin had shared back in 1992, that for Rabin the Palestinian issue was "a barrel of TNT." A ranking U.S. official connected with the talks confirmed in a March 1998 interview that "Rabin in '93 would have preferred to prioritize the Syrian track, but Peres brought him Oslo 'out of a hat.'"

23. Rabinovich, *The Brink of Peace*, 59.

24. Author's interview, Washington, D.C., November 1996. For Rabinovich's description of this document, see *The Brink of Peace*, 59–60.

25. Rabinovich, *The Brink of Peace*, 62.

26. Author's interview, Tel Aviv, March 1998.

27. Author's interview, Washington, D.C., June 1999.

28. Rabinovich, *The Brink of Peace*, 84.

29. Author's interview, Washington, D.C., June 1999.

30. Ibid.

31. This offer was disclosed in an interview Assad gave to Patrick Seale, who reported it in an op-ed piece, "'Full Peace for Full Withdrawal,'" *New York Times*, May 11, 1993, A21. Assad also allowed in this interview that at the end of the peace process there would be "a number of bilateral agreements," though he said he would not support any agreement that infringed general Arab rights.

32. Rabinovich, *The Brink of Peace*, 94.

33. See the chronology presented in Makovsky, *Making Peace*, 238.

34. Author's interview, Tel Aviv, March 1998.

35. Rabinovich, *The Brink of Peace*, 104–05.

36. Ibid., 105.

37. Author's interview, Washington, D.C., November 1996.

38. Author's interview, Washington, D.C., May 1998.

39. Rabinovich wrote that "Rabin told me again that the details of the meeting in his office must remain secret. He would update whoever needed to know about it in the Israeli government (by which he meant first and foremost Foreign Minister Peres)." *The Brink of Peace*, 106.

40. Ibid. Rabinovich notably did not write what his own reaction to the Assad response had been.

41. Author's interview, Tel Aviv, March 1998.

42. Rabinovich, *The Brink of Peace*, 108–09. He also wrote that, "I was back in Washington while Rabin was digesting and contemplating Assad's response. I had been aware of his disappointment with Assad's initial reaction, but it was only later that I learned the full extent of his disappointment" (pp. 106–7).

43. Author's interview, Washington, D.C., June 1999.

44. Makovsky, *Making Peace*, 65.

45. Rabinovich, *The Brink of Peace*, 242. It should not need noting that international humanitarian law unambiguously forbids the deliberate entanglement of civilians in military operations as part of a belligerent's strategic planning.

46. These figures are quoted in Human Rights Watch, *Civilian Pawns: Laws of War Violations and the Use of Weapons on the Israel-Lebanon Border* (New York: Human Rights Watch, 1996), 68. Pages 68–116 give a detailed account of this campaign, as well as of the fighting that continued between these parties in south Lebanon between July 1993 and April 1996.

47. *Ha'aretz*, "A Believer in the Road Already Traveled." Christopher also commented there that, "The Lebanese situation was one in which Syria played an important and many times helpful role in connection with Katyusha rockets."

48. David Hoffman, "Israel Halts Bombardment of Lebanon," *Washington Post*, August 1, 1993; as quoted in Human Rights Watch, *Civilian Pawns*, 38n.

49. Numerous conversations with Dore Gold, General Aharon Levran, and others, 1991–93.

50. Numerous conversations in Syria, June 1992.

51. It was clear to him by the summer of 1995. (See chapter 5.)

52. Author's interview, Washington, D.C., June 1999.

53. For an interesting account of a Clinton phone conversation with Assad just before the signing of the Oslo accords, see Thomas Friedman, "Clinton Says Support of Israel Will Not Waver," *New York Times,* September 11, 1993, 1.

54. David Remnick, "Letter from Jerusalem: The Outsider," *The New Yorker,* May 25, 1998, 93.

55. Author's interview, Washington, D.C., June 1999. Dennis Ross has also recalled that, "There were periods when I pointed out to Rabin that Assad was taking real risks," but that Rabin did not seem convinced; author's interview, Washington, D.C., June 1999. In *The Brink of Peace,* Rabinovich says on a number of occasions, "We were the one taking the risks."

56. Author's interview, Washington, D.C., June 1999.

3. SLOW PROGRESS BETWEEN OSLO AND MAY 1995

1. For more details of the negotiations that led up to the Oslo accords, see Mahmud Abbas, *Through Secret Channels* (Reading, U.K.: Garnet Publishing, 1995); Makovsky, *Making Peace;* and Savir, *The Process.*

2. See *Journal of Palestine Studies* "Fresh Light": 408.

3. Author's interview, Washington, D.C., May 1998.

4. Friedman, "Clinton Says Support of Israel Will Not Waver"; as also repeated in Rabinovich, *The Brink of Peace,* 117–18.

5. Rabinovich, *The Brink of Peace,* 118.

6. Ibid., 119.

7. Author's interview, Washington, D.C., June 1999.

8. William E. Schmidt, "Persecution Ended, Syria's Jews Stage an Exodus," *New York Times,* January 15, 1994, 4. See also "Syria Gives Jews Visas before U.S. Summit," *New York Times,* December 30, 1993, A7.

9. "Leaders Hold News Conference," Syrian Arab Television Network (Damascus), in Arabic, January 16, 1995; as translated in FBIS-NES-94-011.

10. "Gur: Referendum If Peace Price Significant," IDF Radio (Tel Aviv), in Hebrew, January 17, 1994; as translated in FBIS-NES-94-011.

11. Rabinovich, *The Brink of Peace,* 130.

12. Some pro-peace activists in Israel argued at the time that this incident provided an excellent reason for Rabin to close down the households that ultra-extremist Israeli settlers had established in the heart of downtown Hebron, and which were later to cause huge headaches for negotiators on the Palestinian track. Rabin chose not to do so.

13. Author's interview, Washington, D.C., November 1996.

14. Rabinovich, *The Brink of Peace,* 147. In 1999, Rabinovich would write that, "By July 19 [1994], a formula had been found for grafting the lines of June 4 onto the original hypothetical, conditional suggestion made in August 1993"; Itamar Rabinovich, *Waging Peace* (New York: Farrar, Straus and Giroux, 1999), 64.

15. The August 28, 1997, *Ha'aretz* story as cited in Douglas Jehl, "Rabin Showed Willingness to Give Golan Back to Syria," *New York Times,* August 29, 1997.

16. Ibid.

17. In a June 1995, Israeli radio interview, for example, Rabin would refer to "the four main components [of peace] which are, for me, one single package, a four-legged table that cannot stand on three legs. Our ability to sign a peace treaty depends on each of these legs." See "Rabin Comments on Progress on Syrian Track—Says No Treaty Until All Conditions Met," IDF Radio (Tel Aviv), in Hebrew, June 11, 1995; as translated in FBIS-NES-95-112.

18. Author's interview with Ambassador Moalem, Washington, D.C., November 1996.

19. Author's interview, Damascus, March 1998.

20. See Rabinovich, *The Brink of Peace,* 147.

21. Author's interview, Washington, D.C., November 1996. Rabinovich wrote that Assad's agreement to a two-stage withdrawal had been signaled to Rabin a few days earlier in the course of Secretary Christopher's shuttle between the two countries. See *The Brink of Peace,* 147.

22. Author's interview, Damascus, March 1998. See also Homeidi's article, which charts how Syria's official media changed its portrayal of Israeli leaders in a positive direction in this period, and later would change it somewhat back; "Syrian Political-Informational Rhetoric: The Hardening Resumes with Netanyahu," *Al-Wasat* (London), no. 292 (January 9, 1997), 28–30.

23. "Assad and Clinton Speak: Shared Quest for Peace," *New York Times,* October 28, 1994, A21.

24. Douglas Jehl, "Clinton Reports Progress in Talks in Syrian Capital," *New York Times,* October 28, 1994, A1.

25. Ibid., A20. There are of course various cultural influences at work in such a judgment. What appears to an American reporter who perhaps is more used to sound bites as "a lecture" may appear to a Syrian policymaker as a reasoned exposition of his nation's point of view. One other indication of the difference between Syrian perceptions and those of *New York Times* journalists (in this case, the editorial staff) was the map published on page A9 of the paper's November 1, 1991, edition. While the map clearly indicates through crosshatching that the West Bank is "occupied by Israel," it omits this in the case of Golan.

26. Ibid.

27. Author's interview, Washington, D.C., November 1996.

28. Author's interview, Washington, D.C., June 1999.

29. Rabinovich, *The Brink of Peace*, 174.

30. Author's interview, Washington, D.C., November 1996.

31. "Rabinovich on Shahak–al-Shihabi Meeting," *Davar* (Tel Aviv), June 30, 1995, 5; as translated in FBIS-NES-95-127. See also, "Syria Reportedly Blames Barak for Talks' Failure," *Ma'ariv* (Tel Aviv), in Hebrew, February 12, 1995, 2; as translated in FBIS-NES-95-029. In his 1998 memoir, Rabinovich voiced no such implied criticism of the Israeli side. See *The Brink of Peace*, 174–75.

32. Author's interview, Damascus, March 1998.

33. Author's interview, Washington, D.C., June 1999.

34. Rabinovich, *The Brink of Peace*, 174.

35. Ibid., 163. It is significant that Rabinovich's next observation, immediately after recounting this, was that "It was a low moment in the negotiations [with the Palestinians] over Oslo II."

36. Author's interview, Washington, D.C., June 1999.

37. Reconstruction of the clauses of the "Aims and Principles" document, using the text published in Israel: "IDF Views Understandings Paper," *Ha'aretz* (Tel Aviv), June 30, 1995, A2; as translated in FBIS-NES-95-127. The emphasized words were rendered in English in the (otherwise Hebrew) *Ha'aretz* text. See also the slightly freer reconstruction of the original attempted in Aluf Ben, "Israel-Syria 'Understandings' Before Talks Detailed," *Ha'aretz* (Tel Aviv) June 29, 1995, A1, A14; as translated in FBIS-NES-95-125.

38. Author's interview with Eitan Haber, Tel Aviv, March 1998.

39. Ibid.

40. Author's interview with Yehuda Harel, Merom Golan, March 1998.

41. On July 2, 1995, *Ha'aretz* published the results of a nationwide poll of Jewish-Israeli opinion indicating that such a hope might indeed prove to have some foundation. In a poll conducted at the end of May 1995, 61.1 percent of those polled favored retaining control of Golan even if that meant giving up a peace accord with Syria. One month later, that figure had dipped to 50.2 percent, with 41.7 percent now saying they would be prepared for a full withdrawal in exchange for a full peace. See "Poll Shows 'Significant Shift' on Golan Withdrawal," *Ha'aretz* (Tel Aviv), July 2, 1995, B3; as translated in FBIS-NES-95-129.

42. On June 23, for example, Syrian vice-president Abdel-Halim Khaddam said the following about reports that Syria had recently reached an "agreement" with Israel: "If an agreement had taken place, at least it would have been announced, and in Washington. But there is much talk about many things that are untrue." See "Syria's Khaddam Sees Major Difficulties with Israel," *Al-Sharq Al-Awsat* (London), June 23, 1995, 3; as translated in FBIS-NES-95-122. This quotation raises an intriguing question regarding the degree to which Assad, Sharaa, and the peace negotiators were keeping Khaddam informed of developments in the talks with Israel.

43. For example, on May 26, 1995, Rabin was still telling Israeli television that "there is a dispute between us and the Syrians over where the peace border will run." See Israel Television Channel 1, "Rabin on Syria Talks, Dismantling Settlement"; as translated in FBIS-NES-95-103.

44. Author's interview, Washington, D.C., May 1998.

45. Author's interview, Washington, D.C., May 1998. See also *Journal of Palestine Studies*, "Fresh Light": 403.

46. Author's interview, Washington, D.C., March 1998.

47. See "Book Claims Rabin Promised al-Assad Full Golan Withdrawal," *Yedi'ot Aharonot* (Tel Aviv), September 11, 1996, 1, 19; as translated in FBIS-NES-96-178.

48. Author's interview, Tel Aviv, March 1998.

49. Author's interview, Washington, D.C., March 1998.

50. Extract from *The Brink of Peace* in *Al-Sharq Al-Awsat* (London), April 24, 1998, 16.

51. For a thoughtful consideration of the preference of both Assad and Rabin for a cautious pace, see Tzvi Bar'el, "What the Letter of Credit Will Say," *Ha'aretz* (Tel Aviv), Mar 15, 1995, B1; translated as "Syrian Peace Seen as Vital for New Strategic Status," FBIS-NES-95-051.

52. Author's interview, Damascus, March 1998.

4. CHIEFS OF STAFF II: INSIDE AND OUTSIDE THE NEGOTIATING ROOM

1. Israel Television Channel 1, "Rabin on Syria Talks, Dismantling Settlement."

2. Ibid.

3. See "Israeli Offer of 'Symbolic Withdrawal' Rejected," MBC Television (London), in Arabic, May 25, 1995; as translated in FBIS-NES-95-102. The Syrian leadership's focus throughout the negotiations was firmly on the nature of the final status: President Assad never had much time for Western concepts of "confidence building."

4. "[Peres] Views Price of Peace With Syria," *Ha'aretz* (Tel Aviv), in Hebrew, May 26, 1995, A2; as translated in FBIS-NES-95-102.

5. Ibid.

6. Shim'on Schiffer, "Peres: No Wish To Keep 'Syrian' Golan Heights," *Yedi'ot Aharonot* (Tel Aviv), in Hebrew, May 28, 1995, 8; as translated in FBIS-NES-95-103.

7. "Peres Denies Golan Heights Statement," Qol Yisra'el (Jerusalem), in Hebrew, May 28, 1995; as translated in FBIS-NES-95-103.

8. "Radio Cites Rabin, Peres Statements on Peace," Syrian Arab Republic Radio (Damascus), in Arabic, May 31, 1995; as translated in FBIS-NES-95-104.

9. See also Homeidi, "Syrian Political-Informational Rhetoric."

10. Shim'on Schiffer, "Rabin Reveals Content of Clinton Phone Call," *Yedi'ot Aharonot* (Tel Aviv), in Hebrew, June 8, 1995, 1, 16; as translated in FBIS-NES-95-110.

11. "Ministers Attack Peres Remarks on Golan, Syria," Qol Yisra'el (Jerusalem), in Hebrew, May 28, 1995; as translated in FBIS-NES-95-103.

12. See, for example, "Netanyahu on Syria, Jerusalem Issue, Levi Rivalry," Qol Yisra'el (Jerusalem), in English, May 27, 1995; as reprinted in FBIS-NES-95-104.

13. "'Golan Report' Newsletter," (Internet version), in English, May 1995; as reprinted in FBIS-NES-95-120.

14. "Israel Warned of 'Provocative' Visits to Golan," Syrian Arab Republic Radio (Damascus), in Arabic, May 28, 1995; as translated in FBIS-NES-95-103.

15. Rabinovich, *The Brink of Peace,* 165–67.

16. "'Golan Report' Newsletter."

17. Qol Yisra'el (Jerusalem), in Hebrew, May 29, 1995; as translated in FBIS-NES-95-103, at end of item headed "Rabin Says Talk of Referendum 'Premature.'" The bill was submitted to the Knesset on July 26. The vote on it was 59 to 59, so it failed to pass. See "Damascus Reports Knesset Rejection of Golan Bill," Syrian Arab Republic Radio (Damascus), in Arabic, July 26, 1995; as translated in FBIS-NES-95-144; and "Coalition, Opposition Claim Victory in Golan Vote," *Ma'ariv* (Tel Aviv), in Hebrew, July 27, 1995, 3; as translated in FBIS-NES-95-145.

18. "Shahak To Demand Demilitarized Zone to Damascus—Issues, Emphasis at Talks Previewed," *Ha'aretz* (Tel Aviv), in Hebrew, June 21, 1995, A1; as translated in FBIS-NES-95-119.

19. Nehama Dowek, "IDF Position on Golan Seen as 'Most Important,'" *Yedi'ot Aharonot* (Tel Aviv), in Hebrew, June 13, 1995, 3; as translated in FBIS-NES-95-113. Nearly all public opinion polls conducted on war and peace issues inside Israel test the opinion only of Jewish Israelis. This practice ignores the views of that one-sixth of Israel's citizens who are of non-Jewish (mainly of Palestinian Arab) ethnicity. It is hard to see why, in any democratic reckoning, the views of this latter group of citizens should be ignored. For comparable results, see also the figures reported in Aluf Ben, "Peace Index Shows Increase in Support for Process," *Ha'aretz* (Tel Aviv), in Hebrew, April 5, 1995, B2; as translated in FBIS-NES-95-066; and "Poll: Majority Oppose Peace for Settlement Evacuation," *Ma'ariv* (Tel Aviv), in Hebrew, May 30, 1995, 1–2; as translated in FBIS-NES-95-104.

20. See "Knesset Summer Session Opens in Jerusalem—Rabin Speaks," Israel Television Channel 3 (Jerusalem), in Hebrew, May 15, 1995; as translated in FBIS-NES-95-094.

21. See "Katyushas Land in Galilee; No Casualties," Qol Yisra'el (Jerusalem), in Hebrew, May 31, 1995; as translated in FBIS-NES-95-104.

22. See "IDF Analysts: Hezbollah To Step Up Attacks," *Ha'aretz* (Tel Aviv), in Hebrew, June 20, 1995, A4; as translated in FBIS-NES-95-119.

23. Aluf Ben, "Rabin Receives Reports on Syrian Action on Hezbollah," *Ha'aretz* (Tel Aviv), in Hebrew, June 19, 1995, A3; as translated in FBIS-NES-95-117.

24. Ibid., emphasis added.

25. Ibid., emphasis added.

26. "Rabin Orders IDF to Deploy in SLA Outposts," Qol Yisra'el (Jerusalem), in English, June 25, 1995; as transcribed in FBIS-NES-95-122.

27. "Lubrani Warns of Retaliation for Hezbollah Shelling," Israel Television Channel 2 (Jerusalem), in Hebrew, June 25, 1995; as translated in FBIS-NES-95-122, emphasis added.

28. See, for example, "U.S. Official Cited on Hezbollah's Future Roles," Voice of Lebanon (Beirut), in Arabic, June 18, 1995; as translated in FBIS-NES-95-117.

29. For an exploration of these issues by the apparently well-informed writer Zayn Hammud, see his article in *Al-Shira'* (Beirut), January 15, 1996, 18–23; translated as "Article Views Hezbollah-Syria-Iran Relations," FBIS-NES-96-012.

30. "Khaddam Interviewed on Peace, U.S. Embargo on Iran," Voice of the Islamic Republic of Iran (Tehran), in Arabic, June 24, 1995; as translated in FBIS-NES-95-123.

31. "Iran Asked to Support Plan to Disarm Hezbollah," *Al-Sharq Al-Awsat* (London), June 25, 1995, 1, 4; as translated in FBIS-NES-95-123.

32. "Requirements for Success of Talks Reiterated," Syrian Arab Republic Radio (Damascus), in Arabic, June 27, 1995; as translated in FBIS-NES-95-124. Two days earlier, a Syrian radio commentary had dwelt at length on the responsibility of the Americans for the success of the upcoming talks. See "Radio Stresses U.S. Efforts in Washington Talks," Syrian Arab Republic Radio (Damascus), in Arabic, June 25, 1995; as translated in FBIS-NES-95-112.

33. "Rabin Comments on Progress on Syrian Track," Israel Television Channel 1 Network (Jerusalem), in Hebrew, June 10, 1995; as translated in FBIS-NES-95-112. The idea that peace might itself be a component of security, of course, had been a constant in Syrian discourse throughout.

34. Israel Television Channel 2 (Jerusalem), in Hebrew, June 10, 1995; as translated in FBIS-NES-95-112.

35. "Rabinovich Previews Chiefs of Staff Meeting," Qol Yisra'el (Jerusalem), in English, June 24, 1995; as reprinted in FBIS-NES-95-122.

36. "Syria Rejects U.S. Proposal for Troops on Golan," *Ma'ariv* (Tel Aviv), June 28, 1995, 3; as translated in FBIS-NES-95-124.

37. Author's interview, Washington, D.C., November 1996.

38. Author's interviews, Washington, D.C., November 1996 and June 1999.

39. Rabinovich, *The Brink of Peace*, 181.

40. See "'Text' of IDF Planning Document on Golan Security," *Yedi'ot Aharonot* (Tel Aviv), in Hebrew, June 29, 1995, 4–5; as translated in FBIS-NES-95-126.

41. Ibid., section 7 a.

42. Ibid., sections 7 b, 7 c, 8, and 11; original emphasis.

43. Ibid., section 9.

44. Ibid., sections 12–16.

45. Ibid., section 17. Israeli airman Ron Arad had been missing in action after being shot down over Lebanon in 1983. It is not clear whether the document's reference was intended to be about any other MIAs.

46. Rabinovich, *The Brink of Peace*, 181.

47. Ibid.

48. "'Still Very Big' Gaps in Israeli-Syrian Talks," Qol Yisra'el (Jerusalem), in English, June 28, 1995; as reprinted in FBIS-NES-95-124.

49. "Netanyahu on 'Concessions' Shahak to Propose," Qol Yisra'el (Jerusalem), in Hebrew, June 27, 1995; as translated in FBIS-NES-95-124.

50. "Beilin Says Netanyahu Claims 'Inaccurate,'" IDF Radio (Tel Aviv), in Hebrew, June 27, 1995; and "Rabin's Bureau: Netanyahu Discloses 'Nonsense,'" Qol Yisra'el (Jerusalem), in Hebrew, June 27, 1995. Both translated in FBIS-NES-95-124.

51. "[Netanyahu] Reiterates Claims on Concessions," Qol Yisra'el (Jerusalem), in English, June 28, 1995; as transcribed in FBIS-NES-95-124.

52. "Rabin: No 'Written Guidelines' for U.S. Talks," Qol Yisra'el (Jerusalem), in Hebrew, June 28, 1995; as translated in FBIS-NES-95-125.

53. "Rabin, Peres: Netanyahu Document Stolen from Army," Qol Yisra'el (Jerusalem), in English, June 29, 1995; as transcribed in FBIS-NES-95-125.

54. *Yedi'ot Aharonot*, "'Text' of IDF Planning Document."

55. Rabinovich, *The Brink of Peace*, 182–83.

56. Ibid., 183. Rabinovich writes here that the second day of discussions occurred June 29, but other records indicate it was June 28. On page 185, he writes, "A final session was held on the morning of the 29th in the Oval Office."

57. Rabinovich, *The Brink of Peace*, 184–85.

58. Author's interview, Washington, D.C., January 1998. Some days after the end of COS II, respected Israeli journalist Shim'on Schiffer cited what he claimed was "a classified report summing up the points of agreement in the talks . . . in Washington sent over the weekend to decision makers in Jerusalem by Professor Itamar Rabinovich," stating that "'agreement emerged to receive early-warning information by aerial means and to implement confidence-building measures pertaining to the issue.'" The text that Schiffer quoted did not make clear whether the Israeli side had agreed that aerial early warning would be *sufficient*. See "Agreement Emerging with Syria on Aerial Early Warning," *Yedi'ot Aharonot* (Tel Aviv), in Hebrew, July 10, 1995, 1, 19; as translated in FBIS-NES-95-131.

59. Author's interview, Washington, D.C., November 1996.

60. Author's interview, Damascus, March 1998.

61. Author's interview, Washington, D.C., March 1998.

62. Author's interview with Ambassador Rabinovich, Tel Aviv, March 1998.

63. Author's interview, Washington, D.C., March 1998.

64. "Second Document Leaked: Problems in Talks Noted," Israel Television Channel 1 (Jerusalem), in Hebrew, June 29, 1995; as translated in FBIS-NES-95-127.

65. See Aluf Ben, "IDF Views Understandings Paper," *Ha'aretz* (Tel Aviv), June 30, 1995, A2; as translated in FBIS-NES-95-127.

66. Ibid., 50.

67. "Peres Comments on 2d Army Document," IDF Radio (Tel Aviv), in Hebrew, June 30, 1995; as translated in FBIS-NES-95-127.

68. "Commentary: 'Total' Withdrawal 'Vital' to Peace," Syrian Arab Republic Radio (Damascus), in Arabic, June 30, 1995; as translated in FBIS-NES-95-127.

69. Author's interview, Washington, D.C., January 1998.

70. "Rabinovich on Shahak-al-Shihabi Meeting," *Davar* (Tel Aviv), in Hebrew, June 30, 1995, 5; as translated in FBIS-NES-95-127.

71. "Shahak on 'Dialogue' with Syrians," IDF Radio (Tel Aviv), in Hebrew, June 30, 1995; as translated in FBIS-NES-95-127.

72. Author's interview, Tel Aviv, March 1998. The present author's own inquiries in Israel in early 1998 likewise turned up no firm leads, except for a hint from one well-placed source that the person within the IDF General Staff who leaked the two documents may have done so believing that they would end up in hands other than Netanyahu's.

73. Author's interview, Washington, D.C., January 1998.

74. Author's interview, Washington, D.C., January 1998.

75. Rabinovich, *The Brink of Peace*, 185. Rabinovich also wrote that Moalem was "unhappy with the summary that Ross had prepared" (p. 187). He gave no source for this assertion, but what did seem clear was that Ross's tactic of recording the agreements made at Israeli-Syrian encounters was not a perfect solution to the problem of maintaining clear and uncontested communications.

76. Author's interview, Washington, D.C., March 1998.

77. "Radio Links Visit, Israeli 'Escalation,'" Syrian Arab Republic Radio (Damascus), in Arabic, July 10, 1995; as translated in FBIS-NES-95-132.

78. Author's interview, Washington, D.C., March 1998.

79. "Rabinovich: Syria Talks 'on Hold' for Military Accords," Qol Yisra'el (Jerusalem), in Hebrew, July 10, 1995; as translated in FBIS-NES-95-131.

80. "Radio on Early-Warning Stations," Syrian Arab Republic Radio (Damascus), in Arabic, July 11, 1995; as translated in FBIS-NES-95-133.

81. Author's interview, Tel Aviv, March 1998.

82. Author's interview, Washington, D.C., June 1999.

83. Author's interview, Washington, D.C., June 1999.

84. Author's interview, Tel Aviv, March 1998.

85. Author's interview, Damascus, March 1998.

86. "Foreign Ministers Address Meeting," Syrian Arab Republic Radio (Damascus), in Arabic, July 29, 1995; as translated in FBIS-NES-95-146.

87. Rabin, *Rabin: Our Life, His Legacy,* 273. Leah Rabin goes on to give a vivid description of the hate-filled rhetoric that right-wing Israelis were directing against her husband for his pursuit of the peace process.

88. "Third Way Council to Prepare for Elections," Qol Yisra'el (Jerusalem), in Hebrew, October 24, 1995; as translated in FBIS-NES-95-206.

89. Author's interview, Tel Aviv, March 1998. Israeli reporter Orli Azulay-Katz has written that "at a certain stage Rabin decided to moderate the pace to achieve an arrangement with Syria. He thought that it would be wise to let Israelis first get used to the Oslo arrangements with the Palestinians and only then to start the arrangement with Syria—perhaps hold a meeting before the elections and sign a document of principles, but no more." See "Book Claims Rabin Promised Al-Assad Full Golan Withdrawal," *Yedi'ot Aharonot* (Tel Aviv), September 11, 1996, 1, 19; translated in FBIS-NES-96-178.

90. Author's interview, Washington, D.C., June 1999. Warren Christopher has noted that "there have been very important collateral benefits from the Syrian negotiation. One collateral benefit was the fact that that track was under serious negotiation causing the Syrians not to block other progress." The other "collateral benefit" he mentioned was the help the Syrians gave in dealing with "the Katyusha problem." See *Ha'aretz,* "A Believer in the Road Already Traveled."

91. Author's interview, Tel Aviv, March 1998. As Haber told it, indeed, he made this call the very day before Rabin was killed.

92. Author's interview, Tel Aviv, March 1998. See also what Rabinovich says about this in *The Brink of Peace,* 239.

93. For an early report of this, see Aluf Ben, "Syria Proposes 10:6 Demilitarization Ratio," *Ha'aretz* (Tel Aviv), in Hebrew, July 3, 1995, A1, A8; as translated in FBIS-NES-95-127.

94. "Israel Rejects Offer for 10:6 Demilitarization," Israel Television Channel 1 (Jerusalem), in Hebrew, July 3, 1995; as translated in FBIS-NES-95-128.

95. "Security Arrangement 'Leaks' Seen Weakening Position," Syrian Arab Republic Radio (Damascus), in Arabic, July 5, 1995, quoting that day's issue of *Tishreen;* as translated in FBIS-NES-95-128.

96. See "Israeli-Syrian Multilateral Talks Held in Geneva," Qol Yisra'el (Jerusalem), in Hebrew, June 30, 1995; as translated in FBIS-NES-95-128.

97. "Poll Shows Rabin's Popularity Rising," Israel Television Channel 2 (Jerusalem), in Hebrew, July 1, 1995; as translated in FBIS-NES-95-127. The poll showed Rabin leading Netanyahu 43 percent to 42 percent, with 15 percent undecided. Three months earlier, the report noted, a similar poll had shown Rabin trailing the opposition leader 40 percent to 45 percent.

98. "Poll: Left Wing to Keep Strength in Election," *Ma'ariv* (Tel Aviv), in Hebrew, November 1, 1995, 19; as translated in FBIS-NES-94-214.

99. See "Rabin Said Delaying Progress with Syria until April," *Davar Rishon* (Tel Aviv), in Hebrew, October 30, 1995, 1–2; as translated in FBIS-NES-95-210; and "Al-Shar' Blames Israel for 'Standstill' in Talks," Oesterreich Eins Radio Network (Vienna), in German, November 2, 1995; as translated in FBIS-NES-95-215.

5. PERES TAKES OVER

1. Rabin, *Rabin: Our Life, His Legacy*, 10.

2. Author's interview, Washington, D.C., March 1998.

3. Author's interviews with Ross, Washington, D.C., March 1998; and Rabinovich, Tel Aviv, March 1998.

4. Author's interview, Washington, D.C., March 1998.

5. Rabinovich, *The Brink of Peace*, 199.

6. Ben Kaspit and 'Ada Kohen, "Peres Said Desiring Accord With Syria Before Elections," *Ma'ariv* (Tel Aviv), in Hebrew, November 7, 1995, 32; as translated in FBIS-NES-95-216.

7. "Savir: Syria Talks 'Slow, Indirect, and Petty,'" IDF Radio (Tel Aviv), in Hebrew, November 9, 1995; as translated in FBIS-NES-95-217.

8. See, for example, Bart Beirlant, "Peres: 'Peace More Important' than Election Win," *De Standard* (Groot-Bijgaarden), in Dutch, November 3, 1995, 2; as translated in FBIS-NES-95-214.

9. "Peres on Egypt, New Government, Rabin's Murder," ESC Television (Cairo), in Arabic (with Peres speaking in English), November 8, 1995; as transcribed in FBIS-NES-95-217.

10. "Al-Shar', Musa [actually, Rifkind] Hold News Conference," Syrian Arab Television (Damascus), in Arabic, November 8, 1995; as transcribed in FBIS-NES-95-217. See also Michael Sheridan, "Al-Assad Said 'Ready to Move Ahead,'" *The Independent* (London), November 9, 1995, 1; as reprinted in FBIS-NES-95-217. Sheridan reported (though without direct attribution to Rifkind) that many of the British minister's impressions of how Assad had reacted to the news of Rabin's killing were similar to those that Dennis Ross was later to notice.

11. "Beilin on Syrian Call for Negotiations," Israel Television Channel 2 (Jerusalem), in Hebrew, November 8, 1995; as translated in FBIS-NES-95-217, emphasis added. Clearly implied in Beilin's words, too, was the idea that he was referring to a full withdrawal from Golan.

12. Ibid.

13. Author's interview, Tel Aviv, March 1998.

14. "Flying high and fast" was the phrase that Peres himself sometimes used to differentiate his approach to the Syrian track from its opposite, "flying low and slow."

15. Author's interview, Tel Aviv, March 1998.

16. Ibid.

17. Author's interview, Tel Aviv, March 1998.

18. On November 11, one opinion poll published in Israel reportedly revealed that when asked, "Whom would you vote for if elections were held tomorrow?" 56 percent of Israelis said Shimon Peres, while 22 percent said Likud leader Netanyahu. Regarding the peace, 74 percent of those polled said they supported it. See "Peres Interviewed by French Television," TF-1

Television Network (Paris), in French, November 12, 1995; as translated in FBIS-NES-95-219.

19. Author's interview, Washington, D.C., March 1998. This person also noted that the strength of Peres's new emphasis on the Syrian track meant that things that should have been done on the Palestinian track during these few weeks were not all done, and that it contributed to the growing tension in Israeli-Palestinian relations.

20. Author's interview, Washington, D.C., June 1999.

21. Author's interview, Washington, D.C., March 1998. The question of whether Rabin had in fact kept Peres fully informed about the Syrian track was evidently a sensitive one for Peres. In his interview with the present author, Peres claimed that it was "nonsense" to say that after Rabin's death he had found papers on the topic which surprised him. Rabinovich evidently considered that Rabin had kept some of the pertinent facts from Peres. When asked by two newspaper reporters at the end of 1995 whether he had been informed of all developments on the Syrian track, Peres replied, "Why I should tell you?" See "Peres on New Government, Peace Talks," *Ma'ariv* (Tel Aviv), in Hebrew, December 1, 1995, 2–5; as translated in FBIS-NES-95-232.

22. Author's interview, Washington, D.C., June 1999.

23. Author's interview, Tel Aviv, March 1998.

24. "Peres Notifies Knesset of Cabinet Formation—Presents Cabinet, Vows To Continue Peace," Israel Television Channel 3 Network (Jerusalem), in Hebrew, November 22, 1995; as translated in FBIS-NES-95-225.

25. "Netanyahu Addresses Knesset, Faults Accords," Israel Television Channel 3 Network (Jerusalem), in Hebrew, November 22, 1995; as translated in FBIS-NES-95-226.

26. Author's interview, Tel Aviv, March 1998. Savir said with some pride that President Assad would later tell Secretary Christopher that "this man understands us."

27. "Savir Views Peace, 'Positive Signs' From Syria," MBC Television (London), in Arabic, November 24, 1995; as translated in FBIS-NES-95-227.

28. 'Amid Khuli, "Does Peres Mean What He Says?" *Al-Thawrah* (Damascus), in Arabic, November 25, 1995, 1; translated under the title, "Paper Urges Peres To Match Words With Deeds" in FBIS-NES-95-229.

29. "Peres on New Government, Peace Talks," *Ma'ariv* (Tel Aviv), in Hebrew, December 1, 1995, 2–5; as translated in FBIS-NES-95-232.

30. "More on Katyushas; Rabin Criticizes IDF," Qol Yisra'el (Jerusalem), in Hebrew, July 9, 1995; as translated in FBIS-NES-95-131. That evening, Chief of Staff Shahak told Israeli television that "our mistake also contributed to today's incidents. Yesterday, we fired at the wrong place in al-Nabatiyah, but *that happens in the kind of war we are fighting there.*" See "Chief of Staff on Situation in North," Israel Television Channel 1 (Jerusalem), in Hebrew, July 9, 1995; translated in FBIS-NES-95-131.

31. See Qol Yisra'el, "More on Katyushas." The IDF also often seemed to be operating under broadly reciprocal guidelines. Any attack launched against northern Israel would meet with a response in which protection of civilians was virtually ignored.

32. "Rabin Asks Levin to 'Shut Up' on Hezbollah," *Ha'aretz* (Tel Aviv), in Hebrew, July 16, 1995, A3; as translated in FBIS-NES-95-136.

33. "Rabin on Lebanon, Syria, Palestinian Track," Israel Television Channel 1 Network (Jerusalem), in Hebrew, November 1, 1995; as translated in FBIS-NES-95-212, emphasis added.

34. "Israelis Fire Phosphorous Shells in South," Agence-France Presse (Paris), in English, November 30, 1995; reprinted in FBIS-NES-95-230. The casualties from the latter attack were not reported there.

35. "Ministers on Syrian Link to Katyusha Shellings," IDF Radio (Tel Aviv), in Hebrew, November 28, 1995; as translated in FBIS-NES-95-229, emphasis added.

36. "Peres: Syria Responsible for Hezbollah," IDF Radio (Tel Aviv), in Hebrew, November 28, 1995; as translated in FBIS-NES-95-229.

37. "Minister Or: Rules of Game in Lebanon May Change," Israel Television Channel 1 (Jerusalem), in Hebrew, November 28, 1995; as translated in FBIS-NES-95-229.

38. Ibid.

39. "Editorial Views Israeli Escalation in Lebanon," *Al-Ba'th* (Damascus), in Arabic, November 30, 1995, 1; as translated in FBIS-NES-95-232.

40. For further exploration of these issues, see "Peres on New Government, Peace Talks," *Ma'ariv* (Tel Aviv), in Hebrew, December 1, 1995, 2–5, passim; as translated in FBIS-NES-95-232.

41. "Peres Empowered To Decide on Lebanon," *Ha'aretz* (Tel Aviv), in Hebrew, November 30, 1995, A1, A2; as translated in FBIS-NES-95-230. This report named some of the ministers who had taken part in the consultation, and identified which of them had supported and which opposed Shahak's request. It did not, however, give a full record of which ministers were present.

42. "'Agreement in Principle' Sought in Syria Treaty," Israel Television Channel 1 Network (Jerusalem), in Hebrew, December 5, 1995; as translated in FBIS-NES-95-234.

43. See also the reference to this point in Sever Plotzker, "No Surprises Expected," *Yedi'ot Aharonot* (Tel Aviv), in Hebrew, December 10, 1995, 2; translated under title of "Paper: Peres To Urge Clinton To Back Off on Syria" in FBIS-NES-95-237.

44. Author's interview, Washington, D.C., June 1999.

45. "Peres' Agenda for Clinton Meeting Previewed—To Present Detailed Syria Proposals," Israel Television Channel 2 (Jerusalem), in Hebrew, December 8, 1995; as translated in FBIS-NES-95-237. This report indicates that Peres's long-standing predilection for "secret talks" and summit-level meetings still continued.

46. See "Peres on Syria, Palestinians, Talks With NRP," IDF Radio (Tel Aviv), in Hebrew, December 9, 1995; as translated in FBIS-NES-95-237.

47. "Peres Comments at White House News Conference," Israel Television Channel 1 Network (Jerusalem), in English, December 11, 1995; as transcribed in FBIS-NES-95-238.

48. "Peres Comments on Syria Proposals, Condemns Iran," *Ha'aretz* (Tel Aviv), in Hebrew, December 13, 1995, A1, A10; as translated in FBIS-NES-95-239.

49. "Talks With Lebanon To Resume in 'Next Few Days,'" *Ma'ariv* (Tel Aviv), in Hebrew, December 13, 1995, 6; as translated in FBIS-NES-95-239. The possibility of some degree of overinterpretation on this issue, on the part of the Israelis or others, cannot be ruled out.

50. Patrick Seale, "Syria and Israel: No Progress towards Peace," *Middle East International* (London), December 19, 1997, 18.

51. Author's interview, Washington, D.C., January 1998.

52. Author's interview, Washington, D.C., May 1998. Moalem has also said, "All parties agreed at that time that we would complete the negotiation before autumn 1996, before the Israeli and American elections"; author's interview, Washington, D.C., June 1999.

53. "Christopher: Syria-Israel Talks To Resume 27 Dec.," Syrian Arab Television Network (Damascus), in Arabic, December 16, 1995; as translated in FBIS-NES-95-242.

54. "Al-Shar', Buwayz View Peres's Ten-Point Plan—Damascus TV Version of Comments," Syrian Arab Television Network (Damascus), in Arabic, December 19, 1995; as translated in FBIS-NES-95-244. Rabinovich, however, described the ten-point plan as having been Secretary Christopher's; see *The Brink of Peace*, 207.

55. Syrian Arab Television Network, "Al-Shar', Buwayz View Peres's Ten-Point Plan." Sharaa also noted, however, that "This does not negate the concept and understanding reached in the summer of 1993. That understanding stipulated that the resistance has a legitimate right to defend its land inside Lebanese territory."

56. "Syrian Announcement on 'Quiet' in Lebanon Doubted," IDF Radio (Tel Aviv), in Hebrew, December 20, 1995; as translated in FBIS-NES-95-244.

57. "Peres Denies Giving Timeframe of Months on Golan," IDF Radio (Tel Aviv), in Hebrew, December 20, 1995; as translated in FBIS-NES-95-244.

58. "Delegation Head on Upcoming Syrian Talks," Israel Television Channel 1 Network (Jerusalem), in Hebrew, December 20, 1995; as translated in FBIS-NES-95-245.

59. *Journal of Palestine Studies,* "Fresh Light": 406.

60. "Delegation Head on Upcoming Syrian Talks," Israel Television Channel 1 Network (Jerusalem), in Hebrew, December 20, 1995; as translated in FBIS-NES-95-245.

61. "Peres: 'Will Give Up the Atom' If Peace Achieved—Additional Details on Statements," Israel Television Channel 1 Network (Jerusalem), in Hebrew, December 22, 1995; as translated in FBIS-NES-95-247.

62. "Mubarak, al-Assad Hold News Conference in Cairo," Arab Republic of Egypt Radio Network (Cairo), in Arabic, December 23, 1995; translated in FBIS-NES-95-247.

63. Ibid.

64. "Beilin 'Taken by Surprise' by al-Assad's Remarks," IDF Radio (Tel Aviv), in Hebrew, December 24, 1995; as translated in FBIS-NES-95-247.

6. THE WYE PLANTATION TALKS:
A HOPEFUL NEW EXPERIMENT INTERRUPTED

1. Author's interview, Washington, D.C., March 1998.

2. Author's interview, Washington, D.C., January 1998.

3. Ibid.

4. Author's interview with Ambassador Moalem, Washington, D.C., June 1999.

5. Savir, *The Process*, 271; emphasis added. Moalem has more or less echoed the sentiment in the first paragraph's italicized passage. In late 1996 (when, admittedly, the circumstances were already significantly different), he would tell an interviewer that, "We are not in a hurry. If the Israelis are not in a hurry, we are not"; *Journal of Palestine Studies*, "Fresh Light": 410.

6. Author's interview, Washington, D.C., March 1998.

7. Ibid.

8. Savir, *The Process*, 274.

9. Ibid., 275.

10. *Journal of Palestine Studies*, "Fresh Light": 406.

11. Author's interview, Tel Aviv, March 1998.

12. *Ha'aretz*, "A Believer in the Road Already Traveled."

13. "Rabinovich, Savir Comment at End of Round," Israel Television Channel 1 Network (Jerusalem), in Hebrew, January 5, 1996; as translated in FBIS-NES-96-008. In this interview, Rabinovich seemed very eager to defend his pre-Savir record in the talks.

14. "Syria's al-Mu'allim: Talks 'Serious, Useful,'" Syrian Arab Television Network (Damascus), in Arabic, January 5, 1996; as translated in FBIS-NES-96-008.

15. Interview with Ambassador Moalem, May 1998. For an account of Rabinovich's confirming that this incident had indeed occurred, see, "Rabinofitsh ta'-tarif bi-innu isra'il ta'ahhudat lisuriyati insihaban min al-julan," *Al-Hayat* (London), June 5, 1998, 1, 6.

16. Author's interview, Washington, D.C., June 1999.

17. Savir, *The Process*, 273–281.

18. Author's interview, Washington, D.C., June 1999.

19. Savir, *The Process*, 281.

20. "Barak on Syria, Need for Christopher Visit," IDF Radio (Tel Aviv), in Hebrew, January 11, 1996; as translated in FBIS-NES-96-010.

21. "Barak Doubts Results of Wye Plantation Talks," Israel Television Channel 1 Network (Jerusalem), in Hebrew, January 26, 1996; as translated in FBIS-NES-96-019.

22. Author's interview, Washington, D.C., June 1999.

23. "Syrian Paper Comments on Maryland Talks," SANA (Damascus), in Arabic, January 27, 1996; as translated in FBIS-NES-96-019.

24. "Syrian Press Criticizes Recent Israeli Statements on Golan," *Al-Thawrah* (Damascus), in Arabic, January 28, 1996, 9; as translated in FBIS-NES-96-020.

25. Author's interview, Washington, D.C., March 1998. It may be relevant to note at this point that traditionally, Singer (like Barak) had been associated more with Rabin's approach to peacemaking than with Peres's.

26. "Hezbollah Aide on Syria, Internal Issues," *Al-Sharq Al-Awsat* (London), in Arabic, December 27, 1995, 5; as translated in FBIS-NES-95-250.

27. "Two Katyusha Salvos on Galilee; Officials React—IDF: Attacks Could Have Halted Talks," Israel Television Channel 1 Network (Jerusalem), in Hebrew, December 30, 1995; as translated in FBIS-NES-96-001. It is not clear from the report whether or not Christopher knew of the prior attack on Qabriha when he called Sharaa.

28. "Sources Confirm Syrian Restrictions on Hezbollah," Israel Television Channel 1 Network (Jerusalem), in Hebrew, January 15, 1996; as translated in FBIS-NES-96-010.

29. "Lebanon: Hezbollah Claims Ability To Develop Katyusha Rockets," MBC Television (London), in Arabic, January 16, 1996; as translated in *Foreign Broadcast Information Service/Daily Report: Terrorism* (hereafter FBIS-TOT) 96-005-L.

30. See "Vice President Habibi's Visit to Syria Viewed," Voice of the Islamic Republic of Iran, First Program Network (Tehran), in Persian, February 27, 1996; as translated in FBIS-NES-96-040. The visit was rescheduled during February, after Syria's relationship with Israel had started to sour.

31. Ron Miberg, "This is How Hit-Men Operate," *Ma'ariv* (Tel Aviv), November 3, 1995, 8, 9; translated as "Mosad Decision-making on Assassinations Viewed" in FBIS-NES-95-214. See also "Rabin Ordered Al-Shaqaqi Attack," *Der Spiegel*, November 6, 1995, 168–172; as translated in FBIS-TOT-95-023-L.

32. Author's interview, Damascus, March 1998.

33. Savir, *The Process*, 283.

34. See ibid., 279.

35. Baris Doster, "The Turkish-Syrian Dispute as Part of the Middle East Peace Process: The Problem Hinges on Water," *Nokta* (Istanbul), in Turkish, January 13, 1996, 56–59; translated as "Turkish-Syrian Disputes Examined," in *Foreign Broadcast Information Service/Daily Report: Western Europe,* FBIS-WEU-96-032.

36. Ibid.

37. Alain Gresh in *Le Monde Diplomatique* (English Internet edition), December 1997.

38. Savir, *The Process,* 281. The logical connection between the first two of these sentences is not clear, unless Savir judged that Peres had shared the assessment (attributed by Savir to the Syrians) that he could not "discipline" the wayward Labor politicians.

39. Author's interview, Washington, D.C., January 1998.

40. Author's interview, Washington, D.C., November 1996.

41. "Peres Comments on Progress of Syria Talks, Elections," Israel Television Channel 1 (Jerusalem), in Hebrew, January 31, 1996; as translated in FBIS-NES-96-022.

42. Author's interview, Washington, D.C., March 1998. See also Hemi Shalev, "Christopher Is Not Excited," *Ma'ariv* (Tel Aviv), February 9, 1996, 8; translated as "Israel: Peres, U.S. Maneuver Over Peace, Early Elections" in FBIS-NES-96-028. Shalev wrote that Foreign Minister Barak had told "anyone who would listen" during his visit to Washington at the time that keeping the elections to the later schedule would give the opposition the opportunity to tie up the government in endless Knesset filibusters.

43. Savir quoted in Gresh, *Le Monde Diplomatique.*

44. Rabinovich, *The Brink of Peace,* 224.

45. *Journal of Palestine Studies,* "Fresh Light": 402.

46. Author's interview, Washington, D.C., June 1999.

47. Author's interview, Tel Aviv, March 1998.

48. "Peres Announces Early Elections," Israel Television Channel 1 (Jerusalem), in Hebrew, February 11, 1996; as translated in FBIS-NES-96-029.

49. Savir, *The Process,* 282.

50. In 1998, Mufaz would replace Shahak as the IDF's chief of staff.

51. Interview with U.S. participant, April 1998.

52. Savir, *The Process,* 282.

53. "Israel's Netanyahu on Elections, Likud Platform," Israel Television Channel 2 (Jerusalem), in Hebrew, February 5, 1996; as translated in FBIS-NES-96-026.

54. Nahum Barne'a, "His Early Experience, His Late Age," *Yedi'ot Aharonot* (Tel Aviv), in Hebrew, February 12, 1996, 1, 23; translated as "Peres, Netanyahu Election Tactics Compared," in FBIS-NES-96-029.

55. Savir, *The Process,* 284.

56. "Syrian Paper: U.S. Listing as Terrorism Sponsor 'Paradox,'" SANA (Damascus), in Arabic, March 2, 1996; as translated in FBIS-TOT-96-011-L.

57. "Al-Mu'allim, Syria Times Condemn Jerusalem Bombings," Radio Monte Carlo (Paris), in Arabic, February 28, 1996; as translated in FBIS-NES-96-040. A Palestinian-Jordanian journalist soon afterwards criticized Damascus for, as he judged it, telling the truth about its position when it denounced the bombings in English, while lying to Arabic-language readers when it expressed "sympathy verging on actual support" for the bombings, in the Arabic press; Salih al-Qallab, "Denouncing in English; Supporting in Arabic," *Al-Dustur* (Amman), in Arabic, March 2, 1996, 20, 24; translated as "Jordanian Writer Assails 'Schizophrenic' Syrian Stand on Bombings" in FBIS-TOT-96-011-L.

58. "Commentary—Hamas Attacks Spell 'Political Death' for Peres," Voice of the Oppressed (Ba'labakk), in Arabic, March 6, 1996; as translated in FBIS-NES-96-045.

59. Voice of the Islamic Republic of Iran, "Vice President Habibi's Visit to Syria Viewed."

60. Salwa al-Ustuwani, "Habibi Stresses 'Iran's Absolute Support' for Palestinian Opposition Factions," *Al-Sharq Al-Awsat* (London), in Arabic, February 29, 1996, 1, 4; translated as "Syria: More on Habibi Meeting With Palestinian Oppositionists" in FBIS-NES-96-041.

61. For many more details of Israeli-Turkish relations and their impact on Syria, see Gresh, *Le Monde Diplomatique*. It was Gresh who reported there that the defense cooperation agreement had been negotiated by Rabin. For Rabinovich's account of this agreement, see *The Brink of Peace*, 223–24.

62. Gresh, *Le Monde Diplomatique*.

63. Rabinovich, *The Brink of Peace*, 223–24. In light of Israel's efforts to keep the pact with Turkey secret, it seems disingenuous of Rabinovich to ask, as he did here, "If the Syrians so deeply distrusted the Israeli-Turkish partnership being formed, why was Moalem not instructed to raise it with Savir, or why did he not do it of his own initiative?" Rabinovich's insistence that the pact with Turkey had no anti-Syrian edge can also be read in light of his earlier recollection that Rabin once told Ross that Assad's apparent inflexibility in the negotiations arose "because he felt free from pressure and it was a pity that one could not talk to *Iraq*" (p. 188, emphasis added).

64. Author's interview, Washington, D.C., January 1998.

65. Savir, *The Process*, 284.

66. Author's interview with Ambassador Moalem, November 1996; and Savir, *The Process*, 285.

67. This is the author's strong impression from numerous conversations in Syria and Israel in March 1998.

68. One senior U.S. official involved with the talks, who admitted that Assad had responded well to the new approach introduced by Peres, also expressed the judgment that Assad may have chosen to be forthcoming on the "symbols of peace" that Peres asked for, mainly as a way of avoiding having to make hard choices in the security domain.

69. Author's interview, Tel Aviv, March 1998.

7. DISINTEGRATION

1. "Rabinovich Foresees 'Indefinite' Freeze in Syrian Talks," IDF Radio (Tel Aviv), in Hebrew, March 6, 1996; as translated in FBIS-NES-96-045.

2. Author's interview, Damascus, March 1998.

3. IDF Radio, "Rabinovich Foresees."

4. "Beilin on Conditions for Lebanon Withdrawal," Israel Television Channel 1 (Jerusalem), in Hebrew, March 22, 1996; as translated in FBIS-NES-96-058.

5. Author's interview, Washington, D.C., March 1998.

6. Author's interview, Washington, D.C., May 1998.

7. "Delegation to Peace Talks With Israel Returns Home," Syrian Arab Television Network (Damascus), in Arabic, March 6, 1996; as translated in FBIS-NES-96-046.

8. "Appeals Against Terrorism, Jointly and Individually, by Former Adversaries," *New York Times*, March 14, 1996, A10.

9. "Israel's Peres Sums Up Peacemakers Summit," Israel Television Channel 1 (Jerusalem), in Hebrew, March 13, 1996; translated in FBIS-TOT-96-009-L.

10. "Syria's al-Shar' Comments on Sharm al-Shaykh Summit," Syrian Arab Television (Damascus), in Arabic, March 14, 1996; as translated in FBIS-TOT-96-009-L.

11. Author's interview, Washington, D.C., November 1996.

12. Between 1982 and 1984, those Lebanese groups also confronted an American military presence in Lebanon which, though originally deployed in a peacekeeping role, rapidly became entangled in partisan intra-Lebanese disputes. See Cobban, *The Making of Modern Lebanon*.

13. For a Syrian reaction to that move, see the excerpt from the Syrian daily *Al-Thawra* carried by SANA (Damascus), in Arabic, March 2, 1996; translated as "Syrian Paper: U.S. Listing as Terrorism Sponsor 'Paradox,'" in FBIS-TOT-96-011-L.

14. "Motives of Sharm al-Shaykh Summit in Question," Syrian Arab Television Network (Damascus), in Arabic, March 12, 1996; as translated in FBIS-TOT-96-009-L.

15. "Paper Condemns Terrorism, Defends Damascus-Based Factions," Radio Monte Carlo (Paris), in Arabic, March 16, 1996; as translated in FBIS-NES-96-053.

16. Itamar Rabinovich said that information available to him at the time indicated that, after Peres had announced early elections the Syrians were "not happy," but that after Israel withdrew from the peace talks, Assad "opened the arms spigot for Hezbollah." Author's interview, Tel Aviv, March 1998.

17. "Peres Sees 'No Choice' But To Give Hezbollah 'a Beating,'" IDF Radio (Tel Aviv), in Hebrew, March 21, 1996; as translated in FBIS-NES-96-056.

18. Author's interview, Tel Aviv, March 1998.

19. IDF Radio, "Peres Sees 'No Choice.'"

20. Author's interview, Tel Aviv, March 1998.

21. "Peres Receives U.S. Demand To Avoid IDF Action in Lebanon," Israel Television Channel 1 (Jerusalem), in Hebrew, March 19, 1996; as translated in FBIS-NES-96-055.

22. See Salwa al-Ustuwani, "Syria Expresses Satisfaction With Saudi Position," *Al-Sharq Al-Awsat* (London), in Arabic, March 16, 1996, 3; translated as "Aide Hails King Fahd Speech, Criticizes Forum's 'Weak' Results," in FBIS-NES-96-054.

23. "Al-Assad, Mubarak Hold News Conference," Syrian Arab Television (Damascus), in Arabic, April 2, 1996; as translated in FBIS-NES-96-065, emphasis added.

24. Ibid.

25. "Hezbollah Chief Threatens Retaliation for Civilian Deaths," Voice of Lebanon (Beirut), in Arabic, March 30, 1996; as translated in FBIS-TOT-96-013-L.

26. "Israeli Warplanes To Train in Turkey," *Turkish Daily News* (Ankara), in English, April 4, 1996; as reprinted in *Foreign Broadcast Information Service/ Daily Report: Western Europe* 96-067.

27. Alain Gresh has written that the Israelis (who had apparently started the military talks with Turkey under Rabin) would have preferred to keep the cooperation agreement secret for some time longer. It was the Turkish military establishment, under pressure from the U.S. Congress to clean up its human rights record, that was eager to disclose the relationship in order to win kudos in Congress. See Gresh, *Le Monde Diplomatique*.

28. "Editorial Criticizes Israeli-Turkish-Jordanian 'Alliance,'" SANA (Damascus), in Arabic, April 9, 1996; as translated in FBIS-NES-96-070.

29. Savir, *The Process*, 276, 279.

30. See "'Change' in Peres Stance on Hezbollah; Or Discusses Options," FBIS-NES-96-071, emphasis added.

31. Ibid.

32. Quoted in Human Rights Watch, *Israel/Lebanon: "Operation Grapes of Wrath," The Civilian Victims* (New York: Human Rights Watch, September 1997), 22.

33. "Peres on Possible Cease-Fire in Lebanon," Israel Television Channel 2 (Jerusalem), in Hebrew, April 19, 1996; translated in FBIS-NES-96-078.

34. "Army Chiefs Discuss Lebanon Operation, Accord," IDF Radio (Tel Aviv), in Hebrew, April 27, 1996; translated in FBIS-NES-96-083.

35. SLA Radio cited in Human Rights Watch, *Israel/Lebanon*, 33. In a twisted piece of logic, this broadcast concluded, "He who warns is excused."

36. IDF Radio, "Army Chiefs Discuss," emphasis added. The risk of "overshooting the mark," or as Rabin had referred to many months earlier, "making mistakes," is one present in any war—and increases, obviously, as the scale of the campaign increases.

37. Author's interview, Tel Aviv, March 1998. Peres was incorrect in stating that no one was killed anywhere else but at Qana. See Human Rights Watch, *Civilian Pawns*, 59–67.

38. Author's interview, Tel Aviv, March 1998.

39. "Al-Hariri Views U.S. Offer, British Stance," Radio Lebanon (Beirut), in Arabic, April 16, 1996; as translated in FBIS-NES-96-074, emphasis added.

40. By the time the fighting ended, these other mediation hopefuls, whose efforts made varying degrees of difference to the ultimate outcome, would include France, Jordan, Morocco, the European Union, and Russia.

41. Elaine Sciolino, "In the Face of Horror, Diplomacy Stays Muted," *New York Times*, April 19, 1996, A12.

42. Patrick Cockburn, "A War the Israelis Can All Support," *The Independent* (London), in English, April 18, 1996, 17; reprinted as "Israeli Campaign on Lebanon Explained," in FBIS-NES-96-076.

43. "Peres Orders IDF To Resume Full-Scale Operation," *Yedi'ot Aharonot* (Tel Aviv), in Hebrew, April 23, 1996, 1,10; as translated in FBIS-NES-96-079.

44. "Commentary Dubs Israel's Peres 'Killer of Children,'" Syrian Arab Television (Damascus), in Arabic, April 24, 1996; as translated in FBIS-NES-96-082.

45. Ibid.

46. Ibid.

47. "Restricting the Violence in Lebanon," *New York Times*, April 27, 1996, A8.

48. Just before the news conference at which the announcement was made, Peres reportedly offered Christopher some sparkling wine made by Israeli settlers in Golan. See Steven Erlanger, "No Formal Peace," *New York Times*, April 27, 1996, 8.

49. "Peres on Aspects of Cease-Fire Document," Israel Television Channel 2 (Jerusalem), in Hebrew, April 26, 1996; as translated in FBIS-NES-96-083.

50. "Likud Chairman Netanyahu Attacks Lebanon Accord," Channel 2 Television (Jerusalem), in Hebrew, April 26, 1996; as translated in FBIS-NES-96-083.

51. "Labor Party Issues Platform," Israel Information Service (Internet version), in English, May 15, 1996; as reprinted in FBIS-NES-96-101-S.

52. "Likud Issues Platform," Israel Information Service (Internet version), in English, May 15, 1996; as reprinted in FBIS-NES-96-101-S.

53. "The Third Way Issues Platform," Israel Information Service (Internet version), in English, May 15, 1996; as reprinted in FBIS-NES-96-101-S.

54. "Meretz Issues Platform," Israel Information Service (Internet version), in English, May 15, 1996; as reprinted in FBIS-NES-96-101-S.

55. "Peres on Qana, Peace Process, Elections," *Al-Sharq Al-Awsat* (London), in Arabic, May 17, 1996, 17; as translated in FBIS-NES-96-098.

56. Samuel Lewis has also pointed to Peres's extremely lackluster performance in the major television debate against Netanyahu, which made Peres look "tired, arrogant, old, and snippy." Author's interview, Washington, D.C., June 1999.

57. Numerous conversations with Dore Gold, 1991–93.

58. Ignacio Cembrero, "We Will Recover Golan Heights, Whoever Governs Israel," an interview with Farouq Sharaa, *El Pais* (Madrid), May 20, 1995, 6; translated as "Syria's Al-Shar' on U.S. Role in Peace Process," in *Foreign Broadcast Information Service/Daily Report: Western Europe* 95-099.

59. Israel Television Channel 1, "Rabin on Lebanon, Syria, Palestinian Track."

60. "Mubarak, al-Assad Hold News Conference," Arab Republic of Egypt Radio Network (Cairo), in Arabic, June 3, 1996; as translated in FBIS-NES-96-108. See also the interesting details in Arye Bender and Menahem Rahat, "Likud Drafts 'Softer' Government Guidelines," *Ma'ariv* (Tel Aviv), June 11, 1996, 16; as translated in FBIS-NES-96-113.

61. "Netanyahu Government Presents Basic Guidelines," Government Press Office (Jerusalem), in English, June 17, 1996; as reprinted in FBIS-NES-96-118.

62. The monitoring group got under way throughout 1996. On December 12, 1996, it reportedly found the IDF responsible for recently shelling two Lebanese villages with deadly "flechette" shells that injured six civilians. "It was the third successive case in which the group has held Israel responsible for shelling a southern Lebanese village," Reuters reported. *Washington Post*, December 13, 1996, A47.

63. "Syrian Envoy Says No Talks Without Israeli Pledge on Golan," *Yedi'ot Aharonot* (Tel Aviv), in Hebrew, July 14, 1996, 19; as translated in FBIS-NES-96-137.

64. See, for example, Ze'ev Schiff, "Syria Agreed to Foreign Troops on Hermon," *Ha'aretz* (English Internet edition), May 28, 1999.

65. See Ze'ev Schiff, "False Information Influenced Israel's Moves with Syria," *Ha'aretz*, (English Internet edition), December 3, 1997. "False Information Pertained to al-Assad War-Peace Intentions," Israel Television Channel 2 (Jerusalem), in Hebrew, December 3, 1997; as translated in FBIS-NES-97-337. Gil's motivations seemed to include political ones: Before being called back to the Syria job, he had been an organizer for the extreme right-wing Moledet Party (see Haim Baram, "The Patriotic Traitor," *Middle East International*, December 19, 1997, 8). The discovery of Gil's activities raised disturbing questions about the politicization of Israel's oft-vaunted intelligence assessments, many of which are shared with the U.S. government.

66. See, for example, figure 1 in Asher Arian, "Israeli Public Opinion on Lebanon and Syria, 1999," *Strategic Assessment* 2, no. 1 (June 1999): 19. The data show that from 1997 through 1999, the proportion of adult Jewish Israelis favoring a unilateral withdrawal from Lebanon rose from 41 percent to 55 percent. The views of Palestinian Israeli citizens were not recorded, but they could also be expected to be predominantly in favor of withdrawal.

67. The *New York Times* has cited figures showing that in the 1999 elections, Third Way captured only 14.8 percent of the votes of the Israelis in Golan itself, and a far lower proportion nationwide, while in a post-election poll, 42 percent of the Israelis in Golan expressed themselves ready to leave in exchange for a full peace with Syria and compensation from the Israeli government. See Deborah Sontag, "Sadly, Golan Settlers Concede Peace Could Mean Eviction," *New York Times*, June 14, 1999, A1, A6.

68. Impressions noted, and utterance heard, during research visit to Israel, March 1998.

69. Author's interview, Damascus, March 1998.

8. THE PAST AS PRELUDE

1. Author's interview, Washington, D.C., June 1999.

2. Author's interview, Washington, D.C., June 1999.

3. For more details of changes in the strategic balance between Israel and Syria, 1978–89, see Cobban, *The Superpowers and the Syrian-Israeli Conflict*, chapter 2.

4. Roger Fisher and William Ury dealt at length with the value to a negotiator of his side's "Best Alternative to a Negotiated Agreement" (BATNA). Using a "game-playing" model of negotiations, they wrote, "The better your BATNA, the greater your ability to improve the terms of any negotiated agreement. . . . The desirability of disclosing your BATNA to the other side depends on your assessment of the other side's thinking. If your BATNA is extremely attractive— if you have another customer waiting in the next room—it is in your interest to let the other side know. If they think you lack a good alternative when in fact you have one, then you should almost certainly let them know. However, if your best alternative to a negotiated agreement is worse for you than they think, disclosing it will weaken rather than strengthen your hand." Roger Fisher and William Ury, *Getting to Yes: Negotiating Agreement without Giving In* (Boston: Houghton Mifflin, 1981), 109.

5. Savir, *The Process*, 271.

6. Israel had long sought to benefit from a deliberate ambiguity in the wording of Resolution 242's call for Israeli withdrawal from "occupied territories," as opposed to "the occupied territories." Now, Syria was employing an exactly similar ambiguity with regard to the status of its peace option.

7. The difference between these two generally indirect forms of quiet communication among leaders is that track-two diplomacy is conducted by people who are not government officials and are entirely deniable as emissaries. (Indeed, they may have started their contacts quite separately from any official diplomacy.) Thus, the Oslo contacts between Israel and the PLO started quite outside the official domain, then became informally used by Peres as a mechanism for track-two signaling. Finally, when Uri Savir, a government official, became personally involved, the Israeli government's involvement in them was no longer easily deniable, and they continued to serve as a back channel until their existence was publicly disclosed.

8. *Journal of Palestine Studies*, "Fresh Light": 408.

9. The present author had been instrumental in helping to bring the Syrians into this forum, but she had resigned from the effort before the lapse in judgment surrounding Olmert occurred. At least some of the Syrian participants suffered significant professional consequences at home.

10. See chapter 2.

11. Conversation with the author, Washington, D.C., June 1999.

12. The surprises that Schiff mentioned in particular in this connection were Rabin's assassination, the suicide bombs in Israel, and Peres's failure to win re-election. Author's interview, Tel Aviv, March 1998.

13. Those who have expressed this judgment include Secretary Christopher and Ambassador Rabinovich.

14. Author's interview, Tel Aviv, March 1998.

15. Author's interview, Washington, D.C., June 1999. Warren Christopher has stated that Assad "felt he had been emancipated by the fact that the Palestinians had moved themselves." See *Ha'aretz*, "A Believer in the Road Already Traveled."

16. This latter model of "coordination" was not one that either the Palestinians or the Jordanians were ever tempted to enter into—as Assad himself seemed to recognize, with a rare flash of public self-awareness, in the remarks he made about "custodianship" at the press conference just before the opening of the first round at Wye. See chapter 5.

17. Rabinovich, *The Brink of Peace*, 79. William Quandt has pointed out that this model of it being the job overwhelmingly of the Arab interlocutor to reassure the Israeli public, but not the other way around, may have become entrenched in Israel after President Sadat's notable efforts on this score in the late 1970s. But in this, as in many other things, as the Israeli negotiators were coming to learn, Assad was not Sadat. Conversation with the author, Charlottesville, Virginia, June 1999.

18. *Journal of Palestine Studies*, "Fresh Light": 407.

19. Author's interview, Damascus, March 1998.

20. Author's interview, Damascus, March 1998.

21. Reported by Ze'ev Schiff, writing in *Ha'aretz*, January 19 and 24, 1997, and cited in Shlaim, *The Iron Wall*, 566.

22. Author's interview, Washington, D.C., January 1998.

Index

Helena Cobban is a writer and researcher with twenty-five years' experience of writing about Middle Eastern affairs, and an adjunct scholar at the Middle East Institute in Washington, D.C. This book builds directly on experience she gained as a Middle East–based correspondent in the 1970s, and on research she did for her 1991 book, *The Superpowers and the Syrian-Israeli Conflict,* and her 1997 monograph, *Syria and the Peace: A Good Chance Missed.* In the early 1990s, Ms. Cobban spent two years on the directing staff of the nongovernmental group, the Initiative for Peace and Cooperation in the Middle East. There, she helped initiate a pathbreaking effort at building common ground among citizen-participants from many Middle Eastern countries, including Syria and Israel, on a broad range of issues connected to peacebuilding.

Fluent in French and Arabic, Ms. Cobban is a member of the Middle East Advisory Committee of Human Rights Watch, of the International Institute for Strategic Studies, and the Editorial Advisory Board of the *Middle East Journal.* For many years now, she has contributed regular columns on global affairs to the *Christian Science Monitor,* and to the London-based daily, *Al-Hayat.* Her numerous other publications include a book on the Palestinian Liberation Organization (1984), and an award-winning country study of Lebanon (1985). In early 2000, the University Press of Virginia will be publishing her next book, *The Moral Architecture of World Peace.*

United States Institute of Peace

The United States Institute of Peace is an independent, nonpartisan federal institution created by Congress to promote research, education, and training on the peaceful management and resolution of international conflicts. Established in 1984, the Institute meets its congressional mandate through an array of programs, including research grants, fellowships, professional training, education programs from high school through graduate school, conferences and workshops, library services, and publications. The Institute's Board of Directors is appointed by the President of the United States and confirmed by the Senate.

Chairman of the Board: Chester A. Crocker
Vice Chairman: Max M. Kampelman
President: Richard H. Solomon
Executive Vice President: Harriet Hentges

THE ISRAELI-SYRIAN PEACE TALKS: 1991–96 AND BEYOND

This book is set in the typeface New Aster; the display type is Univers 65. Cover design by The Creative Shop of Rockville, Maryland. Interior design by Mike Chase. Page makeup by Helene Redmond of HYR Graphics. Map designed by Michael Sonesen. Copyediting and proofreading by EEI Communications, Inc. of Alexandria, Virginia. Peter Pavilionis was the book's editor.